BRINGING DOWN AMERICA: An FBI Informer with the Weathermen

Larry Grathwohl   Frank Reagan

Introduction to the 2013 Edition

In 1969, Larry Grathwohl stepped out of his life and into the role of an informant for the FBI. At the time, Grathwohl was a 22-year old army veteran and young father, back home in Cincinnati after serving as a paratrooper in Vietnam and a drill instructor at Fort Knox. He was working on a loading dock when he crossed paths with two hippies. The hippies (who were members of the Weathermen) were recruiting people for a violent protest in Chicago. They invited Grathwohl to join them at what would turn out to be a deliberately staged riot against the police – the infamous Chicago "Days of Rage" protests.

Grathwohl alerted his father-in-law, who was a retired Cincinnati police officer. He met with police and FBI agents and agreed to infiltrate the Weathermen as an informant. Working at great personal risk, Grathwohl insinuated himself into the Weathermen just as its leaders were making the decision to abandon their legal identities and disappear "underground." He joined them there, moving between cities, squatting in bare apartments, and trying to alert his FBI handlers as he watched Bill Ayers, Bernardine Dohrn, and other Weather Underground terrorists plan mass casualty bombings and plot communist revolution.

Forty-four years later, we are very lucky to have this memoir, which is Grathwohl's record of his time undercover. First published in 1976, *Bringing Down America: An FBI Informer With the Weathermen* is necessary reading for understanding the violent history and real ambitions of the Weather Underground, a task that is now more important than ever.

For, in the decades since they emerged from hiding, the leaders of the Weathermen have pulled off their most audacious feats: they negotiated a return to society, avoided legal consequences for their most serious crimes, and rose to influential positions in academia and politics – all without renouncing their anti-American ideology or apologizing for the acts of terrorism they committed against ordinary Americans. Today, the former Weathermen continue to wage war on *fascist-imperialist-Amerika* from inside institutions they once targeted with dynamite.

It almost goes without saying that they are more powerful now than they ever were in their bomb-throwing days:

- **Bill Ayers** is in his third decade as a national leader in the movement to radicalize the training of schoolteachers. His dream of turning children into activists for "social justice" and transforming K-12 classrooms into the "motor-force of revolution" is rapidly coming true. He is greeted as a hero at education schools, where his radical ideas rule the curriculum.

- **Bernardine Dohrn**, the former miniskirted terrorist who notoriously cheered the murder of 8-months pregnant Sharon Tate, Tate's unborn child, and other victims of the Manson Family, now bills herself as an advocate for children. What she really does is agitate against schools and juvenile courts that use "zero tolerance" and other discipline to bring order to the lives of children growing up in violent communities. Dohrn's activism is a continuation of the Weathermen's longstanding antipathy towards law enforcement. Yet, in her private life, she enjoys the privileges of being a professor of law at Northwestern University and a high-ranking officer in the American Bar Association.

- **Eleanor Raskin** (née Stein), who has ties to the 1970 bomb plot to kill soldiers and their dates at Fort Dix that ended with the deaths of three Weathermen, and who fled authorities again in 1979 after a raid of her apartment uncovered bomb making materials, became a law professor at Albany Law School, a "human rights" professor at S.U.N.Y. Albany, and a New York State administrative judge specializing in "transnational environmental law."

- **Jeff Jones**, Raskin's husband and co-defendant in the 1979 case, is even more politically accomplished: despite his history of bombing government buildings. Jones is now head of the New York Apollo Alliance, a highly influential coalition of labor leaders and environmentalists who helped draft President Obama's 2009 Recovery Act.

- **Mark Rudd, Howie Matchinger, Susan Rosenberg, Judith Clark, Naomi Jaffee, David Gilbert, Laura Whitehorn, Cathy Boudin, and Cathy Wilkerson** have also reinvented themselves as prominent "social justice" activists. Some of them discovered literary talents behind bars and won outsized praise for their poetic denunciations of America and the police. Rosenberg, Boudin, and deceased fellow terrorist and cop-killer Marilyn Buck all received prestigious P.E.N. awards for their hate-filled poems and anti-American writing.

These days, Ayers, Dohrn, and other prominent Weather Underground leaders avoid hard questions about their terrorist pasts by wrapping themselves in the mantle of "social justice." It is an old trick but one that still works in all the places that matter, like the editorial page of the *New York Times* and university hiring committees.

Their continued success, however, relies on a fragile social pact: no member of the Weathermen must ever tell the truth about what they really did.

For, if even one person were to deviate from the official story, something more than a few tenure appointments would be at risk. High-ranking members of the political Left, including several with ties to President Obama, would be facing potential murder investigations. And more than a few journalists would need to explain why they had been participating in a four-decade cover-up of the real history of the Weather Underground.

A great deal depends on everyone staying silent now. This is why Larry Grathwohl's book is so important: Grathwohl challenges the web of lies the Weathermen have gotten away with shilling in the media for decades. The story Grathwohl tells may at first seem familiar, but it's not. *Bringing Down America* is the real story of the Weathermen.

The current "official version" of the Weather Underground story is a lie of several parts. The first lie is that the Weathermen were merely a student antiwar group. The second lie is that the Weathermen never killed or injured anyone, with the exception of the three members of the organization who blew themselves up assembling a bomb. The third lie is that the Weathermen never targeted people with their bombs, only empty buildings and other "symbolic" targets.

And the fourth lie, which is a relatively recent addition to the official story, is that the Weather Underground itself was not really a terrorist organization at all. The author of this curious claim appears to be Ayers himself. In his memoir, *Fugitive Days*, Ayers objects to ever having been labeled a terrorist: "[t]errorists intimidate, while we aimed only to educate," he raps, in his characteristically inane prose style.

In a 2010 joint blog post, Ayers and Dohrn expanded on the theme: "the Weather Underground carried out a series of illegal and symbolic acts on property," they wrote, "some 20 acts over its entire existence, and no one was killed or harmed; the goal was not to terrorize people."

This is not true, but few in the media have challenged them in recent years. The more vigorously the Weathermen deny ever having been violent, the more vigorously certain prominent figures in the media have stepped up to absolve them – even of crimes the terrorists themselves once proudly claimed. One example from 1970 illustrates this collusion of lies between the media and the terrorists: of course, it is from the *New York Times*.

On June 9, 1970, a powerful bomb exploded in the New York City Police Department headquarters. The next day, the *New York Times* reported that seven people were injured in the blast. The bombing was preceded by a Weatherman communique from

Bernardine Dohrn, titled "Declaration of a State of War." Immediately following the explosion, the Weather Underground took responsibility for it. In *Fugitive Days*, which was published in 2001, Bill Ayers even brags about the Weathermen's "defiance and hyperbole" in announcing that specific bombing in advance.

Yet by 2008, after news reports linked Ayers to presidential candidate Barack Obama, the *New York Times* changed its tune about the 1970 bomb. *Times* editors permitted Ayers to publish an op-ed insisting that neither he nor other Weathermen had ever targeted or injured people:

> I never killed or injured anyone. . . . We did carry out symbolic acts of extreme vandalism directed at monuments to war and racism, and the attacks on property, never on people, were meant to respect human life. . . . But it was not terrorism; we were not engaged in a campaign to kill and injure people indiscriminately, spreading fear and suffering for political ends.

Perhaps the paper of record could return to its own stacks to correct the story now.

The media's abdication of responsibility in reporting the history of the Weather Underground has enabled the Weathermen themselves to recount their actions in memoirs and media stories – always in ways that cast them as both heroes of the people and victims of a fascist state.

Taking advantage of shifting public moods, the Weathermen began manipulating the press from the moment they broke away from the mainstream anti-war movement. By 1970, at the height of radical chic, the photogenic Bernardine Dohrn presided over Weatherman press conferences in high-heeled boots and leather miniskirts, playing up her sexuality as she threatened acts of terrorism on the evening news.

Later, as the Vietnam War drew to a close, the Weathermen adjusted their message to emphasize the "sacrifices" they were personally making by staying in hiding. In 1975, Dohrn, Ayers, Kathy Boudin, Jeff Jones, and Cathy Wilkerson even starred in a feature-length film titled *Underground*.

Filmed in secret, with the participants facing away from the cameras for dramatic effect, *Underground* gave the media-savvy fugitives a new cause to trumpet: their own existence hiding from the police. They were now the vanguard of radicalism just for existing.

Although few people actually watched *Underground*, which consists of hours of stoned, anti-American agitprop, it excited A-list Hollywood celebrities. Warren Beatty, Shirley MacLaine, Jack Nicholson, and Mel Brooks rushed to support director Emile de Antonio when the federal government attempted to seize footage of the film to search it for clues to bring the Weathermen to justice. De Antonio postured as a victim of censorship while calling the government's action "the kind of advertising you can't buy."

Just as Dohrn's leather miniskirt was the perfect symbol of the Weathermen's *Bonnie and Clyde* image in the Sixties, the trumped-up First Amendment battle over *Underground* became the perfect vehicle for dramatizing the Weather Underground's assertion that, by the mid-1970's, they alone were carrying the torch against *Amerikan-racism-and-imperialism* while other antiwar protesters "sold out" after Vietnam.

They changed their tune yet again when they emerged from hiding a few years later. As they climbed to success in the 1980's, the era of *The Big Chill* and other Sixties nostalgia, reporters again came calling.

By 1990, Bill Ayers was being depicted as a celebrity academic who had nonetheless "stayed true to his principles." An admiring profile in *Chicago Reader* described Ayers as "willing to sacrifice his wealth and privilege for just causes" while "mesmerizing" his students with movement stories. Yet, when one student asked Ayers about the buildings he had bombed, he pretended to have forgotten, "like Reagan" he said, to the reporter's amusement.

Such whitewashing of the Weathermen's crimes became entirely routine in the media. In a fawning, 1993 profile, the *New York Times* depicted Bernardine Dohrn as merely an earnest anti-war activist who had broken a few store windows before embarking on a career in child protection, a career that was being hampered by reactionary jurists who refused to grant her a bar license.

In the pages of the *Times*, where two decades earlier she had declared war on American, Dohrn was now just a working mom juggling career and home, "fixing stewed cherries" for a sick son as she battled "misogyny" in the courts.

She even dared to complain that the negative publicity she had received in the Sixties was merely the result of "sexism." "[I] stepped out of the role of the good girl," Dohrn suggested to *Times* reporter Susan Chira, who cooed approvingly about the "pearls-and-pin-stripe-suited" woman behind the "caricatures." Most of the female leaders of the Weather Underground are prominent feminist activists today, to the shame of the feminist movement.

On September 11, 2001, publicity for Ayers' memoir, *Fugitive Days*, coincided horrifically with the terrorist attack on the World Trade Center and the Pentagon. A photograph of Ayers and Dohrn appeared in the *New York Times* that morning under the headline "No Regrets for a Love of Explosives." The couple received harsh criticism from some quarters, but others in the media issued defenses of the couple, arguing that criticizing them for celebrating terrorism was somehow unfair.

Instead of the career-ending event it should have been for Ayers to be crowing in the *Times* about his happy memories of bombing the Pentagon as military personnel pulled their burned-alive colleagues from the building's rubble, the 9/11 terrorist attack became yet another opportunity for Bill Ayers to grandstand about feeling persecuted for being Bill Ayers – just as he had done when his three terrorist colleagues killed themselves constructing a bomb in a Greenwich Village townhouse in 1970.

In 1970, as the townhouse lay smoldering, Ayers had had the foresight to pin blame for the mass-casualty bomb being constructed solely on his "fallen" comrades, even as he ostentatiously mourned them. In doing so, he absolved himself and all the other surviving Weathermen of any responsibility for a bomb plot that would have murdered hundreds of innocent young people.

And this lie – the lie that only the three Weathermen who

died in the blast were involved in the Fort Dix mass murder plot – is the central lie that holds together all the rest of the lies Weathermen tell today.

It is the lie that Bill Ayers, especially, cannot do without. He has told it too many times; he has built his reputation as a national education leader on it.

***Bringing Down America* demolishes this central Weathermen lie** – that Bill Ayers and the other surviving members of the Weathermen never targeted people with their bombs. Grathwohl was a young man when he infiltrated the Weathermen, but he saw them clearly for what they were: not peace activists, but aspiring Marxist revolutionaries whose members had trained overseas with America's enemies.

The Weathermen were, by their own admission, not anti-war, but pro-Communist victory – in Vietnam, America, and elsewhere. In open emulation of Che Guevara, their hero, they spoke of creating "two, three, many Vietnams," followed by "the violent overthrow of the bourgeoisie [and] the establishment of the dictatorship of the proletariat," as Ayers, Dohrn and Jeff Jones wrote in their 1974 manifesto, *Prairie Fire: The Politics of Revolutionary Anti-Imperialism.*

Grathwohl documents how the Weathermen organized themselves into small groups, called "focals," directed by a central "Weather Bureau." Weather Bureau members wielded absolute psychological control over others. Subordinates practiced karate chops and spied on each other while Weather Bureau members such as Dohrn, Mark Rudd, Jeff Jones and Cathy Wilkerson flew to Cuba and Cambodia for guerrilla training and meetings with the Viet Cong.

Within months of infiltrating the Weather Underground, Larry Grathwohl was living in a Weatherman collective in Detroit; enduring Maoist-inspired "criticism/self-criticism" sessions; witnessing joyless acts of "monogamy crushing" sex, and feigning knowledge of explosives as Bill Ayers plotted to bomb the Detroit Police Officers Association Building and Detroit's 13th Police Precinct Station.

Luckily, it was easy to undermine Ayers' sophomoric attempts at bomb making. "Ayers thought of me as an expert in explosives and weapons because I had fought in Vietnam," said Grathwohl, "In addition, I was a greaser; therefore I was used to violence" ("Greaser" was a pejorative for lower-class men).

Between 1969 and 1970, the Weathermen engaged in several missions to kill people, including the New York City Police Department Headquarters bombing, attacks on police cars and courthouses, bombs detonated in public places, armed rioting that caused scores of injuries, and the firebombing of Justice John Murtagh's home as his wife and children slept upstairs.

Then on March 6, 1970, Bill Ayers' girlfriend, Diana Oughton, and two other Weathermen accidentally blew themselves up as they assembled a bomb in a townhouse basement in New York's Greenwich Village. The nail-packed anti-personnel bomb that killed them was intended for soldiers and their dates at a dance for noncommissioned officers at Fort Dix.

The townhouse explosion is remembered today as an iconic moment in late-60's radicalism. But it is only one part of a larger and more damning story about the Weathermen, a story that has been carefully buried by Bill Ayers and others, with help from their friends in the media.

One week before the townhouse explosion, police guided by Larry Grathwohl's intelligence reports discovered two other Weatherman bombs. These bombs, thankfully, failed to detonate.

One bomb was planted inside Detroit's 13th Police District Station, the other in an alley between the Detroit Police Officers Association Building and a busy urban restaurant. These were the bombs Bill Ayers had been planning in the Detroit collective: 44 sticks of dynamite, aimed at police and civilians alike.

If any of these three bomb plots had succeeded – the one at Fort Dix and the two in Detroit – hundreds of innocent people would have died. Soldiers, their girlfriends and wives, police officers, civilian workers, and random passers-by in New Jersey and Detroit would have perished at the hands of Bill Ayers and other Weather Underground terrorists. As historian Harvey Klehr observed in 2003, "[t]he only reason they were not guilty of mass murder is mere incompetence. I don't know what sort of defense that is."

But instead of acknowledging what might have happened if these bombings had succeeded, journalists have allowed the media-savvy Weathermen to turn the story of the townhouse bombing into a story about themselves. For four decades, the Weathermen have used the deaths of their colleagues in the townhouse explosion to deny their own involvement in the Fort Dix bomb plot and to bury their other crimes. Due to prosecutorial problems, the charges filed against Ayers and others in the Detroit case were ultimately dismissed, but their culpability should not be forgotten.

Unfortunately, in the years since 9/11, the media has only grown more irresponsible. In 2003, the Weathermen scored their most high-profile propaganda victory to date: a professionally produced documentary that was slickly repackaged by taxpayer-funded PBS as an interactive teaching tool for America's schoolchildren.

On the PBS website for the film, *Weather Underground*, the Weathermen are portrayed as anti-war activists who put their lives on the line for peace and to oppose racism. The website even features Bernardine Dohrn giving students a tour of her "underground hideout on the San Francisco Bay," adorned with smiling photos of Dohrn and Ayers and accompanied by admiring questions for them, such as: *Was it easy to go underground? Is possible for old farts to go underground? Do you see the same kind of passion that you had . . . in your students?*

No mention is made of the bomb factory the Weather Underground maintained near this hideout, where the fingerprints of several Weathermen were identified among an ominous array of explosives and disguises. Nor does the PBS "teaching tool" mention the 1970 nail-bomb murder of San Francisco Police Sergeant Brian McDonnell, a murder which, Grathwohl reports, Bill Ayers attributed to Dohrn herself.

Ayers himself is described on the PBS website merely as a "school reformer" who "lived underground for ten years," as if he had been an adventurer rather than a fugitive from the law. The PBS curriculum represents the triumph of the "official version" of the Weather Underground story, propaganda funded by the government and packaged for new generations.

And as this book goes to press, actor and director Robert Redford is releasing _The Company You Keep_, a new, pro-Weatherman film that depicts the terrorists as tormented souls who spend their dotage performing good deeds and regretting the consequences of their political "sacrifices" on their own children's lives.

This latest re-invention of the Weathermen as caring parents – and victims of a government that is willing to destroy their fragile families in pursuit of vengeance for long-ago crimes – may be the most offensive re-invention of the "terrorist cult" (as David Horowitz calls them) to date.

For, the Weathermen were, above all else, dedicated to destroying the institution of marriage itself. Their revolutionary Marxist ideology accurately defined bourgeoise family life as the ultimate impediment to revolution, to be corrected by expanding the post-revolution state's reach into private family relations.

The most important story Grathwohl tells in this memoir is ultimately the story of the Weathermen's efforts to seize control of other people's private lives. "Smashing monogamy" with enforced sexual pairings and sexual abuse of vulnerable members; celebrating murder and rape, and forcing the young mothers among them to give up custody of their children in order to prove their commitment to Marxist revolution were all part of the Weathermen's political agenda, as was their efforts to devalue reproduction itself, which was viewed as a perpetuation of white supremacist culture and male supremacy in general.

These Weatherman stories are not the ones featured on PBS websites and in films by Robert Redford. And yet, they represent the actual triumph of their ideology today.

Bill Ayers, the "school reformer" being greeted by cheering crowds of teachers-in-training ought to be a vision that chills the hearts of anyone who cares about the future of our country, or the future of the family. "Calling Bill Ayers a school reformer is a bit like calling Joseph Stalin an agricultural reformer," as Sol Stern acidly observed in 2008.

Of course, the effects of "smashing monogamy" have fallen, as usual, on those in society who could afford them the least: the socially vulnerable, minorities, broken families, and the poor.

The affluent leaders of Weather Underground always made sure that they were insulated from the chaos they orchestrated in other people's lives.

~~~

Larry Grathwohl was a young American veteran who came home from one war to find America's enemies waging social and paramilitary war on America's streets. He "signed up" for a second time, fighting alongside police and FBI agents who deserve to be remembered as heroes for risking their own lives to protect the public from people like Bill Ayers and Bernardine Dohrn.

Grathwohl became a witness to battles much larger than those being fought with dynamite and manifestos. His Sixties story is the story of what really emerged from the youth movement's accelerating rush into revolution, drug use, promiscuity, and violence. His efforts to protect female Weathermen like "Melody," who was "re-educated" by the group to abandon her four year-old child, and Dianna Oughton, who was barreling towards self-annihilation, haunt him to today.

Bringing Down America, Frank Reagan's sensitive rendering of Larry Grathwohl's experiences, deserves a place alongside other classic Vietnam war memoirs and memoirs about the "chilly scenes" of disintegration of American culture in the 1970's. It is a story that people like Robert Redford, Bill Ayers, and Bernardine Dohrn continue to work hard to suppress.

Tina Trent, March 29, 2013

Original Foreword

I lived with the members of the Weather Underground for many months. It was during this time that I came to know them not only as individuals but as an organization as well. A good many of these people I grew to like, and I'm sure I would have established an enduring friendship with some of them if the circumstances had been different. Their fixation with violence to bring about political change is what forced me to view them as a threat to myself as well as others.

I have been asked a great many times if I still feel that the Weather Underground is a threat. The answer is yes. The reason is simple; they are still among us, placing bombs when it suits them and providing other underground organizations with guidance through their communiques and other published writings.

These are a highly dedicated group of people who are willing to give their lives if necessary to fulfill their objectives. They work as hard at being revolutionaries as you and I do at our jobs. It is not unusual for them to go for days without eating. To live in dirt and filth is rule rather than exception.

Political discussions, which take place daily, often lead to criticism/selfcriticism sessions. This brainwashing process is used to reinforce political beliefs and reaffirm revolutionary commitment. During these sessions individual weaknesses are attacked over and over until the individual either acquiesces to self-criticism or is purged. At the end of this process the individual ceases to think as an individual and begins to think in the collective WE. No one is exempt from this process and must be ready not only to criticize but to be criticized as well.

The Weather Underground has broken our laws many times and will continue to do so until caught and brought to justice.

This is not a question of political persecution, but rather one of criminal prosecution.

Everything in this book is based on fact. However, in telling the story we have changed the names of certain participants who were of minor importance (through the use of pseudonyms). In most cases, these individuals were under age or subsequently quit the movement.

ACKNOWLEDGMENTS

I would like to thank Clark Murrish and Don Riestenberg for the help and guidance they gave me when I first started to infiltrate the Weatherman organization in 1969. Also my thanks to author William Craig (Enemy At The Gates) for helping Frank and me get this project started; and to Ed O'Flynn for his ideas and insights that were of significant help.

A special note of thanks to Frank's wife, Rita, and my wife, Sandi, for giving so much of their time and understanding when it was needed. I also have to single out my mother, Mary Richard, sisters and brothers, Joey and Sean Richard, Mrs. Mary Jo Nienaber and Mrs. Theresa Davis for the intimidation they endured when I was publicly accused of being a Weatherman, and also Frank H. Reagan, Sr., for his counsel and advice.

There were many others who have made many contributions and have chosen to go unnamed; to them I also wish to express my gratitude.

October 23,1975 Larry Grathwohl

Original Introduction

I pushed open the door of the small, second-class Washington, D.C hotel, stepped out onto the sidewalk, and started walking toward the Dirksen Senate Office Building on First Street. Jay Sourwine, chief counsel of the Senate Investigating Committee, was waiting there for me.

I glanced back at the hotel and smiled. The government certainly wasn't going to go broke if it put all its guests up for the night in places like that.

"It's close to our office," Sourwine had said the night before when dropping me off at the hotel. I guess it was his way of apologizing for it. "Maybe I'm being too critical," I thought to myself. After all, Sourwine had driven all the way out to Dulles Airport to meet me. And the subcommittee was giving me $25 a day for expenses, plus a round-trip air ticket from California, even though I would have been willing to pay my own way just to tell my story before the Senate group.

Guy Goodwin, Chief of Internal Security for the Justice Department, arranged for my appearance before the subcommittee headed by Senator James O. Eastland of Mississippi. Officially, the unit was named the Subcommittee to Investigate the Administration of the Internal Security Act and Other Internal Security Laws of the Committee on the Judiciary, United States Senate, Ninety-Third Congress. I was invited to appear on October 18,1974.

My testimony was to begin at 10 o'clock. I left the hotel early so that I'd have time to think as I walked over to the Dirksen Building. It was a chilly morning, but the crisp air was invigorating. It helped to wake me up. I was apprehensive. I wanted to get my thoughts straight so that the subcommittee would have the whole story. This was the first time I was telling it for the public record. My only other official appearances had been before grand juries, whose records are secret.

The subcommittee had been investigating revolutionary activities in the United States, but most of their information came from secondary sources or was only speculation. My information was firsthand. I had infiltrated one of the country's most dangerous underground revolutionary groups: the Weathermen, or Weather Underground, as they are now called. *

I know their strength, how deeply they have penetrated our society. I know how they think, how they are guiding other revolutionary groups toward their long-range goal of overthrowing the U.S. Government. I can attest to their fanatical dedication to executing this plan.

If nothing else, I wanted to impress upon the Senators how forceful this dedication is. It's the same dedication that spurs on members of the Al Fatah, the IRA, the Viet Cong, or any other internationally infamous terrorist organization. I wanted to show that these radicals are as dedicated to the violent overthrow of the government as the Senators are dedicated to reelection, yet I wanted to get these points across without sounding like an alarmist.

The facts were on my side. Each year since 1970 there have been 2000 bombings in the United States, the great majority of which are attributed to revolutionary groups, according to FBI statistics, which are supported by statements from Weathermen. Prior to the emergence of violence-prone revolutionary groups in the late 1960's, bombings were a rare form of crime.

Most of the targets are either major corporations or federal, state, and local buildings. So far, 1974 was just like the other years. Weathermen, for example, took credit for bombings in the Health, Education, and Welfare Office in San Francisco, the Los Angeles State Office Building, and the Gulf Oil Corporation offices in Pittsburgh. Gulf was attacked because the Weathermen convicted the company of committing enormous crimes against

---

*Editor's Note: The organization was originally referred to as Weatherman (singular). But the plural usage, Weathermen, then came into vogue among members. With the rise of Women's Lib in the 1970's the preferred terms are now Weather People or Weather Underground.

70 countries in the world by exploiting their people and their resources.

But Weathermen weren't alone in taking credit for bombings this year. The Americans for Justice, the Armed Revolutionary Front of Puerto Rico, the World Liberation Front, and the People's Forces had already boasted of terrorist acts in 1974. The Americans for Justice placed two pipe bombs at the Shell Oil chemical plant in San Ramon, while the New World Liberation Front attacked a subsidiary of ITT. Of course, not all bombing plans are successful. The police in Warren, Michigan prevented possible violence by uncovering a cache of 55 fire bombs. And these are just five of the 25 revolutionary groups active on a national scale. Even individuals get into the act. This year a lone revolutionary planted several bombs in Los Angeles, one of which exploded at the airport, killing three people. However, only the most dramatic acts attract national attention.

The Symbionese Liberation Army burst onto the national scene by kidnapping 19-year-old Patty Hearst of the Hearst newspaper family on February 4, 1974. This act won praise from Weatherman leader Bernardine Dohrn in letters to San Francisco newspapers. Miss Dohrn wrote, "Their action has unleashed an astonishing practical unity among people's organizations." Then, with Patty an apparent convert, the SLA robbed a bank and finally engaged in a bloody shootout with the FBI and Los Angeles police that was viewed on national television.

Six members of the SLA were killed; this spurred the Weathermen to blow up the state building in Los Angeles for revenge.

Although the SLA was first heard of when it took credit for gunning down an Oakland, California school superintendent with bullets dipped in cyanide poison in 1973, its tactics are well-known to other revolutionaries. Violence, such as kidnapping and assassination as committed by the SLA, are the common tools linking all radical groups. The Chicano Liberation Front joined the SLA in murder by killing the police chief of Union City, California. A sniper shot the chief as he left a community meeting at a church. Later the Chicano Liberation Front took credit for the assassination.

Bombings, murder, and kidnapping are recommended procedures. Any reader of The Mini-manual of the Urban Guerrilla knows that kidnapping even a nonpolitical person such as Patty Hearst has tremendous propaganda value.

As one of the Weathermen I was told to study the Mini-manual as well as Revolution in a Revolution, another handbook on terrorist tactics. And now the Weathermen have published their own handbook, Prairie Fire, a 1974 political statement from the Weather Underground.

The 186-page document is a reaffirmation of the organization's dedication to destroying the United States. The book describes their current objectives as follows: "We are communist women and men, underground in the United States for more than four years. ... Our intention is to disrupt the empire ... to incapacitate it ... to attack from the inside. ... The only path to final defeat of imperialism and the building of socialism is revolutionary war."

Weathermen predict that they will have ample opportunity to carry out these plans during this decade. They instruct readers of Prairie Fire to "organize poor and working people. Go to the neighborhoods, the schools, the social institutions, the work places. Agitate. Create struggle. ... "

Because of the numerous incidents of politically oriented violence in the United States and the obviously increased strength of various revolutionary groups, FBI Director Clarence M. Kelley called urban guerrillas and terrorists a "major threat to the internal security of the United States." In a speech in Indianapolis on October 9, 1974 he said: "The Weathermen and other guerrilla groups have openly declared war on America."

I thought of these recent developments as I walked toward the Dirksen Building. My story was important for the Senators to hear, because I could tell them how the Weathermen have built up a successful underground operation and how their network of thousands of sympathizers — including ministers, lawyers, college professors, students, community leaders — help them travel from city to city without detection. These sympathizers, some of whom are duped into helping Weathermen, but most of whom believe in the same goals, provide hiding places, money, and food. I existed in this underground. I met many of these sympathizers. Weathermen worked hard to establish this network, and that is why they are so successful in eluding capture.

Because my thoughts were so occupied with Weatherman activities, I was walking along without paying much attention to my route. At one street crossing, I almost walked off the curb into a turning taxicab. A piercing yell from the driver jarred my attention back to the present.

Once inside the lobby of the Dirksen Building, I paused a moment to brush my hair back. The wind had ruffled it. I checked my tie to be sure it was straight. I wanted to make a good impression on the subcommittee. I smiled at my appearance: shirt, tie, jacket, slacks. If the Senators had only seen me during my Weatherman days — in an old army fatigue jacket and dungarees! I pushed the elevator button.

When I reached the hearing room, Sourwine and Al Tarabochia, the committee's chief investigator, were waiting for me.

The room was impressive. It was furnished with large oak tables and chairs, the type you'd expect to find in a judicial setting. A very long table occupied the center of the room. Pads of yellow legal paper, pencils, and water pitchers were all neatly in place. A large picture of George Washington in the midst of other political leaders hung on the back wall.

Sourwine briefed me on the proceedings. Then, just before 10 o'clock, Senator Strom Thurmond of South Carolina came into the room to swear me in as a witness. I took a seat at the table and began my story.

Chapter 1

First Contact

My first contact with the Weathermen was a chance meeting on September 21, 1969 in Cincinnati, Ohio when two of them tried to recruit me "to help get the pigs in Chicago."

It was a lazy Sunday afternoon, and I had decided to go to Calhoun Street, which was about six miles across town from where I lived. When you don't have any plans, Calhoun is as good a place as any to go. It runs parallel to the University of Cincinnati campus and is crowded with bars, hamburger shops, and small restaurants. During the summer, there are always a lot of people hanging around.

I was lucky. The third car to go by my family's house picked me up. The driver was going across town, so he drove down Route 125, across the little Miami River to Columbia Parkway, and pulled the car over to the curb near the intersection of Taft and Vine to let me out. I thanked him. It was only a short walk to Calhoun.

When I reached the corner, I saw Bob Brewer talking to three other guys. I had known Brewer for years. We had put away a few beers together the previous Wednesday night.

I recognized the faces of the other three, but couldn't think of their names. I had been in at least one class with each of them last year at the University of Cincinnati.

"Welcome," Brewer said when he saw me.

"How ya doin', man?" I said.

"Surviving. Although Thursday morning I wasn't quite sure."

We both laughed and then he added, "You know everybody, don't you Larry?"

"Hell, yes. How you doin'?" I shook hands all around, and we stood there a few minutes while we filled each other in on our summer. Soon we decided to move over and sit on the steps leading up to a large church on the corner of Calhoun and Ohio streets, facing the campus and a Shell service station.

"How about those New York Mets?" someone said.

"The bastards might even beat Atlanta and go into the series."

"No way. They were lucky to get this far. The only real player they got is Seaver."

When we ran out of opinions on why the Mets were leading the league and should not have been, we drifted aimlessly into and out of other topics.

A slight breeze began blowing. I watched it move an old candy wrapper that had been lying nearby. It floated off the steps and landed gently on the sidewalk. Then the breeze nudged it over the curb and into the middle of the road. As I waited for the next move of the wrapper, I saw them: two hippies crossing the street toward us. As I watched, I reached into my pants pocket to see how much change I had. It was impossible to be on Calhoun Street and not be approached for money by at least one hippie. Some asked for half a dollar, but most settled for a quarter. A lot of them were dropouts or just loafers who found they could survive without answering to society as long as they lived near the campus.

The couple that came toward us was really odd-looking. I reached up and tapped Brewer on the arm. "Get out some coins, man. Look what's coming." The girl was tall and very thin. Her long brown hair fell below the collar of her blue blazer. She wore very tight Levi's that did nothing for her figure. A small white canvas bag hung from her shoulder. She was pale and not very attractive.

Her companion was a mean-looking guy. He was slightly shorter than she was, and he wore an old army fatigue jacket. From the looks of it, he never took it off. His Levi's were tucked into a pair of work boots. But what made him really stand out was the large hunting knife strapped to the outside of his right calf. I watched the knife come closer. The way he walked, it seemed as though he couldn't make up his mind whether to be a hippie or a Hell's Angel.

Up close the girl looked very young, about 17 or 18 years old. Her companion was about 23, but looked 40. His eyes were sunken, and his cheeks were drawn tight; he looked emaciated. But he had a cold stare that said he wouldn't be afraid to use his knife. He had a bundle of newspapers tucked under his arm and offered one as they reached the steps.

"Only a quarter," he said. I shrugged. Why not? At least this time I would be getting something for my money. He took my coins, stuffed them into his jacket pocket, and offered newspapers to the others. But they didn't want to buy any.

I glanced at the newspaper. It was tabloid size, and the front page was like a large comic strip. In bold red letters across the top was a headline: "CLASS WAR." On the bottom of the front page was the name: The Fire Next Time.

I looked up at the guy who had just sold it to me and at his girl friend. A couple of freaks, I thought. Brewer was looking over my shoulder at what I was reading.

"What is all that crap?" he said.

The guy, who was called Outlaw, ignored Brewer's remark, and asked instead, "You goin' to Chicago to help get the pigs?"

The question was directed at all of us.

"What do you mean?" I asked.

"Come on, man. Where have you been hiding? The action. The national action in Chicago." Outlaw was amazed at our ignorance of what he was talking about. He turned to his companion: "Give them a flyer, Joyce. These guys are really straight."

Joyce slipped the canvas bag off her shoulder and pulled it open. She took out some leaflets and gave one to each of us. In large letters, the leaflet headlined: "BRING THE WAR HOME."

The text called for withdrawing our troops from Vietnam, Latin America, all other foreign countries, black and brown communities, and the schools. Then, again, in large type, it read:

Chicago October 11

ALL POWER TO THE PEOPLE

After looking over the leaflet, Brewer remarked: "You're a little late, aren't you? Nixon already announced the first cutback in troops last week."

Outlaw turned on Brewer. "You believe that f—in' shit? You believe that fascist in Washington? He wants that war. He has to win to support the capitalistic pigs in Saigon. Just the same as he has to support the other capitalistic puppets in Latin America against the people. The suppressed people around the world."

Outlaw turned from Brewer and looked at me. "You like your buddy here? You dig the war, too?" I didn't know how to answer. Of course I didn't like the war. It didn't make any sense to me, but then I wasn't sure it made much more sense arguing with Outlaw. "No," I replied. "I didn't say I liked the war."

"If you're against the war, you belong in Chicago with us," Joyce said. "You have to bring the war home. We have to fight here, not in Vietnam. Our fight is against racism and suppression. Against the capitalism that makes us slaves."

"Listen to her, brothers. Right on, Joyce," Outlaw said. "We're going to Chicago. And we're going to get the pigs before they get us."

I don't know why, but I answered immediately: "If you don't go to Chicago, the pigs can't get you." They didn't get my attempt at humor. They didn't even smile. They looked as if we were to be pitied, as if we were very naive.

Then they explained. A National Youth Action was being held in Chicago, October 8 through 11, to prove to the Chicago police that they couldn't get away with the "Fascist tactics" they had used the summer before against demonstrators at the 1968 Democratic National Convention.

During that convention the New Left had organized a large demonstration in Chicago to protest the war in Vietnam. But the demonstrators ran into a confrontation with the Chicago police, who were determined to keep the convention city peaceful — at any cost or by any means. The battles between the police and demonstrators were well reported on television and in newspaper accounts. I thought the police had reacted too viciously, even though I assumed they were provoked at times. Professional policemen should be able to handle any situation, even extremely tough ones like those demonstrations.

As a result of the battles, eight activists of the New Left movement had been arrested and charged with conspiracy to incite a riot. The trial of the Chicago Eight, as the defendants were now known, was scheduled to begin in three days, on September 24, 1969.

The eight activists on trial were Rennard (Rennie) Davis and Tom Hayden, both founders of the Students for a Democratic Society; David Dellinger, editor of Liberation magazine; John Froines, an assistant chemistry professor at the University of Oregon; Abbott (Abbie) Hoffman, a founder of the Youth International Party (Yippies); Jerry Rubin, cofounder of the Yippies; Lee Weiner, a sociologist at Northwestern University; and Bobby Seale, a leader of the Black Panther Party. Soon after the trial began, however, the judge declared a mistrial for Seale, reducing the number of defendants to seven.

Outlaw and Joyce said the national youth action in October would center worldwide attention on the trial. "We'll have thousands with us in Chicago," Outlaw promised. "But this time that pig Daley and his henchmen won't get us. We'll be prepared. Last year we weren't. But this will prove to the pigs that we can organize, that we're not afraid of them. We'll prove we're ready to fight for our freedom. Even die if necessary." To die for a cause was a romantic concept. I wondered if Outlaw and Joyce had ever seen death, if they had ever witnessed real suffering.

The conversation continued, and what fascinated me most about Outlaw and Joyce was their seriousness and apparent dedication. They were young. They hated America. They couldn't have seen very much of it, yet they hated it, and their faces showed that they believed every word they said. They were complete political animals. It wasn't their words that bothered me; it was their attitude, the unflinching way they spoke of violence and open confrontation with the police.

"The time is right, man," Outlaw said. "Look what we did in Pittsburgh a couple of weeks ago."

"That was the women," Joyce interrupted. "We had 60 women marching in downtown Pittsburgh. White women supporting the black liberation struggle."

She said the group went to the South Hills High School, chanting "Ho Lives" and "Free Huey" while carrying a National Liberation Front flag. "We painted 'Vietnamese Women Carry Guns' and 'Jail Break' on the sidewalks and walls of the school. The women ran through the high school yelling 'jail break.' Eventually, 26 were arrested for inciting a riot and for assault. The whole thing was part of a guerrilla action to commemorate the death of Ho Chi Minh. He had led the Vietnamese people against the French and the United States. It was only right that we should have a guerrilla action in Pittsburgh against the racist trade unions and worthless high schools. We won in Pittsburgh, and we're going to win in Chicago."

As soon as Joyce finished, Outlaw started talking again. "You can't fight us, man. You might as well join us. We're gonna get the pigs. If we have to, we're gonna tear down the colleges and high schools. Last year was nothing compared to what is goin' to happen this year. And it's not gonna be restricted to campuses."

He told me to open the newspaper I had bought earlier. "Turn to page five, man. Right there. Look. It will give you some statistics to think about. See. There were major rebellions and insurrections even on military bases across the country. Read, man. Black GIs refusing to go to Chicago. Prisoners rioting at the Presidio stockade and at Fort Dix and Fort Riley. It's there for you to read. That's what our movement is all about. We're supporting the suppressed, no matter where they are, even if they're in the army. We'll get the GIs to turn their guns around. To f — the army. We want them to come to Chicago, too. Anybody who is against the pigs. We're gonna tear it all down. Chicago is only a start."

The more he talked, the more amazed I became. He mentioned that he was part of a group called the Weathermen. They weren't planning a demonstration in Chicago: they were planning an attack — an open, publicized assault on the Chicago police and any private property they could get near.

By now Outlaw was repeating himself. The sun was going down, and I slipped on my jacket as it started to get cooler. Outlaw seemed to sense he had lost our interest. "Look," he said. "Think about what we told you. A lot of people from Cincinnati are going to be in Chicago next month."

Then Joyce offered Brewer one of the newspapers. "Take it," she said. "We'll make it two for a quarter." She asked us to read the papers very carefully. Then she added: "Look. We're having a meeting next week. Why don't you come? It's at the Unitarian Church next Sunday. We're starting with a movie at 7 o'clock."

"You mean The Sound of Music?" Brewer interrupted. He was smiling broadly. Joyce continued as if she hadn't heard the remark. "Come to the meeting. Maybe you'll learn something."

They turned and started walking away. When they were about 15 paces from the church steps, Outlaw turned around, waved his arm at us with a clinched fist, and shouted: "Off the pigs!" Then they both disappeared around the corner.

"Think they're serious?" I asked Brewer as we watched them go. "Heavy stuff," he commented, "but they're probably high on grass. There's a lot of freaks in this area." I rolled up the newspaper I had bought and shoved it into my jacket pocket. "They're weird but scary."

"What's scary about a couple of creeps yelling revolution?"

"I was thinking about that guy who was kidnapped in Brazil a few weeks ago by a gang of terrorists." "You mean the U.S. ambassador?" "That's right. Anyway, when he was released, he said he tried to tell the terrorists who kidnapped him that there were other ways besides violence of getting their political objectives. And the terrorists said : 'F — you. Violence is the only way.'"

Brewer looked at me incredulously. "What the hell has a group of South American nuts got to do with those creeps? South America has a revolution a day. It's a way of life down there."

"That's not the point. The point is that, all through the statements they were making, they kept referring to the Third World and suppression in Latin America. If they keep thinking about South America, they might start copying some terrorist tactics."

At this point Brewer grabbed me by the arm. "You read too much," he said. "Let's go get a beer."

"Best idea you had all day."

We walked across the street and around the corner to the Scene, a small bar off Calhoun Street. We went inside and looked around, but we didn't know anyone. We sat at the bar and ordered a couple of beers.

"Working early tomorrow?" Brewer asked after he had drained off half the glass.

"Yeah. I have to go in early." I had a summer job on the loading platform at McAlpine's Department Store in downtown Cincinnati to earn money for school. As we sat at the bar talking, I took the newspaper out of my pocket and opened it up. "Did you get a good look at this before?"

Brewer glanced at the front page. It had a cartoon strip showing first the face of a character firing a machine gun while screaming: "Eat leaden death imperialistic reactionary — business administration major!" Then the bottom panel showed a bushy-haired guy slugging a pig wearing a policeman's helmet while saying, "Taste the sweetness of destiny, racist pig."

Inside, one headline read: "The Time is Right for the Violent Revolution." Another headline claimed that "The Time is Right for Fighting in the Streets."

"Look at this stuff," I said. "It's full of crap," Brewer replied. "What are you carrying it around for? Christ, I threw mine in the basket outside."

We sat quietly for awhile. Maybe Brewer was right. Maybe Outlaw and Joyce were just creeps, a couple of kooks trying to play revolutionaries. Still, something about them worried me.

I was still thinking about the encounter when I arrived at work the next morning. Monday is always a busy day on the loading ramp at McAlpine's Department Store. The work isn't challenging, but you're always busy, so the day goes by quickly. Better yet, the dock manager said he would do me a favor and let me arrange my working hours around my class schedule during the school year. It was a real break.

After work, I went home to change clothes before going to see my wife, Donna, and our two-year-old daughter, Denise. We had been separated since January. I guess we had married too early, and neither one of us was really willing to work at marriage, even though we loved each other. The whole situation was more than we could handle, and Donna had taken Denise and gone back to live with her parents. I visited them a couple of times a week.

Donna's father, Don Riestenberg, had been a policeman for many years in Cincinnati before becoming a bail bondsman. He was a strict law-and-order man who didn't have any patience with people who criticized America. He had always been more like a father to me than a father-in-law, and I respected his judgment, even if he was too conservative politically for me at times. He was a big, burly man more than six feet tall and weighed 230 pounds. I understood that he had been a hell of a good cop in his day.

When I got to the Riestenberg apartment, Don met me at the door. Donna had gone out on an errand with her mother, and after looking in on Denise, who was asleep, Don and I had a beer. He asked me what was going on, and I told him about the job and school, which meant I could help support Donna, and I told him about the meeting we had had the day before with Outlaw and Joyce. I had the newspaper in my pocket and I showed it to him. I watched the expression on his face as he flipped through the pages. First there was curiosity, then a frown. When he got to the last page, he turned the newspaper over and went through it again. Finally he looked up at me.

"Where did you get this?"

I told him Joyce and Outlaw had been selling it on the streets.

The more I told him about them the angrier he became. He went into a tirade about the permissiveness of people in authority toward radical groups at the expense of the law-abiding majority of citizens. According to Don, this was how the radicals had closed Columbia University in New York the year before. Only recently, there had been terrorist action in Columbus, Ohio, just 50 miles away, that had caused two deaths, injured 37, and caused a lot of property damage. Now it was obvious that the radicals were going to try the same thing in Cincinnati.

"What are you going to do about it, Larry?" he asked me. "You're always popping off about the apathy in this country and how it hurt you and your buddies in Vietnam."

I didn't know what to say. He was right about what I felt. I had spent seven straight months in the field with the 101st Airborne in Vietnam, most of the time under fire. My own platoon had taken more than 25 percent casualties, and I believed that a lot of my buddies wouldn't have had their arms and legs blown away or had their lives completely wasted if we had been able to fight the war properly. And the reason we hadn't been able to fight was that the Americans who stayed at home didn't support the men in the field. Many a time we had been fired at by North Vietnam troops and Viet Cong from across the Cambodian border and we hadn't been allowed to fire back — even though we were taking casualties. It had been a hell of a situation and here was Don, asking me what I was going to do about it.

Just as Don was asking me to tell my story about the meeting to some friends of his on the police force, Donna and her mother came home.

"Think it over," Don said as he left Donna and me alone in the living room. "Let me know what you decide."

Working at the department store the next morning, I kept thinking about the challenge Don had thrown at me the night before. I didn't want to have the city torn apart by radical demonstrations or the university campus closed down when I was working so hard to earn money to get an education. There was only one thing to do. During a work break I called Don and told him that I would tell what I knew to the police. Don made arrangements for me to meet two friends of his from the police force the following evening at his office. It was a warm, clear evening and, after I quit work, I decided to walk to the meeting. Somehow it didn't seem right that I was going to the police. I had had my own troubles with them as a street-wise gang member growing up in Cincinnati, and my emotions were mixed, to say the least.

Chapter 2

Cincinnati

I was born in Cincinnati on October 13, 1947. My father was a German Catholic, and my mother a Dutch Baptist. My mother is one of 13 children, and she's proud, as is all her family, of her long ties with the history of the country. Her ancestors go back to the Revolutionary War. Many nights either at home or when we visited my grandmother's farm in Somerset, Kentucky, I used to hear the stories of how the family moved westward to the Ohio area, and then how my great-grandmother came by covered wagon to Kentucky. I heard a lot about family heritage and tradition, especially from my mother. "Be proud of your heritage, Larry," she'd say, "and never be afraid to defend it."

I don't know much about my father. He left my mother and me shortly after my brother, Lee, was born, in 1949. It seems he had another wife and decided to return to her instead of staying with us and after he left, my mother, brother, and I moved in with my mother's sister and her husband. They didn't have any children and wanted to adopt my brother and me. Within two years my mother remarried. From my point of view, however, the guy she got wasn't better than the one that left. He wanted my mother to let my aunt keep both my brother and me. Finally, he agreed to let me move in, but only because my mother pleaded that, since I had a history of asthma, I needed extra attention.

That was the beginning of a bad relationship between my stepfather and me.

When I was seven, I went to St. Mary's School. I hated

11

school. Consequently by the time I was in the fifth grade, after two years in the fourth, I was a 12-year-old chain-smoking
member of a gang called the Stompers. To show how tough we
were, we wore black leather jackets, pegged pants, and ducktails,
and we kept a cigarette permanently dangling from our lips. We
got the cigarettes by swiping them from the grocery store.

Cincinnati is a hard-working, conservative city, and the people generally favor a tough line by the police. One thing was
sure, the cops kept us moving. Any time more than two of us
would stand on a street corner or in front of a store or movie
house, the cops would push us along. To avoid being hassled, our
gang used an old abandoned church on Erie Avenue as a clubhouse. A small room downstairs in the basement made an excellent headquarters. It had an old dusty sofa, a desk, and a filing
cabinet. Over the summer we discovered that we were sharing
our clubhouse with a crew of city workers, who drove their truck
around behind the church and used the main area upstairs to
eat lunch. We had seen them only once, but knew they were frequently there because of the crumpled wax paper, brown paper
bags, and empty beer cans left around.

Then one day, without warning, two policemen barged in on
our cellar. Three of us were sitting around, and these two uni-
formed cops pushed open the door and stalked into the room.
They looked rough and mean standing in front of us. Each had
his right hand clasped on the top of the .38 belted around his
waist, and each carried a nightstick in his left hand. "Line up,
punks" the shorter one growled. I was sitting on the edge of the
desk with one foot on top, and the other dangling down the side.
The taller cop moved toward me rapidly and gave me a shove
that sent me sprawling onto the floor.

"When we say move, we mean move," he snarled. I had
banged my shoulder on the dirty floor pretty hard and took
awhile to get up. "Need some help, Sonny?" the tall cop smiled
down at me. I shook my head. "Then get up against that wall
with your buddies!" The shorter cop had the two other guys
facing the wall and was frisking them.

"What did we do?" I asked.

"Shut up."

From their actions, I expected to be charged with robbing the Cincinnati National Bank. When one of the cops found a penknife in my pocket, he seemed very pleased.

"Where did you get this weapon?" "It's my Boy Scout knife," I said, trying to sound calm and tough. But I was afraid. "Don't be a wise ass," the cop said. After frisking us, they told us to turn around, but to keep our hands up behind our heads.

"We didn't do anything," I said again.

"Nobody ever does," the taller cop said. They pushed us roughly upstairs and into the back of the police car and took us to headquarters.

The ride downtown was quiet except for the constant squeal of the police radio. I couldn't imagine what we would be accused of, and I was afraid to talk with the other two guys. When the car pulled up in front of the police station, the cop on the passenger side jumped out and opened the back door.

"Come on, get your asses out of there," he commanded. We went inside and stood in front of the desk sergeant.

"We found these punks at the old church," the taller cop said.

"Are these the kids that did it?" the desk sergeant asked.

"We figured that's up to the detectives to find out," the shorter cop said. "If nothing else, they were trespassing, and one was carrying a knife."

The desk sergeant mumbled something while writing on a long log. He asked us our names, ages, and where we lived. Then he turned us over to a detective in the Juvenile Division.

The detective questioned each of us separately for about half an hour. He wanted to know how long we had been using the church. Did we know we were trespassing? Who else used it with us? Finally he said we were in trouble because more than $50,000 in damages had been dane to the building, and the new owners were filing charges. He accused us of stealing the pews, doors, brass knobs, fixtures, and lumber that were in the building. I denied it. I told him we used only the basement office.

He wrote a lot of things down in a notebook. Then he said I could call my parents. Since I was only 12, I could be released in their custody. But he said we would have to go before a juvenile court judge the following week. My mother came down to the police station to get me.

We were scheduled to appear in juvenile court the following Tuesday. Fortunately, my mother proved to be a better detective than the cops. An old friend of hers who lived near the church told my mother that she had seen men carry lumber and things out of the church aver a period of a month or so and put them into a city truck. She volunteered to tell the police the same story, but we had to go before the Juvenile Court judge, anyway. The woman testified on our behalf, and the judge agreed to drop the charges, but warned us to stay out of the church and out of trouble.

Despite the judge's warning, I didn't quit the gang. In fact, we stayed together through high school, although we did change our names to the Trojans. Along the way we got into a couple of rumbles in the schoolyard. But in the fall of 1963, we went to a dance at Purcell High School, the all-boys Catholic school that I attended. Girls from other schools were invited to attend our dances, and there I met Donna Riestenberg. Donna was a very pretty brunette. I got mad when someone else asked her to dance, but I didn't get into a fight. I even walked her home.

I began seeing her as much as possible. Meeting Donna was the only thing I liked about high school. I hated most classes, except history. Starting with the Revolutionary War, I read as much as I could. I read The Federalist papers and even the Constitution, but I really devoured biographies, Lafayette in particular. It amazed me that a French nobleman would voluntarily risk his life to help a country fight for its independence. I even read The Communist Manifesto, and I tried Das Kapital, but got bogged down.

I saw Donna frequently during the school years. She was always arguing with me to quit the Trojans, and when another guy from the neighborhood who was about 19 was arrested, she made a point of giving me all the details. He had been shot by the police while running from the back of a supermarket he had broken into. "You're going to end up the same way," she warned.

The incident made me decide to quit school and join the army. I had to get away from Cincinnati, get away from trouble. But I didn't tell my mother until July. At first she didn't believe me.

Then, when I kept insisting on it, she was totally opposed to the idea, even though I would be 17 in October and, with her permission, I could sign up legally. However, I had an unexpected ally. My stepfather argued on my side. "The school can't handle him, so we might as well let the army do it. They might straighten him out." This made my mother cry. But finally she agreed to sign the papers for me after I promised to finish high school in the service. I turned 17 on October 13, 1964 and enlisted on October 19.

Ever since my uncle had given me his World War II army jacket with its patches from the Screaming Eagles paratrooper unit, I had been determined to jump out of airplanes. I guess it sounds strange, but that was what I wanted to do. One of the forms the recruiting sergeant gave me asked for the three branches of the army I preferred. I put 101st Airborne on all three lines and underscored them. I even wrote on the side of the column: "This is my only choice."

Either I got lucky or the person making assignments actually read the application. I got my wish. After basic training, I was assigned to Fort Benning, Georgia for paratroop training and later was assigned to the 101st Airborne. In March of 1965, I made my first jump. It was easy. I followed the leader out of the door without giving it much thought. But on the second jump, I was scared. I had time to ask myself, "What the hell am I doing jumping out of airplanes?" But the $60 a month extra pay for hazardous duty came in handy. And when I got my wings, I was very proud.

During the time I enlisted in the army, went through advanced individual training at Fort Knox, and graduated from jump school, President Johnson began sending more troops into Vietnam. During training it was instilled in us that we were the best fighting force in the world: the best trained, the best fed, the best equipped. We could overcome anybody. With the Vietnam War escalating we knew it was only a matter of time before our unit would be sent to Asia.

I believed that what we were doing was right, but many people didn't. Demonstrations against the war were starting and in April, while I was at Fort Campbell, the Students for a Democratic Society (SDS) organized the first anti-war march in Washington. It drew 15,000 student protestors. It didn't make much difference for me. By June I was in the jungles of Vietnam.

Up to that point, all I knew about war were the stories told by my uncle, the books I had read, or movies in which John Wayne defeated entire divisions of enemy soldiers all by himself. War almost seemed romantic. But once I was in the jungle, I learned that war becomes very personal. The moment I saw a guy get his arm and leg blown off war became a living horror, a nightmare of violence. And it kept up month after month.

I wrote home to Donna whenever I could. She became my link with reality. When I finished my tour in Vietnam, to become a drill instructor at Fort Knox, Donna and I were married. Our daughter, Denise, was born eleven months later, and I extended my tour of duty so that I could finish high school and prepare for college.

I took my duties as drill instructor seriously. No matter how much I hated war or was horrified by it, it was my duty to teach every recruit how to survive what he was going to face in Vietnam. I guess I was a typical DI: hair cut close, boots spit-shined, khakis creased razor sharp, my walk erect. I was part of the army and the army had kept me alive. I might not like its regimentation, but I would follow it.

It was during this time that I was accepted for the fall 1968 term at the University of Cincinnati. I received my discharge and set out to be a freshman in another unreal world.

What strange patterns life takes, I was thinking as I walked into Don's office to meet the police. It was a storefront office, diagonally across from the city and county courthouses; the police station was directly across the street. All the lights were on. The front part had two desks for secretaries, long gone home now, and their typewriters were covered. Large filing cabinets lined the back walls and framed the door leading into Don's office. It was a pretty drab place. But then a man who needs bail money isn't looking for elegant surroundings.

Don was on the phone and he motioned for me to sit down. Before he finished talking, two policemen came in and also sat down. Then Don hung up, introduced us, and I went through my story again. They listened carefully, then questioned me at length. I stressed how worried I was by the total commitment to violence that Joyce and Outlaw had displayed. They seemed to understand.

The meeting lasted for slightly more than an hour. Finished, the cops thanked me and asked if I would meet someone from the police intelligence division the next night. I agreed.

The next night after work, I went to the city hall, where the intelligence division was located, to tell my story to Detective Sgt. Jerry Berry. As it turned out, Berry wasn't as cordial as the other two policemen. During the next 45 minutes, he spent almost all of the time telling me how much he knew about radical activities in Cincinnati. But after awhile I got the impression that he really didn't know much about this new group that called itself the Weathermen. He showed me a lot of photographs, but I couldn't identify anybody. I had met only two of them. Before I left his office, Berry did ask me if I was going to attend the meeting at the Unitarian Church. I said I didn't know. "If you do, give me a full report." That was all.

I then stopped by Don's office to tell him what happened. After hearing my report, Don insisted that Berry really wanted my help, but couldn't come right out and ask me for it. Don interpreted Berry's remarks as proof that he could use any information I could supply. And since Don had known Berry for years, I had to assume Don knew what he was talking about.

Then Don threw me a question that had the hook in it. "Well, are you going to go to the meeting for Berry?"

I said I wasn't sure I wanted to become a police informer. I had enough problems without getting involved in a police matter. Besides, I argued it could easily become very complex. If I got involved, I would have to see it through. That's the way I am. Besides, I said, "I can't afford the time or money to run around chasing radicals."

Don was furious. He said I had always condemned public apathy to him and now I was just like all the other big talkers: I wouldn't back up my convictions. "If you're worried about Donna and the baby," he said, "forget it. I'll take care of them."

I had never seen Don so serious. He was committing himself

to help me and Donna if I would help the police. It was quite a challenge he was throwing in my face. All I could do was promise that I'd think it over.

During the next week, the subject of the meeting was rarely out of my mind. I found my curiosity aroused. So when I next visited Donna, I told Don I would go. I guessed that the least I could do was go to this one session and find out what was going on.

I arrived at the Unitarian Church, a new brick building on Clifton Street, a little after 6 o'clock on Sunday evening. I climbed the few steps leading up to the front door and stepped into a wide vestibule that led directly into the main section of the church. It was much darker inside than out, but I noticed a light shining up from the bottom of a staircase on the left. I looked around for another moment to make sure it was the only light on, then walked over and down the staircase.

Two guys in blue jeans, old shirts, and boots were standing at the bottom. One had his foot on the last step while leaning against the railing. The other guy was slouched against the wall. They were both about 22 years old. At first I expected them to give me some trouble. They were talking quietly, but stopped when they saw me coming down the stairs. The guy leaning against the railing stood up straight.

"How ya doing?" I said raising my hand in front of me. The guy slouched against the wall, while the other fellow asked, "You lookin' for the meetin'?"

"Right."

"Down the hall. Last classroom on the right."

That was all either said. They let me pass. As I walked down the hallway, I thought they were very poor security men, but I guessed they didn't really care.

On either side of the corridor the rooms were dark and empty, but as I approached the last one, I could see a faint light and hear sounds. I opened the door and walked into a revolution on film. A movie screen in front of the room was filled with people screaming and running down the streets, while other guys were running around with machine guns and bombs.

The movie was the Battle of Algiers. I later learned that it had become a recruiting film for revolutionary groups, and it served its purpose very well. While watching it, you had sympathy for the rebels.

After my eyes became accustomed to the dark, I counted 20 people in the room, including myself. Some were sitting on folding chairs, others on the floor. I recognized Joyce (her last name, I later learned, was Green) sitting on the floor up front, but I didn't see Outlaw.

The movie ended, and a guy standing next to the projector snapped on the lights. He was older than the others, probably 28 or 29, and he was big, about six-one, and husky.

As soon as the lights went on, an attractive girl of about 21 got up from a chair and took a teacher's position in front of the classroom. She was wearing tight blue jeans and a denim shirt without any bra. Her name was Karen Ashley, and she began speaking softly, distinctly.

"What you just saw can happen anywhere," she said, pointing to the screen behind her. She paused for effect, then repeated, "It can happen anywhere, even in the U.S."

She looked around the room. The two guys who had been standing in the stairwell when I arrived came into the room and stood along the wall in back.

"That movie is what we're all about," Karen continued. "The French were defeated in Algeria because a small group of revolutionaries had the courage to stand up to the mother country. We have the same courage, and we're going to demonstrate it in Chicago." She became more vehement, more fiery. "We're building an international Liberation Army in America. We support the struggle of the Vietnamese, the Uruguayans, the Rhodesians, the Blacks — All Third-World people who are fighting against U.S. imperialism. We'll join this fight in Chicago. Eight political prisoners are on trial there, and we want them freed. Now. Chicago will be the beginning of a violent revolution."

She paused. Her voice was at a high but controlled crescendo. "A revolution we're going to win." She talked about ten minutes more, then turned the floor over to Rebel Callahan. He was dressed like the others. Blue jeans and old shirts were almost a uniform, a conformity in dress among nonconformists.

Rebel sauntered to the middle of the floor with both hands stuck in his back pockets. It was obvious that he had conducted many meetings before. He had a casual air about him that exuded confidence.

After looking over the audience for a moment, he began: "Okay, you want to know who we are. Who the Weathermen are. I'm here to tell you. We're communists and we dig it." He pronounced the word "communists" slowly and distinctly, pausing to let the meaning take effect. Then he began again: "Communists with a small 'c'. We're not part of the old Communist Party of America. We take orders from nobody, but we support the Third-World people's fight against U.S. imperialism. We support the people." His voice rose on this last phrase, then tapered off again. "We are activists. Young activists. Young because it's up to the youth of America to begin the revolution. We're going to bring down this imperialistic country." Now his voice was at a high pitch as he looked around the room. "It's up to us," he said, pointing at each of us. "Us. The Youth. Not just the college youth. All youth. High school students. Army draftees who don't want to get killed in Vietnam for a lot of fat imperialistic businessmen. The working youth. This is our struggle. All of us. We're the ones who have to change the country. As you can see, Chicago is a national action for all youth and not just college students. We expect many people from the army to be there. We want them to turn their guns around, turn them against the system that's sending them to their deaths. And it's happening. In June, 250 prisoners at Fort Dix revolted, and in July, 584 prisoners at Fort Riley took over the compound for seven hours, ransacking, destroying, defying the pig officers who tried to stop them. These prisoners were aware. Most of them were political prisoners. Young men who didn't want to rush off to Vietnam to die for the capitalists. Many soldiers will join us. The working youth will join us. We will win. We will show the pigs in Chicago that we're prepared to fight."

I was amazed at how skillfully Rebel was using his hands to punctuate sentences and how he let his voice rise and fall for emphasis. He was only my age, but he was a professional agitator. The scene was like a movie about Germany in the early 1930s.

It was frightening. They were determined to cause violence. If these guys ever got a hold of weapons, I thought, they might kill somebody.

Rebel closed his speech by quoting Lin Piao, who said Third-World nationalist revolutions will play a decisive role in the destruction of U.S. imperialism. Then he praised Che Guevara and the violent actions of the Tupamaros in South America, as well as the Viet Cong. He finished by asking us all to attend a rally the next Sunday, October 5, at 10 A.M. at Eden Park. "This rally is extremely important if you're going to Chicago."

After Rebel finished, we broke into small groups to talk with individual Weathermen. I met the two guys who had been standing at the door, Barry Stein and Bill Milton. It turned out that none of the Weathermen at the meeting were from Cincinnati, although they were living here temporarily. Since they all seemed to take orders from the older guy who was leaning against the front wall, I went over to talk with him. He was Gerry Long. I introduced myself.

"I'm glad you could come to the meeting," he said.

Long asked me a few questions about myself. He seemed interested when I told him I was a Vietnam veteran. He wanted to talk about the war and politics. He was very articulate. He talked about the revolution and the need to "raise the level of struggle."

I asked Long about the Weatherman organization. He was one of 11 members of Students for a Democratic Society (SDS) who had written and signed a 16,000-word statement called, "You Don't Need a Weatherman to Know Which Way the Wind Blows," presented during the SDS National Convention in Chicago June 18-22, 1969. It was a call to arms by the more radical members of the SDS. And it defined the radical group's goal as "the destruction of U.S. imperialism and the achievement of a classless world: world communism."[*]

As I learned later, the document had been written to force SDS to take a more violent stand to achieve its goal of social-

---

[*]Karen Ashley, who spoke earlier, also signed this document, as did Bill Ayers, Bernardine Dohrn, John Jacobs, Jeff Jones, Howie Machtinger, Jim Mellen, Terry Robbins, Mark Rudd, and Steve Tappis.

ism in the U.S. It worked. The SDS split into various groups, with the Revolutionary Youth Movement I (RYM I) and Revolutionary Youth Movement II (RYM II) coming out on top. RYM I became known as the Weathermen because of the title of their document. The Weatherman group supported violent action, predicting that a continuing show of violence against the establishment would create a revolutionary awareness among the American people, who would then turn against the government. The RYM II group claimed violence alienated workers, thereby turning them against the movement before they could be indoctrinated to join the struggle. The RYM II advocated nonviolent activity to gain mass support. The Weathermen quickly labeled RYM II the "Running Dogs." The two facets of SDS went separate ways, but only after joining forces long enough to get the Progressive Labor faction expelled from SDS. Both Weathermen and RYM II were angered at Progressive Labor because it did not support the black liberation movement to their satisfaction. Other charges against Progressive Labor were that it had called Ho Chi Minh a traitor and that it had refused to support the National Liberation Front in Vietnam.

These confrontations effectively destroyed the SDS, a group originally formed in 1960 by young radical intellectuals and which by the mid-60s had a national membership of around 100,000. But when the convention broke up on June 22, 1969, SDS was dead.[†] In its place stood the Weathermen, a group hell-bent on violent action. The first task Weathermen assigned itself was to be sure that there would be violence at the National Youth Action-referred to by the Weathermen simply as the National Action-scheduled for Chicago October 8 through 11.

This is what had brought Gerry Long to Cincinnati. He was a member of the Weather Bureau, the national council that directed Weatherman activities. He was checking on the Weathermen in Cincinnati, and he was also supervising activities that were becoming increasingly important as the National Action drew near.

As I was rapping with Long, Barry Stein joined the conversation. He asked me if I was going to Chicago. I said I wanted to,

---

[†]It still exists on some college campuses, but not as a national organization.

but was afraid to take time off from my job.

"I really need the bread, man," I told Long. "We understand," Stein said, "but, hell, don't miss the action. We're going to tear into those f—ing pigs."

Long looked over at Stein. "They're already tearing into the pigs in Wisconsin," he said. There was a trace of a smile on his face. Only two days earlier someone had placed a bomb in the Federal Building in Milwaukee, blowing out parts of the first and second floors. The same day, another bomb exploded at the National Guard Armory in Madison. Nobody was hurt in either explosion, but a lot of damage was done.

Long and Stein talked about the bombings casually. They obviously were very pleased with the action, but it was clear they didn't want to say too much in front of me.

The meeting began to break up. As it did, Joyce Green came over. "Hello," I said. She nodded her head in recognition. "Where's Outlaw?" I asked. She looked at Long and then Stein as if searching for an answer. Then she said, "He's not with us anymore." I got the feeling I shouldn't ask any questions, so I just shrugged and said, "Too bad." She didn't answer. Stein brought the conversation back to Chicago. He asked me not to make any decision until after the rally next Sunday. I agreed.

Since the room was almost empty now, I decided to leave, too.

Once outside, I walked down Clifton Street thinking about the meeting. It had been a weird night, frightening. These people are crazy, I thought. They believe they can blow up the country. How many Weathermen were there? How many in Cincinnati? How many in other cities? How did they get money to live, to travel? The ones I'd met so far didn't seem to worry about money. Apparently most of them were college graduates, but they didn't seem to have jobs. Yet they were free to move around, and everything they did was politically motivated. I couldn't answer my own questions, but I sure was curious.

During the week, I called Sergeant Berry three times before I reached him. He apologized for not returning my calls but I could tell he wasn't sincere. As usual, Berry listened to my description of the meeting without much response. He did express interest in the Eden Park Rally and ended our conversation with the comment, "If you go, give me a report."

Chapter 3

The National Action

Eden Park is a large green area in Walnut Hills, a lower-income black neighborhood. The rally was held near the reservoir at the highest part of the park. From there you look over the Ohio River and across into Kentucky. It's a beautiful, peaceful place. But on Sunday, October 5, 1969 it was turned into a training site for a group of rebels.

I got there about 9:45 A.M. About 15 people were already there when I arrived. I recognized most of them; they had attended the meeting the week before. I sat down on the grass next to a guy named Mark Stivic. The morning dew had already been burned off the grass, and it promised to be a nice day. Stivic was a Vietnam vet, and we talked about the war. He hated Asia, he hated the war, and he hated the United States because of the war.

"This group," he said, referring to the Weathermen, "is where it's at. They'll stick it to this f—ing country."

About 15 minutes later, two cars pulled off onto a nearby dirt work road and parked. Gerry Long got out of the driver's side of the first car. I recognized most of the others as Weathermen who'd been at the church, but there were also three guys I'd never seen before.

Long greeted everybody as soon as he reached us. Then he started the meeting. He was very businesslike, very professional. He sat us in a semicircle in front of him. The three people that I hadn't seen before sat on the outer edge of the semicircle.

Long made a few preliminary remarks about the importance of the National Action in Chicago then told us to line up an arm's length apart for exercises.

I looked around at the others, but they all got up and moved into position.

Long led the exercises. We began with jumping jacks, moved into deep knee bends, touched our toes a few times, and then did some sit-ups and push-ups. Between exercises, Long reminded us that the pigs were fat and out of shape, and we had to be better prepared than they were. Long was probably right. But one exercise session wasn't going to whip them into shape to take on the Chicago police.

After 15 minutes of working up a sweat, Long cut off the exercises and gathered us in front of him again. I was perspiring and breathing pretty heavily. I hadn't worked out like that in quite some time. I flopped down on the grass and leaned back on my elbows. The next part of the program was a karate demonstration. One of the three strangers I'd seen getting out of the cars took over this part of the meeting. The guy made a short speech about karate being an aggressive form of the martial arts, although he stated that most people who practice it in the United States use it defensively. This seemed to annoy him."To get the best results, you have to be aggressive," he said.

He demonstrated the basic karate punch and kick and body position. He told us to stand with our legs a shoulder-width apart, with our right foot back, our knees bent slightly, our backs straight. The toes of both feet should be pointed straight ahead. Then he demonstrated the proper way to make a fist. You open your hand wide and close it starting from the top of your fingers. This formed a tight, hard fist. Once this was accomplished, he told us to bring our right fist up under our arm-pits, close to the body, and to hold the left fist out in front of your eyes. In a fight our arms would move back and forth "as powerful pistons." We had to follow the instructor through the basic positions. The only reason I could think of for this 20-minute karate demonstration was to help build confidence in everybody at the rally. It gave the impression of a well-organized movement.

Then Long took over again. "I want everybody to pay close

attention to our next two guests," he said. "Make mental notes of everything they say. It could save your life, or keep you out of jail next week."

Long had a flair for dramatic statements.

The first person Long introduced was a young lawyer. He seemed to be about Long's age, 28 or 29. He was fairly tall, but thin. His hair was cut shorter than that of most of the people in the group. Unlike the others who were wearing the customary blue jeans, old shirts, and engineer boots, the lawyer was dressed as if ready to play touch football with his fraternity brothers in sweat shirt, brown slacks, sneakers. He didn't advocate violence or editorialize on the National Action. He just stated legal facts. First, he emphasized the consequences of striking, or even shoving, a cop. In Illinois, just touching a cop could be grounds for an aggravated battery charge, which was a felony. He said this was the charge we all had to be prepared to face. Then he went on to explain what would happen if we were arrested. The usual procedure is for the cop to take the person arrested to the nearest precinct. Here, the person is fingerprinted. Then the police records are checked to see if there are any other warrants out for the individual. If there aren't any existing warrants, and the charge is only one such as disorderly conduct, mob action, or resisting arrest — each a misdemeanor — bail can be set immediately. This usually ranges between $150 and $350, he told us. If the person has cash, he can go free. However, he explained that a felony arrest requires a bail hearing before a judge. He stressed the importance of calling a lawyer to help us through any bail hearing.

"A legal staff will be on call in Chicago 24 hours a day," he said. "Use them if you have to." He said we would all be given special telephone numbers so we could contact legal help when we arrived in Chicago. He gave a short course in riot law, but the most important thing seemed to be memorizing the phone numbers for the attorneys.

After the lawyer, Long introduced a young doctor. He was dressed like the lawyer. Before he began speaking, he took a small notebook from his back pocket and opened it. He sounded like a professor lecturing his class. According to the doctor, our biggest problem in Chicago would come from the gas used by the police. This could be tear gas, nausea gas, blister gas, or Mace. He said we should expect a gas attack and be prepared to react to it for our own protection.

The doctor pointed out that many people believe that vaseline can prevent gas burns. "But it doesn't work," he said. "In fact, if you use vaseline and the police use Mace, it can be even worse." As preventive measures for a gas attack by the police, the doctor suggested wearing heavy clothing and a good gas mask, "not a cheap one that will only trap the gas inside." If gassed, we should use mineral oil or alcohol to wipe off the gas. Water would work if used abundantly, he said. "But a little water only makes it worse."

Although the doctor was droning on in a monotone voice, he had everybody's attention. I'm sure there wasn't anyone in the group who hadn't seen newspaper photographs or television reports of police tear-gassing a group of rioters. And since this is what we'd be facing in Chicago, the doctor's message was very practical.

After discussing gas attacks, the doctor turned to other types of injuries. He began with head wounds. "Most scalp wounds bleed a lot, and consequently they look worse than they really are. If you or someone near you has a head wound that is bleeding profusely, don't panic. To stop the bleeding put pressure on the wound with a clean bandage or piece of cloth." He cautioned that all head wounds should be X-rayed at a hospital.

Then the doctor talked about bullet wounds. This was enough to scare me away from Chicago. "Never try to remove a bullet yourself," he cautioned us. "Treat bullet wounds as you would any bleeding injury. Apply pressure to the wound with a clean bandage. Then get the injured person to a hospital as fast as you can." He then went into treating chest wounds as well as stomach wounds.

The doctor was trying to give us a crash course in street medicine. It was ludicrous, and I'm sure he knew it. But on the other hand, I guess he figured that if one tip saved someone's life, this session would be worth it. He stressed over and over that we should only apply enough first aid necessary to get the injured to a hospital.

When the doctor finished, he asked if there were any questions. He got several about gunshot wounds, and somebody asked him to go over the gas protection suggestions.

The doctor finally sat down, and Long took over the meeting again. He thanked the lawyer and doctor for their participation. After he did, the two got up and left the meeting. I watched them until they disappeared around the first bend in the road. I wondered why they had become involved with the Weathermen. They obviously had excellent futures. In a few years they would have everything the people at the rally were rejecting, including money and position in society. It was a really curious situation.

As I was thinking about the lawyer and doctor, Long was reviewing the major points made by both. He stressed that medical assistance teams would be on patrol in the demonstration areas and that lawyers would be on call 24 hours a day. "We expect to have casualties. We expect arrests. But this is necessary." He said that if any of us were injured seriously enough to require hospital treatment, we should treat the pigs at the hospital arrogantly. He said all we were required to do was give our name and address. "Don't tell the doctors anything," he said. "They'll record it, and these records could be used in court against us."

However, he noted that we had one advantage. We were white. "And, so far the pigs haven't been as tough on the whites as they have on blacks."

Then he turned his talk back to motivation and the reasons for the action. "We're going to Chicago to win," he said. "This is the first of many battles. But we can win. The same way the Viet Cong are beating back a half million U.S. troops without the aid of vast technical resources. The Viet Cong have determination and a few simple weapons. And the blacks in this country are battling the same heavy odds that the Viet Cong are. And the blacks will win. We are going to help them win. Our fight is against this capitalistic pig society that is invading Vietnam with its powerful military machine while suppressing blacks at home."

Next, Long stressed the importance of generating the proper publicity from the Chicago action. "This can be a very effective propaganda weapon for us," he said. "We have to keep in mind that everything we do has to be done for the political good of the movement." He said we had to weigh all situations carefully before acting. For example, if we were being busted on a minor charge, we should go peacefully unless there was a crowd around to witness our resistance. And he cautioned us not to harass the pigs if nobody else was around. This would only result in a bust that would serve no purpose. He said that newsmen made the best witnesses for the movement. "If there are newsmen around with cameras, fight all busts," Long stressed. "For the most part, news photos, especially on television, will favor us. Get the pigs to strike back at you; we need the sympathy of the people. And nothing outrages the people as much as seeing the pigs slash at college kids who are just trying to hold a peaceful demonstration."

Long was clear and precise on the value of propaganda. If nothing else, he was determined to capture headlines in Chicago.

After the propaganda lesson, Long went through a checklist of things to bring with us and some things we definitely should leave home. If we went to Chicago by car, he advised us to park it as soon as we got there and leave it alone. "We don't want to be stopped by the pigs unless it fits into our plans. Use public transportation."

Next he told all of us to get a tetanus shot. He said the tetanus shot would help protect us against lockjaw, which was a common result of head injuries. He asked us to buy a helmet, either a motorcycle or army surplus model. If we wore glasses they should be shatterproof and taped to our heads so they wouldn't fall off easily. Contact lenses were out. "And don't be foolish enough to show up in sandals," he snapped. "You need boots or shoes with reinforced tips. And wear heavy protective clothing."

He told us to bring clubs, but no knives or scissors. And most important: "Bring money. As much money as you can. We'll all need it for bail. If you don't use it, a brother or sister will." Money was also essential so that we wouldn't be busted on a vagrancy charge. Then Long cautioned us about Chicago's curfew laws. Everybody under 18 had to be off the streets by 10:30 P.M. on week nights and by 11 P.M. on Friday and Saturday nights.

"Have sufficient identification," he said. "Don't give the pigs an excuse for busting you just because you can't prove your age. Even if you look well over 18, be prepared to prove it. If you can't, the pigs sure as hell will bust you. They'll use any excuse they can to keep us off the streets at night."

As a last note, Long warned us not to bring any grass to Chicago. "If one brother or sister in a group is found with grass, the pigs will bust everybody in the group, which will keep you out of action. No grass. Leave it home."

The sun was beating down on us. I was getting hungry, but nobody mentioned anything about a lunch break. In fact, while I was thinking about my stomach, Long called for another exercise session. This time we incorporated the karate movements we had learned earlier into the program of jumping jacks, sit-ups, and push-ups.

After this round of calisthenics, we had a few more political speeches. But most of it was rhetoric I'd heard before. Barry Stein reemphasized the need for "bringing the war home," and how the "Red Army" will march in Chicago beginning on Wednesday. Rebel Callahan promised that several thousand demonstrators from all over the country would be in Chicago. When these speeches were finished, we broke up into small groups for more political discussion.

About 2 o'clock the meeting disbanded. Long offered to drive me back to the Clifton area. I accepted. All the talk in the car centered on Chicago. I told them I would try to make it, at least for a day. This pleased them, although I had no intention of going. Berry's request to report on the meeting didn't include getting clobbered in some violent confrontation at Chicago, and I wasn't about to volunteer. When we got back to Clifton, Long pulled the car over to let me out near Calhoun Street. He was living with the rest of the Weathermen in a house on Hollister Street, but they didn't invite me to go with them.

I stood on the sidewalk and watched them drive away. They really are fanatics, I thought. Will the Chicago police be ready for what they're planning?

The attack on Chicago was scheduled to begin on Wednesday, October 8. But some of the Weathermen couldn't wait. Late Monday night, when most of Chicago was trying to sleep, an explosion rocked Haymarket Square. A ten-foot-high statue commemorating seven Chicago policemen killed by a bomb blast during a labor riot in 1886 was dynamited. When the dust settled the nation's most famous police monument lay scattered in a thousand pieces around the park. I could picture Gerry Long and Barry Stein allowing themselves a smile when they heard about the bombing. The Weathermen had to be gaining credibility as a revolutionary movement.

The bombing certainly generated response from the establishment. First Mayor Daley declared it an "attack on all citizens of Chicago." Then Sergeant Richard M. Barrett, president of Chicago's Police Sergeants Association, was quoted in the newspapers as saying the dynamiting was "an obvious declaration of war" on the police by the young radicals. Lieutenant O'Neill called for the citizens of Chicago and the nation to "wake up" to the true nature of these radicals. "We're not dealing with a group of harmless kids armed with firecrackers," he said. He was right, but as I read the lieutenant's remarks, I wondered if he really knew how dedicated to urban guerrilla activity the Weathermen were.

As it turned out, blowing up the statue was only a mild introduction to the week's events. At 8 P.M. on Wednesday, 400 Weathermen gathered in Lincoln Park to honor "Heroic Guerrillas" from all Third-World countries. Two of these guerrillas singled out for special praise were Che Guevara, who was "murdered by CIA pigs in Bolivia," and Nguyen Van Troi, a Vietnamese who was hanged after he tried to assassinate Defense Secretary McNamara in Vietnam in 1964.

Around 10 P.M., the Weathermen marched from Lincoln Park. The helmeted mob moved down Clark Street carrying clubs, bats, bricks, and Viet Cong flags on the way to the wealthy Lake Shore Drive section of the city. As the mob passed the North Federal Savings and Loan Bank, someone hurled a brick through the window.

The sound of glass shattering sent the mob running through the streets smashing windows and busting up cars. In some cases, private homes were attacked because they belonged to the wealthy capitalistic establishment. A Rolls Royce was destroyed; when another man came out to protect his Cadillac, he was beaten to the ground.

As the mob ran on, a line of police formed at State and Division streets to stop the rampage. Without hesitation, the Weathermen ran right into them, swinging clubs and fists. As the police fought to control the attack, many of the demonstrators turned and ran down other streets toward Lake Shore Drive. On the way, they armed themselves by picking up bricks and wooden planks from a nearby construction site. More police arrived, and the fight continued. At one point, a cop shot one of two demonstrators who had jumped him. But the battle continued under the rallying cry, "Tear the f—ing state down!"

Police swarmed into the area, cutting off side streets in an attempt to contain the mob. By midnight, they had succeeded. One hundred were arrested, and dozens were injured, while 21 policemen needed hospital treatment. The area was filled with shattered glass and ruined automobiles. The next day the battles were headlined in the Chicago newspapers, while the newswires and television told the story to the rest of the nation. I knew Gerry Long would be pleased with the coverage and delighted with a statement by Stephen Zicher, an assistant corporation counsel in Chicago: "We didn't expect this kind of violence. In the past, there was always a big difference between what the young radicals said and what they actually did."

While the citizens of Chicago were reading about the riots in either The Tribune or The Sun-Times, the Weathermen were gathering at Grant Park. This time the focus of attention was the women's militia. Bernardine Dohrn, a graduate of Chicago Law School, a founder of the Weathermen, and a member of the controlling Weather Bureau, began a short speech by saying: "We are born in 1969 in America behind enemy lines." An hour later, Miss Dohrn and ten other women were arrested for assaulting policemen who were standing in their line of march.

At noon, the Weathermen joined RYM II, the Young Lords, and the Black Panthers in a demonstration in front of the federal courthouse where the Chicago Eight trial was taking place. Three of the demonstrators held a large banner that demanded the immediate release of Bobby Seale, chairman of the Black Panther party, who was one of the eight on trial for conspiracy. Another demonstrator held a sign that read: "Racist Pig Daley, Stop Racist Raids."

Following the courthouse rally, several hundred demonstrators went to the International Harvester Plant to join workers who had gone on strike that morning. The Weathermen's plan to invade high schools that afternoon was cancelled because of the number of police assigned to the schools as guards. According to the Weathermen, the high schools were "prisons, and prisons must be liberated."

Thursday afternoon, Illinois Governor Richard B. Ogilvie announced that he was sending 2500 National Guardsmen to Chicago. Weatherman activity also received criticism from an ally. Fred Hampton, a leader of the Black Panther party in Illinois, publicly condemned Wednesday night's violence. When I read this, I wondered how Gerry Long and the other Weathermen reacted. My guess was that they shrugged it off, saying that Hampton didn't know how to create a revolution.

In an attempt to prevent further bloodshed, the police tried to round up Weathermen who were wanted for Wednesday's demonstration. They arrested 43 in a raid on the Covenant Church. Others attending the meeting escaped from the police. But one news story, more than anything else I read about the violence, reflected Weathermen hatred for the establishment. A police undercover agent talked his way into a Weatherman meeting at the Emmanuel Methodist Church early Friday morning. But once inside, he was recognized by a demonstrator who had been arrested Wednesday night. As soon as the agent was identified, he was punched and kicked to the floor. According to the article, which had a banner headline in The Chicago Tribune, the pastor of the church arrived in time to prevent continued beating of the cop. After the pastor stopped the assault, two Weathermen carried the cop out of the building and threw him into the street. Then all of them split. The pastor called an ambulance, and the cop was taken to the hospital in critical condition.

On Saturday, the Weathermen met at noon in front of the

blown-up police monument in Haymarket Square. Jeff Jones, a member of the Weather Bureau, led this rally. When about 300 Weathermen gathered, they marched from the square to Randolph Street and then onto La Salle. Suddenly, someone screamed, "Break!" The orderly demonstration turned into another mob action. The Weathermen charged down Madison, smashing windows and fighting police. A cop was thrown through a Railway Express office window. Shortly after that, Assistant Corporation Counsel Richard Elrod was knocked to the ground by a group of Weathermen, then kicked in the head and back. He was rescued by police and rushed to the hospital with a broken neck. In addition to the street fighting both the local air force and navy recruiting stations were fire-bombed.

As the Weathermen battled the police, 2500 other demonstrators, including RYM II, the Young Lords, and the Black Panthers, marched five miles from People's Park to Humboldt Park on the west side in honor of Manuel Campos, a slain Puerto Rican independence leader.

By Saturday night, at least $1 million in property damage was reported to the police, three demonstrators had been shot, one city official lay paralyzed, 250 Weathermen had been arrested on charges including felony and attempted murder, and 57 policemen were hospitalized, at least one critically.

Three weeks earlier, Sergeant Berry had asked me a question: "Do you think the Weathermen are serious?" He had his answer.

And this, according to the Weathermen's own statements, was only a beginning.

Chapter 4

The FBI Connection

By Friday, October 17, I was sure the country had forgotten the incidents in Chicago. The New York Mets had won the World Series. Who had time to worry about a group of young radicals? I had a few beers at the Scene that night, and most of the talk was about the Mets. I was looking for Brewer, but he didn't come in.

After I finished my second beer, I left the bar and walked over to Calhoun Street. I saw Outlaw plodding down the street in front of me. I don't think he had changed since I met him a month ago. When he came closer, I stopped him. "How ya doin', man?"

He looked at me with a quizzical stare. He seemed high or drunk. "Got a cigarette?" he said.

I reached into my pocket, took out a Marlboro, and gave it to him. He shoved it into his mouth and, without thanks, asked, "What the f–do you want?"

I reminded him how we had met and asked him if he had gone to Chicago. "Those bastards are crap," he said. "They think they can run your life. You have to take orders or else."

Outlaw was rambling. He told me the Weathermen kicked him out of the house, or collective, they were living in, because he refused to go to work and turn all the money over to them. "They needed some bread and wanted me to go dig a ditch or something for a few days to get it. 'F — you,' I said. 'When I work, I work for me.' So they threw me the hell out."

Outlaw was the type of person who appreciated the violence and goals of the Weathermen, but couldn't be restricted by rules. He was a social misfit, regardless of the society he lived in.

"Those bastards are crazy," he said. I asked him if he'd seen Joyce Green or any of the others recently. He thought I was asking about Joyce for personal reasons.

"She's jail bait, ya know. Hell, she's only 16, and she's a runaway. Her old man's got a lot of bread, and she hates him. Somebody in the group conned her into joining up with them. But she don't mind it. She takes orders."

He asked me if I wanted to go for a drink, but I refused. I didn't want to get stuck paying for him. He took the half-smoked cigarette out of his mouth and flipped it into the street. "F — you," he said, and walked off.

I then went to visit Donna. While she was in the kitchen making me a sandwich, I looked through the newspaper. A short article near the bottom of one of the pages caught my attention. The U. S. Senate had started an inquiry into the activities of the Weathermen. The article said the Justice Department would handle the details.

When Donna came back with my sandwich, I put the newspaper aside. She wasn't interested in the subject of the Weathermen, so we didn't discuss it.

I thought about the Senate inquiry a lot over the weekend. I changed my mind at least a dozen times before I decided to call the Justice Department's office in Cincinnati and tell them what I knew about the Weathermen.

I made the call during my coffee break on Monday. One of the department lawyers listened to what I had to say. He told me to call the FBI. It sounded like the beginning of a runaround, so I went back to work. But later in the afternoon, I dialed the FBI office. When I was finally connected with one of the agents, I started the conversation abruptly. I was sure they must get 100 calls a day from all types of kooks. I didn't want to be put in that category.

"Look," I said, when I heard a voice on the other end of the line, "I read that the Senate is conducting an inquiry into the Weathermen. I have some information. Do you want it or not?"

My opening took him by surprise. He told me to slow down. I outlined my story. "Why not come over and see me tomorrow?" he said. "My name's Murrish — Clark Murrish."

I made the appointment for Tuesday, October 21. I got to the Federal Building about 5:30 P.M. It's a sterile-looking structure with a wide lobby that opens onto two streets. The FBI office is on the sixth floor.

I stepped off the elevator into a waiting area. A counter crossed the far end of the room, and behind it there were two desks with covered typewriters on them. There was a large picture of J. Edgar Hoover on the back wall and an American flag in the corner. A young girl sat behind the desk on the left. When I reached the counter, she asked if she could help me. I told her Clark Murrish was expecting me. She picked up the phone and dialed a number.

Soon the door behind the counter opened and a tall man, bald on top with salt and pepper hair on the sides, stepped into the front office. "Larry Grathwohl?" he asked, looking at me. I nodded, and he unlocked a door in the counter and told me to follow him.

The office looked more like a place for insurance salesmen than the FBI. I had expected to see more than a few rows of desks pushed one next to the other. Each desk was very neat with only an in-and-out basket on top and a chair beside it. There were a few agents in the office; all the rest had gone home.

Murrish had a holster strapped to his belt, but it was empty. He reached one of the desks in the line and motioned me to sit down on a chair beside it. He had a file folder on his desk, which he opened as I sat down. He glanced through some papers inside.

"You have a good service record, Larry," he said without looking up. He obviously had run a quick check on me. "You still at the university?"

"Yes and no," I said. "I'm staying out this semester to earn some money, but I plan to return in the spring." I explained that the semester break would also give me more time to think about what I really wanted to do with my life.

Murrish studied the papers a moment longer before closing the folder. He asked me to tell him the story from the beginning.

He listened without commenting, but I could sense he had a genuine interest in what I was saying. When I finished, he reached back into the file folder and took out a group of photographs. He put them on the table and asked me if I knew any of them. He had photographs of Gerry Long, Barry Stein, and Rebel Callahan.

We talked for about an hour. He asked me why I didn't go to Chicago.

"I didn't want to get my head busted for no reason," I said.

"I don't blame you."

I told him what I had read about Chicago and waited for his comment, but he didn't volunteer any information. He just repeated that the government had an interest in the Weathermen. He asked me if there was anything else, and when I said no, he thanked me for coming in. He picked up the file folder, pulled open the desk drawer, and shoved it into place. Then he removed a key from his pocket and unlocked the middle drawer of the desk. His snub-nosed .38 was lying inside.

"If you remember anything else, Larry, be sure to let me know." "I will," I said. He picked up the revolver and shoved it into his holster. I stood up, and he held out his hand. "Thanks for coming in," he repeated. "I appreciate it." We shook hands, and I left.

Another week went by. I thought about the Weathermen a few times, but I was busy with work. Anyway, I had passed on all the information I had about the movement to the FBI.

When I got home from work on Tuesday, October 28, I had a message from Murrish. It just said, "Please call." The next morning I did, and Murrish told me the Weathermen were meeting that night at the Student Union Building on campus, and he asked me if I would attend. I was glad he asked me to go. At least it proved somebody was trying to analyze what threat the Weathermen were.

The meeting was held on the second floor of the Student Union Building. I went upstairs and down the hall to a classroom. About 20 people were seated behind the desks when I went in. The meeting was getting ready to start, so I took a seat in the back.

A guy named Arlo Jacobs conducted the meeting. He was an imposing person, whose choice of words and delivery were almost perfect. He had graduated from Princeton in three years and won a Fulbright scholarship. He began the meeting by discussing the events in Chicago, which he considered a victory. It was a political success because the Weathermen proved to Chicago and the nation that it was a force to be reckoned with. The television and newspaper coverage alone was worth the action. Jacobs said Chicago could be considered a military victory because of the number of pigs who were hospitalized. He reminded the group that Chicago was the Weathermen's first action, but that it provided invaluable experience. He said the state could be brought down only by armed struggle conducted by urban guerrillas. He said that this type of warfare could be successful only if the participants were tenacious. To emphasize his point, he noted that Simon Bollvar was constantly ridiculed, called insane, and actually expelled five times before he returned to win his first battle in South America. He also cited the success of Fidel Castro after nine years. This country can and will fall, he said. It will take time, but it is inevitable. Chicago was our first step. He said it showed that a broad base for the revolution was developing because white youths took to the streets to support the blacks in their struggle against suppression.

Jacobs opened the meeting for debate, and all the speakers were full of revolutionary rhetoric, all aimed at proving Chicago was successful. I decided to make myself known. It took a few minutes until I finally got the floor. I felt I had to make a short speech in order to gain their confidence. If I just sat quietly in the background listening to everything being said without participating, they might get suspicious of my motives. I didn't know if Murrish would want me to attend more Weatherman rallies, but if so, obviously it would be better if I looked like an active participant.

"I know you people think you did a great job in Chicago. In fact, you've spent the better part of an hour convincing yourselves of this." Then I raised my voice and added, "But I don't." I paused at this point, as the heads of those people sitting in front turned around to look at me. "I think the Salvation Army is better prepared to take over a country. While we're sitting here debating Chicago's success, there's a war going on in Southeast Asia. Guys are getting killed. And what are you doing about it? Nothing. That's what you're doing. You're all full of crap."

If nothing else, I got their attention. I would be known. Jacobs just stared at me. I saw Barry Stein and Joyce Green staring also. When I was through with my statement, Mike Spiegel, one of the guys who had been at the first meeting I attended, jumped up and agreed with me.

"He's right. We haven't done enough. We came here to plan more action, and all we've done so far is talk about Chicago."

Jacobs finally got the meeting back to order and explained its main purpose. Sarcastically, he said he hoped the plans "would meet with the approval of our friend in the back." He said a special seminar on international trade was scheduled the next day between students and businessmen on the same floor where we were holding our meeting. The plan was for us to take over the seminar, which was a perfect forum to air Weathermen political thought on worldwide suppression by the U.S. It would demonstrate that Weathermen were not confined to Chicago, but were active in all cities.

As Jacobs was speaking, I made it a point to look at everybody in the room. Most of them were familiar, and if my guess was right, only one or two were students at the university. The rest were either Weathermen who had come to Cincinnati to recruit or contacts like myself and Mark Stivic, the Viet vet I had met at the rally in Eden Park. I also met another Vietnam veteran, Eddie Schaeffer, at the meeting.

Jacobs ended the session and walked down the aisle to talk to me. Spiegel joined us at the same time. "If you want action, Grathwohl," Spiegel said, "you can get it tomorrow."

Spiegel suggested we talk as we walked outside. While we were leaving, Joyce Green and Mark Stivic joined us. After talking for a while, we walked up toward Calhoun Street. The others were going back to the collective, but they didn't invite me along. Before they left me, Jacobs reminded me to report behind the Student Union in the morning at 10 sharp. I told him I'd be there. I had to pretend to be anxious to join in demonstrations.

Otherwise they would lose confidence in me, and I wouldn't get any information.

I called Murrish in the morning, but he was out of the office. I left a message and then called McAlpine's and told the dock foreman I had a toothache and was going to the dentist. He was annoyed that I didn't give him more notice, but I told him it was difficult to plan a toothache.

It was a poor day for a revolution. It was raining like hell. Still, 16 of us were there on time. As we gathered outside in the rain, Joyce Green unfolded a long canvas wrapping. Inside were six Viet Cong flags. She passed them out. Arlo Jacobs sent Eddie Schaeffer into the building to make sure the meeting was in progress. I was glad to see Schaeffer return with a positive report. At last we'd get out of the rain.

Jacobs gave the order to start. We ran into the building, stormed up the stairs to the second floor, and down the corridor chanting: "Ho, Ho, Ho Chi Minh, the Viet Cong are going to win." We chanted it over and over as we ran along. The few students who were in the hall jumped aside as we went by. At the end of the corridor we yanked open the double doors to the small auditorium and raced inside.

A group of students and businessmen were sitting on chairs in a large circle. They were conducting an informal discussion as part of an economic seminar class. We were circling the group like a bunch of wild Indians around a wagon train, shouting our allegiance to Ho Chi Minh. As we circled, one of the students started to stand up, but as he did, Schaeffer turned his chair over, and he fell into the middle of the group. When we stopped and took stationary positions, one of the businessmen demanded to know what was going on, but Mike Spiegel told him to shut the f–up. He did.

My job was to protect the speaker, who was supposed to be Nancy Chiara. She looked more like a beauty queen than a revolutionist. But Nancy took too long getting started. So Spiegel jumped forward and gave a short lecture on the evils of our capitalistic society. Nobody tried to stop Spiegel from speaking. I think they were all too astonished. When Spiegel finished, we all ran out of the room again and down through the halls shouting,

"Ho, Ho, Ho Chi Minh, the Viet Cong is going to win." Nobody tried to stop us.

We raced down the stairs and out the back door. Then we split. I ended up with Barry Stein and Hal Lincoln. When we saw nobody was chasing us, we decided to go back to the Student Union to see if we got any reaction from the students. We went down to the cafeteria in the basement.

Stein was pleased. "At least that will let the students and administration know we're alive," he said. Lincoln went over to the food counter and got three cups of coffee. I watched a long-haired girl carrying an armful of books come into the cafeteria and look around. When she saw our table, she came over. Barry knew her. I started to get up when she arrived, but nobody else did, so I sat down again.

She sat with us. "How did it go?" she said to Barry. "Good reaction?"

"There will be."

Stein didn't introduce her to me, but he did call her Mary. His conversation seemed more guarded than usual, but I remembered that when I had first met him he had said very little. Mary then got up to leave as abruptly as she had appeared.

Stein turned to Lincoln as she left. "I don't know about that broad," he commented.

Two male students walked by our table carrying coffee. They were talking about the demonstration because we heard them say something about Viet Cong flags. Stein was pleased to hear it.

"They'll learn we're here," he said. He sipped his coffee. When he put the cup down, he looked at me. "You missed Chicago."

"I couldn't get away, but I won't miss the next one." I paused a moment and, when nobody said anything, I continued: "Shit, I read all about it. I liked the way you guys treated that pig who got into the meeting."

Stein looked up from his coffee. "Which one?"

"The one at the church meeting."

Stein smiled. "That mother. He proved how stupid the pigs really are. He comes to the church and gives us a lot of bullshit at the door. So we let him in. We can always use another guy.

Then he stood in the back of the room and started looking all around. I noticed one of our guys sitting in the corner looking at him. Then this guy gets up and walks over to the pig. He stood in front of him and yelled: 'This guy's a pig. I saw him at the pig station last night when they were busting us.'"

"Of course the pig denied it. He started talking fast and making a lot of excuses, when all of a sudden the brother standing in front of him hit the pig on the side of the head with a hard right. The next thing I knew, a few more brothers were punching him, and he tumbled to the floor screaming for us to leave him alone. Then the pastor who runs the church came running in. He started ranting about how he didn't know what type of people we were or he wouldn't have given us the church and all that bullshit. Some brother wanted to stomp him, but we held him back. To keep the pastor quiet, we laid off the pig. A couple of guys picked him up and brought him outside and tossed him into the street. Then we all split. You could never tell what the f—ing pastor was going to do next."

Stein got great pleasure from telling me the story, although he was very careful never to mention names and never to actually say he took part in the beating.

"These pigs thought they were dealing with some panty-ass white kids out on a lark," Stein added, "but I think some of them believe us now. Look at that Daley's lawyer. He was a big shot last year at the convention, but he's not saying much now, is he?" Stein was talking about Elrod, the assistant corporation counsel whose neck was broken.

"I read where they got someone locked up on that," I said.

"Yeah, but they can't prove a thing. The charges will be dropped. We got good lawyers working on it."

When Lincoln and Stein finished their coffee, they stood up. "We gotta get back, man. You did a good job today. We'll be in touch." Then they left.

It was almost noon. I decided to get a sandwich and then go to work.

Chapter 5

Moratorium

Before reporting to work at 1 P.M., I telephoned Murrish. When I told him about my part in the demonstration, he got angry.

"I didn't ask you to start a revolution," he barked. "All I wanted was a report. A simple report. I don't need you running around town playing Trotsky."

I listened without uttering a sound, but I was thinking how the hell did he think I was going to get the information. He'd probably tell me to go to the meetings, take notes, smile politely, and then leave. But if I was needed to find out how far the Weatherman group would really go in supporting their rhetoric, I couldn't find out anything without gaining their confidence. Of all people, Murrish should understand that. When he calmed down, I explained my reasoning. He agreed. Before I hung up, we made a date to meet. Murrish said he would pick me up in front of McAlpine's at noon the following Tuesday.

When I got home that night, my mother gave me a message from Arlo Jacobs. He wanted me to meet him on Calhoun Street around 9 o'clock. It was important. My mother wanted to know who Arlo Jacobs was and what kind of business had to be conducted on a street corner on a Friday night. I told her Arlo was a former classmate who had a flair for the dramatic, and that he probably wanted to borrow five dollars.

When I got to Calhoun Street, Jacobs and Barry Stein were selling copies of the latest issue of The Fire Next Time, for short, Fire. But making sales was secondary. Rapping with anyone

who would listen was the major reason for being on the street.
They had a guy backed against a store window and were firing off
the litany of indictments against the U.S. from its involvement in
Vietnam to its suppression of the blacks. Once the guy had gone,
Stein asked me if I was going to Washington. "Probably," I said.
By Washington, I was sure he meant the moratorium scheduled
for November 13 through 15. A group that called itself the New
Mobilization Committee to End the War in Vietnam (MOBE) was
organizing mass demonstrations in Washington, D.C. and San
Francisco. Actually, the moratorium concept was created by the
Vietnam Moratorium Committee as small peaceful demonstra-
tions in cities and on campuses throughout the country. The first
Moratorium Day was held October 15, and judged a success by
its organizers, as well as by political and religious leaders. But
as MOBE got into the act, the concept expanded to mass demonstrations in the nation's capital and on the West Coast. Attorney
General John Mitchell showed his displeasure by delaying per-
mits to MOBE organizers. He questioned whether the plan was
Communist-inspired and calculated to cause violence. Some for-
merly sympathetic U. S. Senators withdrew their support, but
others remained loyal to the moratorium concept.

I should have given Jacobs and Stein a more positive answer. I hadn't done myself any good in their eyes by not going to
Chicago. If I was going to get anywhere with them, I had to say
yes to Washington. Stein didn't wait for a more detailed answer.

"The ass holes who are organizing these demonstrations are
creeps," said Stein. "They call themselves liberal humanitarians.
The only thing they'll accomplish will be organizing long dull
marches and boring speeches. They're as bad as the shitheads
who are running the country. All they do is talk."

As I listened, it became clear that the Weathermen were going to take advantage of the demonstrations. They had had to
organize the Chicago National Action. This time they could capitalize on somebody else's work.

Finally they got around to asking me if I was available to
help out. I knew they were testing me, to see if I was willing to
go along with them. I had to say yes. The only way I could investigate the Weathermen was to be accepted by them. Therefore, I

had to be prepared to participate in demonstrations and rallies and speak out for the overthrow of the government, even though I didn't believe in it. As long as I didn't provoke any Weathermen into action, I felt perfectly justified. They wanted to tear down the government. I didn't know any other way to stop them. I knew I would be acting on my own, without Murrish's formal approval, but I figured the results would be worth the risk.

"What do you want me to do?" I asked.

"We have some other friends coming intq Cincinnati," Jacobs said. "We were hoping you could take care of them. Maybe get them a ride from here to Washington."

"Who are they?"

"We'll give you the details later," Stein said. "We'll call you."

I stayed with them for a while. They returned to selling newspapers and rapping about politics. By now I was familiar with most of their rhetoric, so I joined in. I felt like a carnival pitchman, but my effort impressed Jacobs. After an hour or so, I asked them if they wanted to go for a beer. They refused. There was too much work still to do. They had no time for drinking beer.

On Tuesday, I decided to conduct an "awareness" poll of the Weathermen. It wasn't as scientific as Gallup's or quite as extensive. Actually, my poll consisted of interviewing Tommy Cash during our coffee break on the loading platform at McAlpine's that morning. Tommy was about my age. He was a navy veteran and had been working at McAlpine's about nine months.

If the Weathermen were interested in me, they had to be interested in Tommy and others like Tommy. Both of us were from the working class, and we were young. According to the Weatherman philosophy, "young people have less stake in a society (no family, fewer debts), are more open to new ideas (they have not been brainwashed for so long or so well), and are therefore more able and willing to move in a revolutionary direction."

Those were some of the conclusions I came to after analyzing the situation. But I was interested in knowing if any of their philosophy was getting through to the working youths. Tommy would tell me.

I waited until we loaded the last car, then we walked inside to the vending machines. Tommy was taller than me and very husky. Although he had been in the navy four years, the closest he got to the war was Hawaii. As he punched out two light coffees in one machine, I pulled the lever a couple of times on another to get two small coffee cakes. We adjourned to the side of the room to enjoy a brief break. I got right into my poll.

"Ever hear of the Weathermen?" I'm sure Gallup would disapprove of such an abrupt beginning, but I didn't have time to lead up to the question.

Tommy took the cup of coffee away from his mouth and looked at me like I was nuts.

"Sure," he said, "What's the matter with you?"

His answer startled me. "What do you know about them?"

"I don't know anything about them, except that guy on Channel 5 never gets the weather right."

Tommy filled his mouth with a large bite of the coffee cake while I held back a snicker. I wasn't laughing at Tommy; I was thinking how he had just pierced Barry Stein's ego without either of them knowing it.

"I don't mean the television weather clods."

"Then who the hell do you mean?"

I briefly described the Weatherman organization.

Tommy was only vaguely aware of the violence in Chicago and had no idea of who started it, except that they were a bunch of long-haired fags who deserved a rap in the mouth. "College pissheads," he said. "How the hell can they start a revolution? I could kick the shit out of half of them myself." He paused a moment, then added: "Even you could probably take out a few of them."

He enjoyed his own remark so much that he almost choked on the coffee cake. Before we could continue our discussion, the supervisor yelled at us: "There's a car outside. Take care of it, will ya?" I stuffed my empty coffee container in the trash can and went out to get the merchandise slip from the customer.

Murrish picked me up at noon. His plain gray car was sitting in a no-parking zone near the building. When he saw me coming, he got out of the car, and we walked around the corner to a small coffee shop. A back booth was empty, so we took it. Since the government was buying, I ordered a hot meat-loaf sandwich with whipped potatoes. Murrish had only a cup of coffee and a Danish. While waiting for the order, I filled him in on my Friday night meeting with Stein and Jacobs. He didn't like the idea that I was planning to go to Washington. He didn't want me to get so involved.

"We'll have enough people there without you," he said.

During lunch, I went over the demonstration at the college again, step by step. Murrish jotted a few things down in a small notebook. He wanted to know if there were any new faces in the crowd. I told him no. He asked if I knew the exact number of students who took part. I didn't, but there weren't many. Most of the protestors were Weathermen. Finally, he removed an envelope from the inside pocket of his jacket, opened it up, and took out several photographs. Most of them showed somebody speaking to a crowd. He had a photograph of Gerry Long and another of Rebel Callahan. Neither had been back to Cincinnati as far as I knew. I flipped Callahan's photo over. There was a brief biography on the back. His full name was Matthew J. Callahan. According to the caption, he had been arrested in February 1969 at Kent State. I shuffled through the other photographs, but I didn't recognize anyone.

"If you see any of them around, let me know." I assured Murrish I would and turned the conversation back to the Washington protest. I explained my reasoning: that only by taking an active part in their activities could I gain access to Weatherman strategy. But Murrish remained adamant. He didn't want me to go. However, he did concede that he couldn't prevent me from going. "Just try to stay out of trouble."

The waitress returned. "Anything else, hon?" she asked, not really caring which one of us answered. We told her no, so she scribbled out a check and dropped it on the table. Murrish left a tip, then paid the cashier. I told him that if I did go to Washington, it wouldn't be before Friday the 14th, which was ten days away. He asked me to keep in touch, especially if I heard any specific details about the demonstration.

Even as Murrish and I were discussing the Cincinnati Weathermen, a Weatherman group from Boston was joining other demonstrators in a wild rampage at MIT. They carried

Viet Cong flags and marched around the campus, eventually forcing the Center for International Studies to close. Then they took over the administration offices, shouting "Let's smash MIT." Then, the next day the same group caused a work stoppage at the school's Missile Guidance System in the Instrumentation Laboratory.

On Monday, November 10 Arlo Jacobs called me again. He asked me to come over to Calhoun Street. When I met Jacobs, he got right down to business. Most of the Weathermen were leaving by car for Washington Wednesday night. But most of the university students who were going to support the MOBE-organized demonstration were leaving by bus from the campus on Friday. He said this group was planning a brief demonstration prior to boarding the buses. "You can imagine how half-assed that will be," he said. "We want you and a couple of other guys to liven up this demonstration if you can."

The other two guys were Weatherman contacts from the University of Dayton in the northern part of the state. Arlo told me to meet them on the Cincinnati campus and go down to Washington with them. It was an obvious test to see what we could or would do. Jacobs didn't say so, but I knew at least one of the Weathermen would be around to watch us.

"That sounds easy," I said. "What do you want us to do?"

"Nothing. Just make sure everything goes all right on the campus and then come down to Washington." "Where will we meet?" "You'll find us when you get there. We'll be where the action is; the jerks from MOBE will be running the dull stuff."

I put in for another half day's work on Friday. I told them I had to go back to the dentist. The supervisor gave me a caustic look, but grunted approval.

As the week unfolded, it turned out that not all protestors were content with marching to Washington. To begin with, a munitions plant in Hanover, Massachusetts was set on fire. Next, a bomb exploded in the yard of the Municipal Electric Power Company in Seattle, Washington, while another bomb was discovered in the city's First National Bank Building. While no one was injured in Seattle, ten people were hurt when a bomb exploded in the Franklyn County Courthouse in Missouri. In New York City, bombs were exploded at the offices of Chase Manhattan Bank, Standard Oil Company, and General Motors and at the Criminal Courts Building.

The New York bombings were well advertised. The news media and the building authorities were warned about a half hour in advance of each bombing. Then a letter was delivered to United Press International explaining the reasons for the attacks. The letter read in part:

> ... the Vietnam war is only the most obvious evidence of the way this country's power destroys people. The giant corporations of America have now spread themselves all over the world, forcing entire foreign economies into total dependence on American money and goods. ... Spiro Agnew may be a household word, but it is the rarely seen men like David Rockefeller of Chase Manhattan, James Roche of General Motors, and Michael Haiden of Standard Oil who run the system behind the scenes. ... The empire is breaking down as peoples all over the globe are rising up to challenge its power. From the inside, black people have been fighting a revolution for years. ...

I didn't know whether the Weathermen had anything to do with the bombings, but the wording of the letter certainly sounded like their philosophy. However, whether they were actually involved or not was academic. The incidents proved that insurrection was increasing. The Weathermen didn't need a large organization as long as others followed them. When I called Murrish on Friday to fill him in on my plans, I asked about the bombings. He was reluctant to talk. He did say there wasn't any reason to believe they were connected.

It was after 4 o'clock when I got to the student union building to meet the two contacts from Dayton, Jim O'Hara and Tom Klein. They were sitting on the wall in front of the building. They were easy to spot. Jacobs told me to look for a guy with bright red hair-that was O'Hara. It was starting to get cold. I was wearing a Levi jacket, but I didn't have a hat or gloves. I introduced myself to O'Hara and Klein, and we rapped for a few minutes before going up the street where the student buses were.

A mock burial ceremony was just beginning as we got there. The funeral services were for the innocent Vietnamese who were killed during the war. Cardboard tombstones lined the grass along the sidewalk. A large banner hanging from a tree proclaimed that the Viet Cong were going to win. The students had a silent procession around the tombstones. As soon as it was over, O'Hara started shouting: "Ho, Ho, Ho Chi Minh." Others joined in. Klein tipped over a nearby trash can and lit it. Soon other fires were going. Then I ripped the banner from the tree and told O'Hara to grab one end. A few other students also took hold, and we raced out into the street, blocking traffic. Other students followed, jamming the street. A traffic cop came running down from the corner, but he couldn't do anything alone. A few newspaper photographers who had been standing around started snapping pictures. Then we ran back and forth across the street as if we were in a snake dance. As we raced past the buses, the students began boarding, chanting as they climbed in. We spent so much time carrying the banner around that we missed getting on the last bus.

Fortunately, one of the coeds who had just taken part in the demonstration was driving to Washington with a girl friend. She offered to take us with her. We accepted, but we should have looked for someone else. The girl was driving a Volkswagen. Not only was it crowded in the back, the heater didn't work. But the girl did have a large supply of grass that she passed around freely. It didn't help. I froze all the way to our nation's capital. What a way to go to a revolution!

When we arrived Saturday morning, the sun was up. We abandoned the car on a side street and found a donut shop for breakfast. An old counterman grumbled as we sat down. "Freaks. Nothin' but freaks all over the place this weekend," he was mumbling to anyone who would listen.

We ordered five coffees, and he splashed them down in front of us. He said he had only plain donuts left. We took one each. It was going to be a long day.

The counterman continued to grumble. A morning paper was open in front of him. The moratorium had begun at 6 P.M. two nights before, on Thursday, November 13, 1969, with a "March Against Death." Beginning in Arlington National Cemetery across the Potomac River in Virginia, the protestors marched back to the District of Columbia past the White House and down to the Capital, almost five miles. Forty-six thousand people took part, each carrying the name of a soldier killed in the war on cardboard signs. As they reached the Capital, the signs were deposited in coffins lined up across from the Capitol steps. The protestors marched in silence with only the funeral drum roll breaking the quiet. The peaceful march took 36 hours.

But on Friday night, the peace had been shattered. Some 150 Weathermen, along with 1000 members of other radical groups, rallied at DuPont Circle. They heard speeches and shouted chants. Then they burst from the circle and raced for the South Vietnamese Embassy, only to run into the waiting District of Columbia police. The police were well prepared. The 3800-man force was put on emergency-duty notice, while 11,000 National Guardsmen and paratroopers had been sent to back them up. The rioters and police battled for about three hours.

The counterman shook his head as he continued to read about the demonstration in the newspaper. "Freaks. The cops should have thrown them all in jail."

We walked over to Pennsylvania Avenue and then down to the Capitol. A crowd was gathering near the coffins that contained the names of the dead American soldiers. According to MOBE plans, the coffins would be carried from the Capitol to the Washington Monument. Later in the day, ceremonies would be held at the monument.

When we got to the Capitol, the two girls left us to look for the group from Cincinnati. Soon we were immersed in a sea of humanity, mostly young people, but many of them were in their late 20s or early 30s. They could have been lawyers, accountants, junior executives, or advertising writers, and they had given up a Saturday in suburbia to protest the war.

Before the march began, Senator Eugene McCarthy made an appearance. He was cheered wildly. He responded with a short lecture. He reminded us that the burden of America rested on our shoulders and that we had to carry it.

O'Hara, Klein and I pushed out to the edge of the crowd and headed on our own to the Washington Monument. I saw some Viet Cong flags and even a few pictures of Uncle Ho, but they were outnumbered by American flags, which were being sold along the way. At the monument, Pete Seeger and Arlo Guthrie were taking part in the ceremony. Then there were speeches by Coretta King, as well as by Senators Goodell and McGovern. They were predictably boring. I wasn't sure what I expected, but it was more than what I was getting; their words were tired. It all seemed to be a mass happening without any meaning.

As we moved away from the monument, we heard other shouts: "F–you, Agnew," and "Two, four, six, eight. Now's the time to smash the state." We moved toward the chanting. A mob of about 5000 was converging on the Justice Department. Many of the protestors wore knapsacks to hide their rocks and bricks. Viet Cong flags were bobbing up and down all over the place. The poles made excellent weapons. I joined in, but it seemed as silly as listening to speeches near the monument. A cadre of police were at each side, but they made no move to close in. We chanted some more. Faces appeared in various windows of the building, and with each one, someone recognized Agnew. He was reputedly inside coordinating all the intelligence data on the demonstration.

The mob didn't stay inactive long. A bottle was hurled at the building. Other bottles, bricks, and rocks started flying. Someone shinnied up the flagpole in front of the building and cut down the American flag amid cheers and whistles. In its place, he raised a Viet Cong flag. As he started down the pole, the MOBE marshals rushed over to capture him, but girls in helmets screamed and kicked at the marshals, and guys in helmets hit them with sticks. "Pig lovers," they shouted at the marshals. "You abandoned the people for the pigs." The attack on the marshals brought the police into action. They fired tear gas canisters into the area, quickly overcoming the mob. The police wore gas masks. The gas that was curling around us was sickening. I started to run from the area. Jim O'Hara and Tom Klein were with me and, along with hundreds of other protestors, we headed up Constitution Avenue. Windows were broken along the way. Bricks were thrown at cars, windshields smashed. Anyone who had cans of spray paint began writing slogans on sidewalks, stores, buildings. Trash cans were grabbed, turned over, and set afire. The mob grew more unruly as it moved along. It had been scattered in many directions, but that seemed only to present more problems for the police. It would have been easier to contain us if we were in one area.

O'Hara and I were still together, but Klein had disappeared. We turned up one street only to see a group of six helmeted people running toward us. Behind them two motorcycle cops were gaining rapidly. The cops soon whirled past and cut in front of the six, as if heading off runaway steers. The six turned, split up, and ran for the cover of the buildings. The cops jumped off their motorcycles and moved in. As they did, two demonstrators ran from a building across the street and banged the motorcycles to the ground. The cops turned. Two other demonstrators were going to throw matches near the gas tanks, but the cops started back. As they did, the original six escaped. O'Hara and I ran off with them.

Two blocks down, a police car came screaming around the corner. Somebody hit it with a brick, and it went into a spin. "Off the pigs," came the cry as the car bounced up over the curb and came to a sudden stop just before crashing into the building. "Pigs!" came another shout, followed by a fusillade of rocks aimed at the patrol car. Other police came up the street, and we were off again.

Broken glass was everywhere. Fires were burning wherever there was a trash can. Walls were covered with paint. I felt like I had been running forever. I also felt like a fool, a very tired fool. Right now, Murrish looked like a genius. Why hadn't I listened to him?

I didn't find Arlo Jacobs or Barry Stein or any other Weathermen from Cincinnati. But I had found the action.

Chapter 6

Joining the Collective

It was a long ride back from Washington, and I got home late Sunday afternoon. I looked like a bum and probably smelled worse. Nobody was home when I got there, so I showered and went straight to bed.

But I couldn't fall asleep. I tossed around, thinking about the demonstration. Maybe I was an idiot for running around Washington like I did. The FBI probably had more people involved than did the Weathermen. What was my part? Nothing. What could I tell Murrish? That I saw a lot of people throw bricks through windows, set garbage cans on fire, turn motorcycles over? I didn't have an overall perspective; I didn't know what effect, if any, the demonstration had. It was certainly violent. But Murrish would know that without me. Why the hell was I going on with this, anyway? So the Weathermen bombed a few buildings. So what? Nobody was killed. Not yet, anyway. They'd be stopped. I wasn't needed. Christ, I was tired. Finally I got some sleep.

I was a half hour late for work on Monday morning. When I walked in at 8:30 A.M., the supervisor was angry. He stuck his head out of his small glass-partitioned office and bellowed to me. "Grathwohl! What do you think we're running here, a country club? You leave early on Friday and stroll in late today. You think we're on the four-day work week or something?"

I apologized.

"Okay, okay," he said. Then he pointed to all the packages

piled up in the back of the room. "You'd better get to work." He turned back into his office, but then popped out again. He looked at me like he was studying a photograph. "You got a relative over at the university?" he said.

"No," I answered, "but I'll be going back in the spring."

"You see the television news Friday?"

I shook my head.

"Some punk college kids ran around with some signs saying they backed the commies in Vietnam instead of our boys. One of them looked like you."

I didn't say anything, and he turned and went away again.

At lunchtime I called Murrish. I made an appointment to see him the next day, November 17, after work. I felt dejected, frustrated. The only thing I seemed to be accomplishing was angering my boss.

Murrish appeared glad to see me. He had left word with the clerk at the front desk to show me right in. I sat down on the chair next to his desk. He swung around and pushed his chair back. There was silence for a moment. Then he said: "Well, what do you have?"

"Probably not much more than you already have."

"I'll make the judgments. You just give me the information."

I went through the entire weekend, step by step. Murrish stopped me occasionally to elaborate a detail or to expand an observation. I concluded my report by saying: "Maybe you were right. You didn't need me in Washington."

He ignored my remark, and asked me if I had heard from any of the Weathermen since I got back. When I told him no, he asked if I could get in touch with them.

"I think so. Barry Stein gave me a telephone number before the demonstration a few weeks ago at the college. He said to call the number if I got into any trouble."

"You still have it?"

"I think so." I looked through my wallet and found it.

Murrish leaned forward. "If you're still serious about continuing, we can use your help. Do you think you can push a little harder to get in with the Weathermen? To be accepted, so that they'll talk to you more?"

I looked at him in amazement. Up to now he had taken information, but he had never asked me to do anything except to attend a couple of meetings. Now the FBI was actually asking me to infiltrate a revolutionary group. How could I refuse? I had gone this far. Don was taking care of Donna and Denise, and my job was enough to keep me in spending money.

"I'll work on it."

"Very good. I'll be expecting to hear from you soon."

The next day I dialed the number Stein had given me. A girl answered. I asked for Arlo Jacobs because he had been the one who called me to go to Washington. After a pause, Jacobs got on the phone.

"Where were you in Washington?" I asked. "I'm running around trashing the city while you're hiding out someplace. What are you guys ... "

"Not on the phone," he snapped, almost in panic. "I've been meaning to call you, but most of us just got back yesterday. We had things to do."

"Bullshit."

There was a slight pause before Jacobs said: "Meet me tomorrow night. We'll talk more specifically then. Be at the Gold Star Chili Bar at eight."

"All right," I said, and hung up.

The Gold Star Chili Bar was a small restaurant on Calhoun Street with about ten tables in the small back room at the end of the counter. It specialized in a spicy chili sauce concoction poured over hot dogs. If you didn't like hot dogs, you could buy another chili concoction that had onions and cheese in it and was served on top of spaghetti. It looked terrible, tasted fine, and cost only 95 cents. It was also the basic diet for a lot of college students who hung out there.

When I got to the Gold Star that night, Barry Stein and Nancy Chiara were waiting for me in the last booth on the far side of the room. I ordered a Pepsi and joined them. Two chili-stained paper dishes with small pieces of hot dog rolls were on the table in front of them. I stared at Nancy on the way to the table. She was a beautiful girl.

"Where's Jacobs?" I asked, playing out the arrogant role I'd begun with Jacobs. "He had something else to do," Stein said, moving over to give me room to sit down. We talked about Washington. Stein was pleased that I had taken part. Without specifically saying he was answering my question to Jacobs, he told me how busy everybody had been in Washington — discussing it like a businessman talking about a successful deal. "We're moving, man. The revolution is now. It's going on all around us. We've come a long way in a few short months."

I looked at Stein. "I still think you talk more than you act."

"Was Cambridge just talk?" Stein asked angrily. A sniper had put a few bullets into a police station wall in Cambridge; in retaliation, the cops raided two Weatherman collectives in Boston, arresting 26 people on charges ranging from attempted murder to criminal sedition.

Stein must have realized that he shouldn't have sounded as if he knew who conducted the attack, because he quickly added: "The pigs will never learn. They can't make those charges stick. Nobody knows who took the shots, but whoever did it believes in the revolution."

"Our lawyers will make fools out of those pigs," Nancy added. "They'll rip the case apart. It's a frame-up, anyway. The pigs are so scared of us, we're getting the blame for everything."

Both of them claimed the actions in Chicago and Washington were developing a broader base among the youth. "We haven't gotten the masses yet," Stein said, "but it's only a matter of time."

Soon they turned the conversation around to Vietnam and me. I told them the war was a horrible scar on the American image: women and children being blown apart, butchered for no reason. This impressed them. I said I was tired of the pigs pushing people around. "When I was a kid in Cincinnati, the pigs pushed us around just because we were poor." I told them the story about being busted by the cops for what the city workers had done. They were intrigued because it fortified their reasons for being part of the movement. According to their philosophy, the Weathermen existed to liberate me from the suppression of the pig establishment. The more I talked about running with gangs and away from cops, the more interested they got in me. They took turns grilling me about my childhood. I told them the pigs pushed me around when I was a kid the same way the pig army was pushing the Vietnamese around.

"Why did you go in the army if you felt that way?" Nancy asked.

"At that time, the army was an escape for me. A way out of Cincinnati. But once I got over to Vietnam, my outlook changed. I hated the destruction we were causing."

I watched their expressions as I talked. What I had said was partly true, but my reasons were different. I got to hate the war all right, because I was tired of watching guys I came over with die for no reason. One time we chased a VC unit over the border into Cambodia, but the captain wouldn't let us go after them. So the VC turned around and fired at us from the other side, killing a couple of guys. All we did was pull back. It was ludicrous.

Nancy asked another question. "After you got disgusted, why did you stay in the army? Why didn't you split?"

"I wanted money for an education, so I figured, why not let the pigs pay for it. I got my high school diploma in the army, and I was going to let Uncle Sam help me through college."

"Right on," Nancy said, delighted that I was ripping off the establishment.

As I continued to talk about Vietnam, I gave the appearance of growing angrier. "Just when I find a group that claims they're really going to tear this country apart, they go soft on me." They knew I meant them. "We're going to tear it apart," Stein said. "But you have to know how we move. How we work."

"I'll be dead by that time," I said sarcastically.

Stein didn't answer me. Instead, he asked me to get up so he could get out of the booth.

"Wait here," he said as he left.

Nancy continued the questioning. She was as dedicated as Jacobs and Stein. Political philosophy fascinated her. She hated the American system. "I want to go to Cuba," she said. "Maybe it will be soon."

Stein returned. "Let's go," he said.

"Where?"

"Over to the house."

I had evidently made it past step one. Stein must have given me good grades on my oral examination.

The collective was in a three-story wooden frame house on Hollister Street. It was the second house from the end of a block in which all the houses looked alike. Fifty years earlier it was probably a fashionable neighborhood, but now two of the houses were vacant, their windows broken. We walked up the front steps, opened a large door, and stepped into a hallway with a staircase on the right. Stein led the way up the stairs. I wondered if the people who lived on the first floor knew who their neighbors were.

A door at the top of the stairs opened into a large, almost empty room. Two old sofas, without legs, were pushed against the wall with an old easy chair across from them. The wooden floor was bare. I could see a sink and stove in the kitchen in the back of the apartment. A dining room was on the right. It contained a scarred kitchen table and two straight-backed chairs. The only light in the living room came from a bulb hanging from the ceiling.

Stein ushered me into the living room and told me to sit down on one of the sofas. I stretched my legs out in front of me and felt very comfortable. A well-worn copy of Regis Debray's Revolution in the Revolution was lying on the floor near me. I didn't see any other books, but there was a pile of newspapers, including Fire and The Berkeley Tribe in the corner. Stein left the room, and Nancy continued to talk about the revolution. I could hear other voices upstairs.

Stein returned soon, and we continued talking about Vietnam and American transgression in other countries such as Bolivia and Argentina. He praised the Tupermaros in South America for their terrorist activities against U.S. imperialist-sponsored government. Our conversation was beginning to become repetitious. "It takes an armed struggle to bring down an armed state," Stein was saying as I got up and walked across the room to the pile of newspapers. I turned from the newspapers and looked across at Stein. "Why did you ask me up here? There's nobody around."

"Don't be so impatient."

We were waiting for somebody; I was sure of that, so I walked back across the room and flopped back down onto the sofa. They asked me many of the same questions they had raised at the Gold Star Chili Bar. I gave the same answers. I knew I was passing step two. About a half hour later, I heard the front door open and close and footsteps on the stairs. I watched the living room doorway.

A short girl bundled up in a stocking cap and parka came through the door, followed by a tall guy in an army fatigue jacket. The girl removed the cap, and her hair fell down almost to the buckle of the belt on her jeans. As she came into the living room, I got a good look at her. She was very attractive. I guessed her age to be about 26. The guy behind her was a couple of years older. I had never seen either one of them. I turned back to look at the girl. I was really taken by her. She wasn't as pretty as Nancy, but she was much more appealing.

Stein got up from the old easy chair and went over to talk with the guy who had just come in. Their voices were low, but I could tell they were talking about me. Then Stein called to me. "Larry, come on over here."

I got up and walked across the room. Stein made the introductions. "Larry Grathwohl, this is Corky Bennett and Naomi Jaffee. They just got in from Chicago."

I shook hands with both of them.

"We've heard a lot about you, Grathwohl" Bennett said. "I'm glad you could make it over here tonight." Then he turned to Stein, "Anybody else here?"

"Spiegel's upstairs."

"Ask him to come down."

Stein went down the corridor. Bennett had to introduce Naomi to Nancy, so I knew she wasn't from this collective. When Spiegel came into the room, Bennett said: "Naomi is joining us here. I want you to tell everybody she's with us."

Naomi had just gotten out of jail in Chicago, where she'd been since the Chicago action on October 8. She described the horrors of the Cook County jail. "It's almost all black or Puerto Rican," she said. "It proves everything we've been saying. The white pig establishment keeps the blacks and browns and poor whites suppressed."

She discussed the conditions in the jail for half an hour more. "The pigs couldn't break us," she said. "We all stuck together. We sang songs. We even got the others, the supposed criminals, to join in with us. The pigs didn't know what to do with us. They know now they have people working for the suppressed. People who care." As she was speaking, Stein brought a couple of jugs of red wine in from the kitchen and passed them around. He also had a loaf of Italian bread.

After Naomi finished reporting on her experiences, Corky Bennett turned to me. "You grew up in Cincinnati, Larry. How do we reach the young people here? What do we do?"

I took my time answering. I tried to figure out what he was looking for. I wanted to come on strong. "For one thing, you people spend too much time talking," I said. "Take me, for example. You call people with my background 'greasers,' but you need us greasers to make the movement work. Yet your basic method of operation, as far as I've been able to determine, is to plan an action to death with meetings. The guys in Cincinnati that I know are too impatient for all that discussion and planning. They don't want to stand around talking. Hell, I've been fighting all my life. Fighting is nothing new to me. But all this talk is. I'm ready to fight, and so are the kids on the street if you give us something solid to fight for, something we know will benefit us and not the pigs who are chasing us around."

I told them their actions in Chicago and Washington were building an awareness of the Weathermen, but I didn't agree with the belief that they were successful. The Weathermen had a long way to go before the general public took them seriously.

"Bullshit," Spiegel shouted. "The pigs know goddamn well how serious we are. And they're going to be taking us a lot more seriously in the future or they'll be dead."

My remark opened up a round of discussions on how violent any future action should be. I detected a slight hesitancy by Bennett to commit himself to agreeing with an all-out campaign of violence. Spiegel and Naomi were for it.

"Cincinnati has been rather quiet," she said. "We haven't been working here that long," Bennett snapped, almost in defense. "Michigan and New York had a head start."

Naomi didn't dwell on that particular remark. She had made her point, which seemed to come across quite clearly, even to me. She had been sent to Cincinnati to evaluate its effectiveness. "Maybe we need more bread to carry on our operations here," she added. "What plans do we have for getting more?" she asked.

"That's not a topic to discuss now," Bennett cut in.

"You're right," she apologized.

At first I thought they were backing off the subject because I was in the room. But then I remembered how Jacobs didn't want to discuss Washington on the phone when I called him the other day. I put the two together and figured they thought the telephone and house were bugged. I was sure the only bugs in the place were the roaches I had seen. By now a number of others who lived in the collective had returned. Arlo Jacobs came in and apologized for not meeting me at the Gold Star Chili Bar. I had seen most of the people in the room either at the demonstration at the campus or at the early meetings I had attended. From the appearance of most of the people in the room, it looked like a convention of hoboes in training.

The conversation centered on a meeting scheduled for the student union building the next night. It was easy for them to get the use of a meeting room, because SDS was a registered student group, and the Weathermen were technically part of SDS. A large crowd was expected. It was the first official meeting of SDS this year.

"We want Naomi to tell the meeting about her experiences in jail," Bennett said. A former SDS district leader who was a student at the university also was expected at the meeting.

"She's living in a dream world," Bennett said. The girl had opposed the ouster of the Progressive Labor Party and the split of SDS into two revolutionary youth movements.

"She's a typical running dog," Spiegel remarked. Then he turned to me, "She's the one who does nothing but talk, Grathwohl."

An agenda for the meeting was drawn up.

"We passing out any song sheets?" Stein asked.

"We got a new one for the book," Naomi said.

This was the first time I had heard about a songbook. Somebody produced a black-covered loose-leaf notebook. It was passed over to Naomi, who held it for a moment, and then gave it to me. "You might want to look at this."

I took the book and flipped through the pages. The latest entries were about the riots in Chicago. One read:

> You thought you could stop the Weatherman
> But up-front people put you on your can.

Then the verse turned to Richard Elrod, the city's assistant corporation counsel whose neck had been broken during the Weatherman attack:

> Stay, Elrod, stay
> Stay in your iron lung;
> Play, Elrod, play
> Play with your toes for awhile.

A very compassionate poet, I thought. Another song had instructions to sing it to the tune of White Christmas. It began:

> I'm dreaming of a White Riot
> Just like the one October 8
> When the pigs took a beating
> And things started leading
> To armed struggle against the state.

Some of the songs were typed on regular three-ring loose-leaf paper, while others had been cut out of a newspaper, probably Fire, and pasted in the book. There were also a list of slogans and a few passages from Revolution in the Revolution.

I handed the book back to Naomi after a few minutes. The discussion about the SDS meeting continued until 2 A.M. Then the group started drifting upstairs to the third floor. Bennett told me he would see me the next night at the meeting, so I took this as a cue that I could leave. I had to get up for work in the morning, and I didn't want to be late again. I said good-bye and left.

The SDS meeting at the student union building drew about 50 students. I was surprised. Evidently the demonstration had done some good for the Weatherman image. As Bennett predicted, the former SDS leader who had supported the Progressive Labor Party began an argument about the violent tactics used by the Weathermen. She claimed the same goal could be reached without violence. Spiegel and Naomi did most of the arguing against her. After the meeting, I asked Naomi if she wanted to go over to the Gold Star Chili Bar for some spaghetti. She accepted. I had two very valid reasons for asking her. First, I sensed that I would need her on my side if I was going to get any place in the Weatherman group. Secondly, if I needed a sponsor into the movement, it might as well be someone who looked like her.

Naomi wasn't satisfied with the way the meeting had gone. She felt it had gotten out of control and that she hadn't done enough to bring it around to the Weatherman viewpoint again. She was probably right. The argument with the SDS leader took the spark out of the meeting, and most of the people left. During the dinner Naomi asked me many of the same questions I had been asked by Spiegel, Bennett, and Nancy Chiara. I poured on the part about the poor kid from the other side of the tracks, and I added a little more bitterness to my remarks about Vietnam. Otherwise, my answers were the same.

I saw the Weathermen on a daily basis after that. I met with them at the house, in the Gold Star Chili Bar, or on the street. Another demonstration was being planned for the campus. There was an internal fight over how violent it should be. One faction, led by Spiegel, was in favor of using dynamite. Bennett resisted this as being too extreme. He wanted to build a larger following before adding violent measures. As a prelude to the demonstration, they were painting slogans on buildings, fences, or any place there was room.

Even though I was in daily contact, I didn't seem to be any closer to actually being invited to join the group. I was still considered a contact, along with Eddie Schaeffer and a few others. This was disappointing. I decided I had to do something more drastic. I settled on conducting my own night action by painting slogans on buildings near Calhoun Street.

I went to a hardware store and got a few cans of spray paint.

There was a side wall of a building off Calhoun Street that was perfect. It was near the Gold Star and sure to be seen by the Weathermen. I was off on Tuesday, so I decided to strike late Monday night. I shoved the spray cans in my coat pocket and went off to rap on Calhoun Street with the others. I found Naomi and spent about an hour with her. She invited me back to the collective, but I made an excuse. Then I went off for a few beers. It was easier going out on night patrol in Vietnam than getting ready to paint a building.

About 1 o'clock in the morning, I moved in on my target. It was a beautiful wall. Unmarked. I advanced on the objective, shielded from the street by the shadows. I started with "OFF THE PIGS!" Then I added: "UP THE REVOLUTION!" Then I stepped back to admire my work. It was beginning to be fun. Then I checked the street to see if anyone was walking around. All was quiet.

I decided to add one more sign. Something a little different. I got out the second spray can and began working. Slowly, so it could be perfect. This one was definitely more creative. "UNCLE HO WANTS YOU!" it said. Then, underneath, I had drawn a finger pointing out toward the street with a Viet Cong flag draped from it. A masterpiece in revolutionary slogan painting. As I admired my work, I heard voices coming down the street. Cops, I thought. I couldn't be caught painting walls; Murrish would never forgive me. I put the spray can quietly on the ground near a trash barrel and moved back into the dark part of an alley on the side of the building. The police paused near the building. I held my breath. The voices moved on. I breathed out and went home to bed. I waited until Tuesday afternoon before going to look for Bennett. I found him and John Harmon at the Gold Star. Harmon was in his late 20s, like Bennett. He was a former minister of some kind, but had dropped his church affiliation and joined the Weathermen when he was in college. I joined them at the table.

"Who the hell needs you, Corky?" I said. "I may start my own movement. Schaeffer is as anxious to get going as I am, and I'm sure there are other vets around who'll support us." Then I told them what I had done.

"That was only a start," I added. "We followers of Uncle Ho will get things moving." Bennett was furious. "You can't do that. You can't go out and conduct an action on your own."

Then Harmon explained. "I don't think you understand. We don't paint walls just for the fun of it. That would be childish. And our main goal isn't to annoy the pigs. It's to get a quick message across to the public. Just the way Schick does by using billboards along a highway. Last night you did what you thought was necessary. And we approve of individuals acting alone. But they have to act under an overall plan. A framework. We don't want to suppress your enthusiasm, but we do want to channel it so we'll all benefit."

He explained that wall painting was a vital part of the communication system. The newspaper, Fire, reached all-the individuals who were in the movement or in sympathy with it, but the only way to reach the general public was by putting slogans on walls.

"We have to compete against hundreds of thousands of capitalistic phrases that go out to the public every day on everything from cereal boxes to television commercials. One method we have of standing out is through sign or poster painting. People aren't going to fight for us if they don't even know we're around."

"We use short phrases so that people will remember them. And they're faster to paint. All we're trying to do is get people to start thinking about what they see painted on the walls. Once we get their attention, they may come looking for more literature."

Harmon was making sense. I had never thought about wall painting in that context before. My aggressiveness had impressed them, though. Two days later, I was assigned to a sub-collective in a house on Vine Street.

Chapter 7

Moving In

Hal Lincoln called me at work on Tuesday, December 2, to tell me to bring my things over to the house on Hollister that night and I would get further instructions about the sub-collective on Vine. After talking to Lincoln, I called Murrish and told him I was moving in with the Weathermen. I said I would keep him informed.

My mother thought I was crazy when I went home after work, packed some clothes in a torn army duffle bag and said that I was moving out. I told her I'd keep in touch, but not where I was going.

"This has something to do with those strange phone calls you've been getting," she said. "I know it does, and I don't like it. Whatever you're doing, I don't like it."

I told her not to worry, knowing it wouldn't do any good, and left.

Barry Stein and Naomi Jaffee were waiting for me when I got to Hollister Street. Naomi explained that we were all going to an important meeting across town, but that I'd be able to drop off my things at the sub-collective on the way. She said Barry Stein was in charge of the people working out of the sub-collective.

The sub-collective was a small three-room apartment in a three-story wooden-frame house on Vine Street that resembled the house on Hollister. Except for five mattresses scattered throughout the room and three old wooden chairs. the apartment was barren. Stein came into the apartment with me. I tossed my duffle bag into a closet in the front hall, took a quick look around, and left. There weren't any other signs of life. We drove into a well-kept residential section of the city. Stein parked the car in front of a long, ranch-style house. Inside, there was expensive Danish-modern furniture and wall-to-wall carpet. The White Panthers were an extremely violent group, organized in Detroit, and they were trying to expand. However, they lacked the natural base that the Weathermen had in the SDS, a registered student organization on many campuses.

The meeting was called to try to arrange a working agreement between the two groups. Naomi said there wouldn't be any talk about merger, but that there should be joint operations to show strength. White Panthers had taken part in the demonstrations in Chicago and Washington. Naomi said strong revolutionary groups can seek alliances for the benefit of the overall struggle. "Only weak groups should mistrust alliances," she warned.

We held the meeting in the family room, which was right off the large living room. The house was chosen for the meeting because it wasn't bugged by the police. Since we weren't in the collective, it was permissible to smoke grass. A number of cigarettes were passed around, but some preferred water pipes.

The primary objective of the meeting was to coordinate a demonstration on the campus the following week. Mike Spiegel was displeased with the raid we pulled on the campus when the businessmen were meeting there in October. "We should have smacked a few heads," he said now.

Spiegel was in charge of the collective, although he was usually overruled by Corky Bennett, John Harmon, and Karen Bittner. The four of them made up the primary leadership council. They ran the Weathermen activities in Cincinnati, but they had to report to members of the Weather Bureau, the national controlling unit. Bureau members stopped by occasionally, as did Gerry Long prior to the Chicago riots. The bureau could also reassign individuals or purge those they thought were not doing the proper job. I had the feeling Naomi had been sent by the Weather Bureau to upgrade Cincinnati's activities, although this was never said. However, I was willing to bet that Bennett and Harmon had the same feeling.

Naomi Jaffee was immediately assigned to the secondary leadership of the collective, along with Arlo Jacobs and Nancy Chiara. When members of the primary leadership were out of town or not available, the secondary leadership took over. Then came three important action groups. They were the Street Collective, Travel Collective, and High School Collective. Members of these smaller collectives had particular assignments. For example, the street collective members worked on recruiting youths from campus and the greaser, or working class, areas. The high school collective was responsible for high school and private school students. The travel collective covered other colleges and schools in the area. As a member of the sub-collective, I could be called on to help a member in any group who needed assistance. I was a trainee. By assisting members from all groups, I would get to know how the entire organization worked. Then, when my training period was over, I'd be promoted into either the high school, travel, or street collective.

Mike Spiegel had one goal during the meeting: convince us that we should stop "f—ing around and go out and blow up the ROTC building."

This brought on various degrees of dissent from Bennett and Harmon and raves of approval from Naomi Jaffee and the White Panthers.

"Violence may turn too many against us," Harmon snapped. "We want a demonstration the other students can join in with us. We can't invite them to join in a bombing."

"We need the students, the workers, the military. We need everybody. As many followers as we can get if we expect to tear down this motherf—ing country," Bennett said, raising his voice.

"I agree with Corky," Naomi said. "We can't afford to turn the students against us. But, at the same time, we have to show them we're deadly serious when we talk about revolution. Why did we take over the SDS? I'll tell you why. Because they had too much talk about a revolution and not enough action. Therefore, we need more violence in the demonstration. Maybe the campus isn't indoctrinated enough yet to support a bombing of the ROTC building, as Corky claims, but we should do more than just talk."

The argument continued to rage. Finally there was a lull as everybody took turns puffing on cigarettes. Naomi then turned the meeting over to other specific aspects of the university demonstration, such as time, place, and theme. She said we could discuss the degree of violence again later, but that she didn't favor any action that the police could bust them for immediately, like blowing up the ROTC building with 100 witnesses. "If we decide to blow it up, we have to do it at a different time under different circumstances."

The bombing issue was dormant, but not dead. Our theme for the campus was "Revolution Now." A revolution was needed in this country to prove to the Third-World people that they had support within the imperialistic mother country. Demonstrations such as ours would give them encouragement so they would continue to fight on. Naomi said Mike Spiegel was going to give the speech during the demonstration. Naomi was going to help write the speech and assigned me to do the research.

As the meeting wore on, other differences with the White Panther leader Perez began to emerge. He didn't think we should identify ourselves in any way with revolutionary groups or revolutionary slogans. He just wanted to come on as a group of university students opposing the war. He didn't want to bring in references to socialist or communistic causes.

I grabbed at these remarks. It was a chance for me to defend Weathermen policy while winning a few points with Naomi. Before any of the others could answer Perez, I told him he was wrong.

"Are you afraid of being called a communist?" I asked. "Or are you ashamed?" Without waiting for an answer, I decided to turn the needle a little. "You're refuting Guevara, Mao Tse Tung, and Ho Chi Minh. They weren't ashamed of being communists. Why should we be?" I knew I had Weathermen approval because nobody interrupted me, except Perez. "The communist party in the U.S. is dead and buried," he shouted. "They were a bunch of old farts who didn't want to do anything. We want action."

We argued the point for about 20 minutes. Finally I lost my temper and bellowed: "You're just a shithead. You haven't been making any sense all night."

When the meeting finally came to an end early in the morning, we had made definite plans to stage a campus demonstration on Tuesday. Perez and other White Panthers would join us.

Going back to the car, Naomi and Bennett were pleased with the outcome. They praised me for taking such an active part. However, Naomi was critical of my heated argument with Perez. "You have to present your points more rationally," she said. "Anger can't win an argument for you. But overall you did a good job."

They dropped me off at Vine Street. I flopped on one of the mattresses and went right to sleep. I was late for work again in the morning.

I spent the first part of the next night working on the speech with Spiegel and Naomi. They used me as a sounding board for certain phrases or lines. If I reacted well, they thought others on the campus would react the same way. While we used the table in the kitchen, other small groups were busy painting signs, mapping out the demonstration area, and collecting spray paint cans. Then, later in the evening, two teams of four each went out on "night actions." My group painted slogans on the walls along Calhoun Street while the other group did a similar job on the campus. We wanted to attract a big turnout.

I dragged myself through work the following day under a constant barrage of cold stares from the supervisor. He didn't say anything, but I knew his thoughts were not friendly.

I planned to take a nap after work, but when I got back to the apartment, there was an urgent message for me to report immediately to the house on Hollister.

When I got over to the collective, the living room was crowded with members sitting on the floor and draped over the chairs and sofa. It was quiet except for Bennett's voice. He was condemning the establishment. I had seldom heard Bennett as vehement as he sounded now.

"The f—ing pigs didn't give them a chance," Benedict was saying. "They went in shooting to kill from the very beginning. They wanted blood, and they got it."

Fred Hampton, a chapter leader of the Illinois Black Panther party, had been killed by the Chicago police during a raid on a

Panther apartment earlier that morning. Mark Clarke, another Panther, was also killed.

The demonstration scheduled for the following week was going to be held the next day instead, to protest Fred Hampton's murder. Everybody was expected to work all night to get things ready. Those with roles in the guerrilla theater would begin rehearsals immediately. The demonstration had taken on added importance. We had to make our protests heard by the pigs who had killed Fred Hampton. The establishment had to be shown that whites as well as blacks were angered by Hampton's death.

I joined Naomi and Spiegel to work on the speech. The theme would remain the same: "Revolution Now," but Hampton would emerge as a cause célèbre for the movement, a martyr whose death had to be avenged. I researched old copies of The Berkeley Barb, Tribe, Village Voice and other newspapers we had in the house for quotes by Hampton. Spiegel was excited. He had concrete material to work with.

We worked well into the night. Spiegel kept changing lines, phrases, paragraphs. Each time he changed it, the speech took on added violence. Naomi, Spiegel, and I walked the streets for a couple of hours, discussing the nature of the violence. The Weathermen had to be in the forefront of the white movement to support the struggle of the blacks to conquer their suppressors.

Spiegel finally left Naomi and me to edit the final draft. We made a few more changes, put the final version of the speech together, and left it on the kitchen counter so that Spiegel could find it in the morning. I was getting ready to leave when Naomi said, "You might as well stay here for the night. It's too late to go back to Vine Street. You'll only have to come back here in the morning."

My supervisor at McAlpine's was going to love that. I could picture myself calling in with the excuse: "Sorry, boss. I need the day off to burn down the campus."

I agreed to stay anyway.

Naomi led the way up the stairs to the third floor. It was dark, but I could make out the outline of bodies scattered all over the floor. I followed Naomi to the end of the room.

"Here," she whispered, pointing down to an empty mattress,

but there wasn't any sheet on it.

"Okay," I said.

She didn't move. "Do you always sleep with all your clothes on?" she asked. I pulled off my shirt and let my trousers drop to the floor. Then I sat on the mattress to remove my shoes. I looked up. Naomi was naked. I pulled the blanket up from the bottom of the mattress, and she crawled onto the mattress beside me. She reached over and touched my shoulder. "Relax," she said. "You're so tense."

I hadn't expected any of this. I half expected it was a put on, a practical joke, like a fraternity initiation. As soon as I touched her, the light would go on, and everybody would holler. I reached for her. She moved over and nobody snapped the lights on.

"You still have some of the straight working-class ideas," she said in a low voice.

"What?"

"You're afraid of f—ing. I mean, you're shocked that we're in bed together tonight. Although you've wanted to f — me since you first saw me, right?"

"Right." She was absolutely right. But it was embarrassing to me making love in a room full of people. I looked to see if anyone was staring at us. It felt like they were.

"We worked hard together all night, Larry. There's no reason why we should break off the relationship just because we're going to bed. We're not getting married. We're just enjoying ourselves after a hard night's work."

How could I refute that reasoning? As I rolled over on top of her, I became less and less concerned about the other people in the room.

When I woke up in the morning, Naomi was gone. In fact, most of the people in the room were already up. I pulled on my pants and went downstairs. Naomi was in the kitchen with Spiegel. Most of the others were in the living room exercising.

I felt slightly embarrassed when I saw Naomi and slightly jealous of Spiegel. I walked over and touched her shoulder, but she just pulled away. "Mike wants to make a few more changes," she said as if we had never stopped working on the speech.

"There's coffee on the counter," Spiegel offered. "But maybe you want to exercise first."

I walked into the living room thinking about Naomi. Maybe I had said something to her that I shouldn't have. I continued to think about her as we did sit-ups, push-ups, deep knee bends, and practiced a few karate movements. It was a morning ritual. The 20 minutes of exercises were usually followed by political discussion, but today the discussion was being waived so that we could concentrate on the demonstration. I was doing my push-ups next to Nancy Chiara. I looked over at her and wondered what kind of job we could share. I might get to enjoy this life after all. There were certain things I decided to leave out of my report to Murrish. He might not understand.

In the middle of a sit-up, it occurred to me that I had to call McAlpine's and make an excuse for not going to work, and then call Murrish to let him know the demonstration was set for 1 o'clock today. I cut my exercises short and went back into the kitchen. I poured a cup of coffee and told Spiegel that I had to check in with the store. "I don't want to lose any bread."

Spiegel said there was a pay phone in a bar on the corner of the street. I told him I'd be right back. My supervisor was furious. I told him I had a slight recurrence of the malaria I had contracted in Vietnam and had to go over to the Veterans Hospital for a shot. I knew he didn't believe me, but he did credit me with having an original excuse. Then I put in a quick phone call to Murrish. I told him I didn't see any explosives in the house, so I presumed we weren't going to blow up the ROTC building as originally discussed. With the switch in demonstration dates, we didn't have the time to plan anything violent. Murrish said there would be agents watching the demonstration, and to alert him if the plans changed. I made both phone calls in five minutes. I didn't want to be gone too long.

An advance party of five people led by Barry Stein went off to the campus at 11 o'clock to pass out literature announcing the demonstration during the break in classes. I left for the campus with Naomi and Spiegel. We talked about Fred Hampton and the Black Panther party all the way down.

The activities began with the guerrilla theater at a quarter to one in the lobby of the student union building. Bennett and

Karen Bittner were in charge of the theater. The idea was to get the students thinking about Vietnam and the U.S. suppression so they'd be more receptive to Mike Spiegel's speech. Nobody wore any costumes, but they did have arm bands to show if they were the Vietnamese or American soldiers. The soldiers carried broom handles for rifles, and the American soldiers stormed a Vietnamese village looking for Viet Cong. When they didn't find any, they massacred all the villagers, including women and children. The more the villagers protested, the faster the American soldiers killed them. As the massacre came to an end, Bennett, wearing an arm band identifying him as General Ky, strode onto the scene, smiling with approval. He had a rope tied to his arms. Behind Ky, pulling the rope to move his arms, was John Harmon, identified as Secretary of Defense Laird. Laird walked over and put his arm around Ky. "Our presidents will be proud of us today," he said to Ky. "This village uprising was a threat to your regime. But we put it down."

"The government will need more money to help restore this village," Ky said smilingly. "We'll see that you get it," Laird said.

The skit was over in 12 minutes. About 50 students had watched from beginning to end without comment. Bennett then invited the audience to step outside and listen to something that was of vital concern to "all of US."

Outside, we had a group of students gathering. Some had come because of the leaflets that were passed out, but most of them were either going or coming from the student union building. Schaeffer was stationed inside the building. As soon as the play ended, he signaled me, and I told Spiegel. Spiegel jumped up on the wall in front of the student building. I took a position just in front of him at the base of the wall. I was responsible for keeping anybody from attacking him while he finished his speech.

Spiegel began dramatically. "Yesterday another assassination was committed in the United States. Yesterday a man of peace was assassinated by the pigs. A man who worked for the people was murdered by a pig assassination squad."

We had members of the Weathermen and White Panthers scattered throughout the crowd. Every so often they'd lead the audience response with shouts of "Right on!" or "Power to the People!" Spiegel was doing an excellent job. If he ever went straight, he could probably run for office. "Yesterday it was Chicago, but tomorrow it may be Cincinnati. We have to stop the pigs now before they kill us like they murdered Fred Hampton."

He eulogized Hampton and made him a symbol of repression around the world. The other Weathermen and White Panthers played their parts well. They cheered at the right time; they hissed at the mention of the Chicago pigs. A stranger viewing the demonstration would say Spiegel was succeeding in generating true student unrest, that the crowd was turning into a violent mob. However, in reality, most of the support was coming from our own people scattered in the crowd, not the students.

I was moving my arms around to keep warm. I noticed a big burly guy moving about in the crowd, and I kept my eyes on him. He moved from the back, through to the front, and then went to the back again. He didn't say anything. He was just watching and listening. Halfway through the speech, the crowd had grown to about 100. It was a good turnout. Two Cincinnati plainclothes cops watched the whole thing from the steps of the student union building. They tried to be unobtrusive, but they didn't succeed.

As Spiegel's speech drew near its conclusion, Eddie Schaeffer opened a sack and passed out cans of spray paint. Some of us already had the cans in our pockets. When Spiegel finished, he threw his fist high into the air and leaped off the wall. He ran over the bridge and down the path toward the ROTC building. The other Weathermen and White Panthers took off after him. I hung back for a few minutes to see who was following. The cops stayed on the building steps, and I lost track of the burly guy who had been moving around in the crowd. About half of the students who had listened to the speech joined in, but it seemed that they were just curious to see where we were going. I ran after Spiegel.

We passed other buildings shouting, "The VC are gonna win!" and "Up the Revolution!" Spiegel led the mob right to the ROTC building. He was the first to start painting a slogan on the red brick walls of the building. Many people looked out from inside the building, but the front door never opened. I was half afraid that Spiegel had a stick of dynamite with him, but he didn't. He seemed content with painting slogans. The attack took about three minutes. Then we split, running in different directions. Later, we all gathered in the living room at the house on Hollister Street to review the action.

"We weren't violent enough."

"The guerrilla theater dragged too much."

"Not enough students took part in the action."

Naomi said we weren't capitalizing on local campus issues enough. We had to take advantage of all rifts between the college administration and the students, the students and the city, or the city and the college. "If we don't have an issue, we'll have to create one."

As we were discussing the action, Stein came upstairs from the hallway and whispered something to Bennett. I watched Bennett go over to the doorway with Stein. Standing there was the girl Mary I had met in the school cafeteria after the first demonstration. I heard Bennett telling Stein that "this should never be allowed." Stein was nodding in agreement while claiming that he had nothing to do with it. Bennett opened the door and looked out, closed it again, and turned into the living room toward me.

He motioned for me to come out into the hall. I got up and joined the conversation. He started to introduce me to Mary, but I said I'd already met her with Stein about two months ago. Mary evidently had been hanging around the Weathermen because she seemed to know everybody by name.

"Mary's made a serious mistake," Bennett said to me. "She brought some guy along with her. Mary claims he's a Vietnam vet and disgusted with the system."

"I don't claim, he is," Mary said strongly.

"All right. He is," Benedict answered. "Anyway, since he's here, we're going to ask him up to talk, but I want you, Larry, and Stein to see him. Give us a few seconds before you bring him up, Mary."

She agreed and disappeared out the door.

Bennett went into the living room and broke up the meeting. Everybody was free to do anything they had to. Bennett, Spiegel,

Harmon, and Karen Bittner went upstairs to talk more about the action on a council level. Naomi stayed in the living room. I sat on the floor, and Stein flopped in one of the old chairs.

Mary brought the guy into the room. It was the same burly guy who had moved through the crowd in front of the student union building. But now, up close, he was older than he'd appeared before. He was in his late 20s, possibly even 30.

We started rapping about Vietnam. He had served two tours, he said, before he got fed up with the entire system: the army and the country. He was back in the states only six months, and this was his first semester in school.

He believed in what the Weathermen stood for and wanted to be part of the demonstrations. "Except I wouldn't have stopped at painting the ROTC building," he said. "I would have blown it up."

He was coming on strong, which was good. Naomi was listening very carefully to him and to my questions. Stein asked him many of the same questions he had grilled me on.

The guy had been in Vietnam all right. I even knew his outfit. In fact, his hair was still growing out from a crew cut that he once had. Most of his references to battles and incidents in Nam were from 1965, when I was there. Mary remained very quiet during our talk.

After awhile, Arlo Jacobs came in and joined us. He asked a few questions, but most of the work was left up to me. I wondered why they'd trust this assignment to me, but decided to take them at face value. This guy was a vet and so was I; therefore, we might have something in common. I began to like him. He evidently had read some of the literature the Weathermen gave out. He was very familiar with Fire. Was he too familiar? It occurred to me that the guy might be a plant to see if I gave anything away to him that I didn't tell the others. I dwelled on this for a moment, then dismissed it. I went around with him again on certain points. He knew Cincinnati better than I did, yet he had been in the city only about six months. After a half hour, I made an excuse to leave the room. I motioned for Naomi to follow me, and we went upstairs to where Bennett was still conducting a leadership meeting.

I think Bennett had forgotten about the guy downstairs, because he hesitated a moment when I interrupted his conversation to talk about Mary's friend.

"What do you think?" Bennett asked. "Mary says he's a good man."

I waited a moment before answering. "He's a pig."

Everybody looked at me in disbelief.

"You sure?" Bennett snapped.

"As sure as I am that you're Weathermen."

"How do you know?" Harmon asked.

"The way he answered questions about Cincinnati, for one. He's probably a vice cop that they pulled off assignments to get in with us." After I said this, I added: "I ran into a lot of those creeps when I was a kid."

"Second, he was in Nam in '65 in a military police outfit. I'm willing to bet he was a cop before he went into the army. His story just doesn't fit." I wasn't absolutely sure he was a cop, but I was positive that he was a plant, which meant Mary had to be one, too. I tried to figure out what Sergeant Berry was trying to pull. Maybe Berry never believed my story.

Spiegel, who hadn't said anything until now, got up off the mattress. "Let's stomp the f — ," he said. "Let's stomp him the same way we took care of that cop in Chicago."

"No, that won't do," Bennett said. "He can't hurt us. But if we stomp him, we'll have all the cops in the city in here within an hour. We got away with it in Chicago because we were just passing through. We'll just have to get rid of him."

"What about Mary?" Naomi asked.

"Maybe she didn't know," I said.

"She had to know," Bennett insisted.

"Corky's right," Spiegel said. "We'll have to cut Mary off too. How much does she know?"

Everybody shrugged. Mary had been hanging around for some time, but today was her first visit to the house. She must have been getting as frustrated as I was, I thought. That poor guy downstairs probably talked her into coming up here to bluff it out.

"Mary has to be taught a lesson," Spiegel said. "We have to

set her up as an example." "True," Bennett said, "but we don't
have to decide that now. The time will come to take care of her."

Bennett started downstairs.

"I'll get them out. But I want it passed around about Mary."
Before he went down the stairs, he turned to me.

"Thanks, Larry," he said.

Spiegel followed Bennett down the steps. I was worried for
Mary's safety. When the time came that they could get political
propaganda from harming her, they'd do so. She was probably
safe until then, especially since she didn't really know very much
about the organization.

I had to get to Murrish so that he could warn the plant and
Mary. I also wanted him to find out what Sergeant Berry was up
to. Jesus Christ, I thought, Berry could end up getting me killed.

Chapter 8

War Council Preparation

For most people, the Christmas season sparks a spirit of brotherhood, but for the Weathermen the month of December meant planning for the National War Council in Flint, Michigan. The conference was scheduled to be held from December 26 to 31.

I had heard about the war council, but I wasn't fully aware of its ramifications until a meeting on December 9. It was on that same day that Naomi told me I'd been moved up from the sub-collective to full collective status. I believe Mary and her friend had a lot to do with my advancement. When I turned the guy in as a pig, my reputation grew.

My duties as a member of the sub-collective were menial, anyway, and I'd been complaining to Bennett about them since first being assigned to the house on Vine Street. All I did was answer the phone, deliver messages, and run back and forth to the store. I was supposedly ripping off food or spray-paint cans, but in fact I was paying for the goods from my paycheck.

Now I was upgraded in rank and assigned to the high school collective with Ray Lansing, Hal Lincoln, and Annie Walton. Naomi was the secondary leadership for this group, so I was sure she had something to do with my assignment. Karen Bittner was the primary leader. The high school collective, it was explained to me, concentrated its activities on high school students. We hung around the schoolyards during the lunch break and after school, rapping with kids. Our opening pitch to male students usually focused on Vietnam: "Why should you be facing death in a country you know so little about?" We took a Woman's Liberation attack for the females: "Why should you earn less when you graduate?"

By personalizing the approach, we got the kids to listen to us. Then we'd give them copies of our newspaper, Fire, or other pamphlets such as reprints of an interview with an 18-year-old American who spent three years in Red China. I tried to picture my brother Joey listening to this leftist pitch. I was sure he wouldn't pay any attention to me unless I had an endorsement from Johnny Bench.

The high school collective concentrated on four schools: each one was given a code name so we could discuss the area freely without worrying about somebody listening to us. Our primary targets were North College Hill High School, called "Rose"; College Hill, named "Throne"; Withrow High School, known as "Bagel"; and Walnut Hills High School, referred to as "Lox."

Although my primary duties lay with the high school group, I was also told that from time to time I would be called on to help members of the street collective in recruiting greasers and college students. The greasers, or members of motorcycle or juvenile gangs, were considered prime candidates for the revolution because of their antiestablishment sentiments.

The night I was promoted, Bennett announced that everyone should be prepared to spend the end of the month in Flint, Michigan at the National War Council.

As a member of the sub-collective, it had been my job that afternoon to go down to the Greyhound bus terminal and pick up the shipment of newspapers. In theory, Fire was printed twice a month at the SDS offices on West Madison Street in Chicago and shipped out to all collectives across the country. However, we never seemed to get two issues a month. Fire was the replacement for New Left Notes, the original publication of SDS. When the Weathermen took over SDS in June, they wanted a more inflammatory format for the "revolutionary newspaper," and a title that fit the new thrust of the organization. Thus, The Fire Next Time was born. Fire was affiliated with Underground Press Syndicate and Liberation News Service, two organizations that sent material to 100 or more underground newspapers in the United

States. Most of these were published near major universities.

Fire was important to us because it kept us informed about happenings in other collectives and served as a constant reminder of our mission: revolution. In addition to the inflammatory news geared to provoking violent action, Fire frequently ran articles concerning guerrilla organizations in other countries. The issue that Bennett was holding contained the second of a two-part series on the Arab guerrillas' fight against the Zionist Jews for Palestine. According to the article, Israel was a "colonial-type creature imposed by forces outside the area" and the Jewish masses "are being led by Zionism toward another disaster."

During the meeting, Bennett used Fire as a visual aid for his inspirational talk about the war council. "Why are we going to Flint?" he asked rhetorically. "Because it's time for action!" As he went on, his speech became more violent. Of course, it was easy to talk about something that was going to take place in Flint, but when it came to making a decision on a specific violent action, Bennett always hesitated, which was to the advantage of Cincinnati and the university. Other cities weren't so lucky. In the last two days, fire bombs had exploded at Rutgers University in New Jersey and at Sam Houston State University in Texas.

Finally, Bennett reached the dramatic climax of his talk. He scooped up a newspaper from the pile, holding it out so we could see the front page. A photograph of a marching mob was in the corner on the left. A drawing of a machine gun was on the right. The headline was a call to arms: "DURING THE 1960s THE AMERICAN GOVERNMENT WAS ON TRIAL FOR CRIMES AGAINST THE PEOPLE OF THE WORLD. WE NOW FIND THE GOVERNMENT GUILTY AND SENTENCE IT TO DEATH IN THE STREETS."

He turned the newspaper around and looked down at the page. "That's what Flint is all about," he said.

"Right on!" came the response.

A lengthy discussion followed. These discussions bored me, but within the Weatherman operational framework they were very important. With each discussion you reiterated your political philosophy, thus reaffirming your commitment to revolution.

The general consensus was that the Weathermen had come a long way since they split from SDS in June, but the war council was needed to organize a greater national direction for the movement.

When the speeches were over, we got down to the mundane aspects of preparing for the revolutionary council: who was in charge of closing the houses, how many cars we would need to get there, what we should take with us. I got the first job: to make sure both houses were closed and that nothing incriminating was left behind.

The formal meeting broke up around 10 o'clock, but most of us sat around and continued to talk. I was rapping with Ray Lansing and Hal Lincoln about the high school collective. They considered it extremely important that a solid foundation be built with the young people.

"Those kids understand more than you think," Lincoln said. He was sitting on the floor with his back resting against the sofa. "The kids can be loyal to the movement. Look at that kid, Jimmy, up in Boston."

Lincoln was referring to a story in Fire about a 16-year-old contact at a collective in Boston. In November the Boston police had busted 24 Weathermen on charges of conspiracy to murder after a sniping attack on a Cambridge police station. One of the individuals arrested was a 16-year-old kid named Jimmy who was associated with the Weathermen, although he wasn't a member of the organization.

According to the Boston police, Jimmy's testimony against the Weathermen linked them to sniping. The article reported that Jimmy was held in "protective custody" for two weeks, during which time he was beaten and bribed. But once on the witness stand, Jimmy turned against the police, claiming they had beaten him until he'd agreed to testify against the Weathermen. Sitting in the courtroom, he pointed to four policemen, saying: "Those four pigs beat me. That big fat one. He put them up to it."

Jimmy was a temporary hero in Weatherman circles. "Goddamn pigs can't even win a frame-up," Lincoln laughed. "If we got more kids like that, we can't lose."

I was sure the story was being told for my benefit. They didn't want me to think I was wasting my time trying to recruit 16-and 17 -year-old kids. I found it hard to believe that we could get many high school kids who were devoted to politics.

About midnight, I excused myself from the discussions and went to bed. I was still holding down the job at McAlpine's, although it was becoming more difficult. The next morning when I got to work, I called Murrish and made an appointment to see him at his office that night. Murrish was interested in my new status in the collective.

I used the phone booth near the loading platform. When I pulled open the door and started back to the working area, I noticed that Tommy Cash had been watching me. As I got back to the platform, he said: "You dealing in numbers? Or pushin' grass or something?"

"What are you talking about?"

"Christ, Grathwohl, you're always on the phone. So either you're a nut about telephone booths or you've got something goin'." I made a mental note to be more careful. I wasn't worrying about Tommy, but I didn't want to stir up any curiosity around the collective. I thought about calling Murrish back and changing our meeting arrangements, but I decided against it because I didn't want to act paranoid.

A car pulled in for a pick-up. After we loaded it, Tommy began talking about the Super Bowl game, and he never returned to my phone habits.

I met with Murrish that night for about an hour. I filled him in on our plans to attend the war council. It was a pretty routine meeting as far as I was concerned, although he did caution me about being more careful now that I was considered a full-fledged member of the Weathermen.

He didn't want me to be leading any of the activities.

I smoked the last two cigarettes in my pack during the meeting. After lighting up the last one, I rolled the pack into a tight little ball and tossed it into Murrish's wastebasket.

"You smoke too much," he said.

I agreed with him, but at the same time I was trying to think of a place to buy another pack. Then I remembered the newsstand in the lobby. When I said good-bye, I hurried out to the elevator. Once in the lobby, I turned toward the newsstand. When I was about five feet away from it, I spotted Joyce Green standing to one side looking through a magazine.

My first impulse was to turn around and walk out. Maybe she hadn't seen me. But what if she had? What if she'd been assigned to follow me? I couldn't take the chance of leaving abruptly. I kept walking toward the stand. Joyce didn't look up from the magazine, so I nudged her. She actually seemed surprised when she saw me. She also seemed embarrassed. Then I noticed that the magazine she was reading was Cosmopolitan.

I ordered two packs of Marlboros and asked Joyce if she wanted anything. She refused. My mind was racing with excuses for my being in the building. Then it came to me — malaria.

"The government is still screwing me," I said. "They make it hard as hell for me to get treatment for the malaria I got in Vietnam, and every once in a while I get a relapse. When I do, I usually go to the Veterans Hospital for treatment. No sense in paying for it myself. But they got some of my papers fouled up, so I had to come down here to straighten it out."

Joyce thought it was wild that I was ripping off the government. On my way out, I had a ridiculous thought. Was Joyce working for the FBI, too? No. Not Joyce.

I was a little apprehensive for the next few days, but nobody questioned me about being in the Federal Building. During the weeks after that, I took a few days off from McAlpine's so that I could work the high school areas with Annie Gordon and Naomi. I had to pretend to be excited about my new assignment.

They decided to break me in at North College Hill High School. We went out to the area just before lunch. I had a stack of newspapers with me. As the students came out for the break, we started rapping with them. I was surprised at the number who were curious or politically aware enough to talk to us.

We hung around the school until the kids were released at 3 P .M. and followed some of them down to a small drugstore. Annie did most of the talking. If she was talking to the boys, she warned them they'd be fighting a useless war for the benefit of Nixon. "You'll stake your life so he can get richer," she said. In talking to girls, she stressed woman's equality. "When you graduate, why shouldn't you have as many opportunities as the boys?"

The next day we went back to the same area. We rapped with the kids who came out during the lunch period. At one time we actually had a crowd of about 15 listening to us. We gave each one a copy of Fire. We didn't keep their attention too long, but I blamed that partially on the cold weather. You can't concentrate on Che Guevara if your feet are getting cold.

As our small group was breaking up, a police squad car pulled up to the curb with a sudden halt. A cop threw open the door and hopped out.

"All right," he demanded, "what's going on?"

The other cop got out of the car a little more slowly, walked around to the back fender and stood watching us. His hand was on his hip. The first cop grabbed a newspaper from my hand. "What's this crap?" "Have one," I said. "They're only a quarter." "Don't be a wise ass." He looked at the newspaper, then crumbled it up in his hand. He looked at all of us, then gave us an order: "Move on. And I don't want to see you handing out this crap around here again. You understand me?"

Annie turned to me. "Let's go," she said. "We don't want any trouble." "That's the right idea, Miss. Keep thinking that way, and you'll be all right."

We left and headed for Walnut Hill High School. We went to a small pizza shop near the school to wait for the kids to start flocking in. We took a booth near the front window. It felt good to be in out of the cold. I had been fairly quiet most of the day, for which I was criticized while we were waiting. I had to be more aggressive, I was told. As the kids began coming into the pizza shop, Anne saw a few she knew and went over to talk to them. Soon she was back at the table. A few minutes later a tall thin boy walked in, saw Anne, and came over to the table. He looked lost in the crowd. Anne invited him to sit down.

His name was Tom Udall. He was a senior, but he was only 16 years old. He was advanced intellectually, but not physically, and from all appearances he seemed out of place socially. He was very aware of current events and was fascinated when Anne explained my background to him. I could see I had an admirer.

After a while another two boys joined us, and we rapped about Vietnam. I told them about my war experiences, and they listened attentively. They were both seniors and were facing the draft if they couldn't stay in college long enough to avoid it.

As we talked, one of the two women who owned the pizza shop kept coming by the table. Both of the women were in their 50s. One worked at the cash register near the front door, while the other served as a waitress. Evidently the one who acted as a waitress was listening to our conversation. Finally she went over and whispered to the woman at the cash register. They both looked back at our table.

I watched them talk for a few seconds. Then the woman at the cash register came from behind the counter, and they both walked over to our table.

"I'm going to ask you to leave," the cash register lady said to us.

"What did we do?" I asked.

The waitress could hardly wait to tell me. "You're corrupting these children, that's what you're doing," she said. She was breathing heavily, and her voice was cracking from restraint.

The other woman was much calmer, but just as determined. "We don't want to make a scene," she said, "but if you don't leave, we're going to call the police."

Two run-ins with the police in one day was too much for me to endure. I agreed to leave. Just then Udall objected.

"They don't have to leave if they don't want to. this is supposed to be a free country."

His sudden outburst stopped the women for a moment. "They're turning your head with their garbage, young man," the waitress said. "Go over to the people your own age."

Udal was going to object again, but Anne Walton stopped him. "It's all right, Tom," she said. "They can keep us out, but they can't keep our ideas out." Anne then made a brief political speech about the repression of ideas, and then we left before the cashier had time to call the police.

We discussed the incident on the way back to the house. Anne was extremely upset. by now others had joined in. Mike Spiegel said some sort of action was necessary against the owners of the shop. "If two old women can chase us away, how the hell are these kids going to believe us about the revolution?" From Spiegel's point of view, he was right. The incident was humiliating.

We decided to return to the shop and paint slogans on the windows and walls of the building. the action was mild, yet would demonstrate to the students that we wouldn't let the two women get away with rebuking us. Anne and I were selected to return. As we went off to the pizza shop, the others took off for the campus. We had actions on two fronts.

Our night actions were increasing, although they were confined to painting slogans and breaking windows. Our main target was the ROTC building. As soon as they scrubbed the paint off, we put it back on.

As the month wore away and we got closer to the council meeting, our discussions on the importance of a national conference increased. These discussions always included a review of our preparations. Our main obstacle was money. We had to transport 14 to 17 people, not counting a few contacts. I offered money from my paycheck. Bennett used this as an example of true comradeship. The possibility of robbing a bank was brought up, but dismissed. It was felt that, to rob a bank, we would need professional outside help, which would be unwise at the present time.

Bennett wanted to go over the specific arrangements, so we planned to meet at the Student Union Building at about 8 o'clock. I was tired of sitting around the house, so I said I was going over to Calhoun Street to rap with some students. Barry Stein said he would come with me. Since I didn't have anything planned, I didn't mind. We picked up a few copies of Fire and left.

As we got a few blocks from the house, I discovered I needed cigarettes.

"Christ, Grathwohl, you're going to turn into a weed," Stein said.

There was a small neighborhood bar on the corner where I

had stopped a few times before for cigarettes. My prior visits were made in the afternoon when only a few of the regular patrons were in the place.

I gave my stack of newspapers to Stein and told him I'd be right out. The long bar was fairly crowded, and off to one side four young toughs were shooting pool on a coin-operated table. One of the guys watched me as I came in through the door. I knew he was staring at my long hair and new growth of beard. The cigarette machine was to the right of the door. I searched through my pockets but couldn't find any change. I had to squeeze past two of the guys who were shooting pool because they were blocking the aisle.

"Excuse me," I said as I brushed by.

"Ain't that something," one of them said. "Jesus Christ sure is polite."

"Aw, Chuck, that's not really Jesus Christ, is it?"

"Who else could it be?"

The remarks brought a few murmurs of laughter from some of the other patrons, but I ignored them. I handed the bartender the dollar bill and asked for change for the cigarette machine. He grabbed it from my hand and flipped the coins onto the bar. As I was picking up the coins, I heard the four guys starting to argue. I turned around and saw one of the guys holding a copy of Fire. Barry Stein was standing in front of him.

"What's this crap?" the guy said. He walked over to the bar, grabbed his beer, and downed half the glass. I started back up the aisle and bumped into the guy who had just finished his beer. "Watch it, man," he said. "Let's get out of here," I said to Stein. I pushed Stein forward, and he opened the door, letting in a cold blast of air. "At least we got some clean air in here," Chuck shouted after us.

I stopped. I had come in for cigarettes, and I was going to get them. "I'll be right with you," I said to Stein, and turned toward the machine. I dropped the coins into the machine and reached down to pick up the cigarettes. When I straightened up, the guy named Chuck was holding out the crumpled newspaper. "Take this shit with you. We don't need any goddamn hippie newspapers in here."

I pushed by and walked to the door. When I opened it, I felt a sharp thud on the back of my head. It sent me spinning forward. My left foot got caught on the door jamb, and I ended up lying out on the sidewalk near the curb. I saw Stein out of the corner of my eye, looking on in amazement. Then Chuck started walking toward me. He was ripping up the newspaper. "I told you to take this crap with you," he said.

I stayed down on one knee but clinched up my fist and shifted my weight forward so I could spring up. When Chuck was about a foot in front of me, he began dropping the torn-up newspaper on my head. I brought my fist up as hard as I could and hammered Chuck in the balls. He let out a horrible scream as he slumped to the ground.

"Let's get the hell out of here," I yelled at Stein. We ran down the street and around the corner. We didn't stop running until we reached the college campus. And neither one of us looked back.

We were both panting hard as we went into the student union building. Our meeting was in a small room on the second floor. As soon as we went through the door, Stein told everybody what had happened. I guessed it was the first street fight Stein had ever seen. He was impressed, and so were the others.

I slumped down in one of the chairs, and Naomi came over behind me. She touched the back of my head very gently. "You sure you're all right?" she asked.

"Sure." Then she pulled her hand away. "You won't be any good to us if you end up in the hospital," she said.

Everybody kidded me a little longer about the fight, then we settled down to discussing our preparations for the war council. Bennett conducted the meeting. He spoke to me first.

"Are both houses ready to be locked up, Larry?"

"Just about. I have the books and newspapers packed in cardboard boxes. I'm going to stash them in a locker at the Greyhound Terminal."

"Okay. But just make sure you're not followed when you go downtown. How about the cars?"

"We'll have about 17 people going with us, so we'll need three cars."

"Who's getting the cars?"

"I am," Stein said. "We have yours," he said to Bennett. "Although the reverend said we could use his station wagon if we left our car with him." "We'll have to think about that," Bennett said.

The reverend was a minister in Cincinnati who was sympathetic to the Weathermen movement. I had seen him only once, but he frequently gave us money, in addition to lending us his car. Spiegel also got money from a Quaker group in town to help us continue our protest against the war, although I was sure they didn't realize the scope of our movement.

"Tom Udall said we could borrow one of his parents' cars," I added.

Bennett was pleased. "That kid's a good contact."

"Do we have enough bread?" Bennett asked.

Naomi answered him. "It's being taken care of. We don't need much. A church in Flint is letting us use its parish school. All we have to do is bring our sleeping bags."

Bennett reminded us to impress on everybody that grass, acid, and smack were prohibited. "Larry, this is one of your duties. I want you to stress the fact that no grass is to be carried. And that means everybody."

I know he was particularly worried about Schaeffer bringing something with him, although he didn't single him out. "The pigs will be watching us very closely," Bennett continued, "and I don't want any of us getting busted on a ridiculous drug charge."

"One other thing. No talking to the press. If they show up, we'll have official statements prepared. Bill Ayers is National Education secretary, and he'll handle all communications with the press."

We got into a general discussion again about why the national council meeting was important. "The council should meld us into a cohesive national movement," Spiegel said. "Up to now our effectiveness has been impaired because we've been fragmented."

When we broke up about 10 o'clock, Naomi came over to me. "I have to talk to you," she said. "I was just going to ask you if you wanted something to eat. We can go down to the Gold Star."

"Good. I'm hungry."

The night seemed colder as we stepped out of the building. The sky was bright with stars, and we could see our breath in front of us. Naomi and I strolled across campus. She didn't talk for awhile, but as we got nearer the other end, she reached out and tugged at my arm. "Wait a minute, Larry. I want to tell you something."

I stopped and turned toward her.

"You know," she said, "we're all committed to the movement."

"I know."

"I mean, we have to do things sometimes to benefit the movement, even though we may not want to do them. My whole life has been built around the revolution. My parents dedicated their lives to the movement, but they did it all wrong. They were too soft. We can turn this into a great socialistic country, Larry."

I took my hands out of my pocket, cupped them under my mouth, and blew on them. She reached up and placed her gloved hands over mine. "This will keep you warm a minute. I'm sorry I got a little carried away. But I want you to understand."

"Understand what?"

"I want you to understand why I do things. You've been involved with us for only a few months. But the movement has been my whole life. And most of the others have been working for one goal for years."

"I think you're dedicated, Larry. We all do. You don't utilize your leadership qualities properly, but you're becoming one of us. However, I think you still cling to some of your middle-class ideas." I started to protest, but she interrupted me. "You may not even realize it, but you do. Your relationship with me for one. We sleep together, Larry, but it doesn't mean anything. It can't. We can't think of ourselves. We have to consider the overall good, and monogamy is bad. You can't work for the whole if you're too involved with one person."

I was anxious to know what she was leading up to. "I'm sermonizing again. I'm sorry. I'll get right to the point. Bill Milton and I are getting married." I pulled back and looked at her. I couldn't believe it. "I don't understand. You just got finished saying..." She cut me short again.

"It's for the movement," she said. "We need money. And we need another car. Milton's parents are anxious to get him married and away from the movement. They're so anxious, they'll do anything. Give him anything. It's an easy-rip-off, Larry. That's all it is."

I stood looking at her, dumbfounded.

"I knew you wouldn't understand. That's why I wanted to tell you. No one has mentioned our marriage because to us it doesn't mean anything. It's just a way to get some bread." She turned and started walking away. Then she stopped again and turned toward me. "This won't change anything between us," she said. Then she walked briskly away. "Come on," she said. "I'm hungry."

Naomi left for Cleveland the next day to meet her new in-laws. I went home to visit my mother and tell her I couldn't be home for Christmas.

Chapter 9

The Council Meets

When I arrived home, my mother stared at me. "You need a haircut," she said. Then she kissed me on the cheek. "And shave off that horrible beard."

I hugged her and told her that I had to leave right away. I could see the shock in her eyes. She didn't say anything right away, but I knew how deeply I had hurt her.

"The only Christmas we missed together was when you were in Vietnam," she said. "I cried and prayed then. But why do you have to leave home now? What are you doing that you can't be with your family at Christmas?"

There wasn't much I could say. I pointed to the Christmas presents I had brought home with me. It was hard to say good-bye.

Then I went to see Donna. She thought what I was doing was crazy. Fortunately Don was there, too, and he gave me some moral support. He also gave me $50 and said he would take care of Donna. He promised to get me more money if I needed it.

A short time later I piled into a 1964 Chevy with Benedict and four others. It was another long, cold trip. The heaters in our cars never seemed to work, so when we arrived in Flint the day after Christmas we were beat. We drove to the Catholic school where we were being allowed to stay. It was closed for the holidays, and we found two U-haul vans in the schoolyard when we arrived. They had been rented by the Seattle collective, which used them as sleeping quarters during the trip. There were cars from other states: California, New York, Illinois, Massachusetts, Maryland, Colorado, and Pennsylvania.

Inside the school, the various collectives were assigned to different classrooms. In ours, the desks were piled along the walls so we could spread our sleeping bags on the floor. Naomi was already there, rapping with a group from Boston. I was glad to see her and her friends. They had a large box of peanut butter crackers and a case of Coke. That was our dinner.

Before we went to sleep, Bennett gave each of us a pass to the conference identifying us as members of the Cincinnati collective. Contacts were given passes identifying them as friends, but they would have to be accompanied by one of the Weathermen to get in. The conference itself was set up on an informal schedule that depended on small group rap sessions that would cover specific topics. And while most members of the Weather Bureau were scheduled to address the assembly, no specific times were established.

The meeting took place in an old ballroom in Flint. Its decorations were somber. A large papier-mache gun hung down from the ceiling, its crooked barrel pointing down at a photograph of President Nixon. A slight draft circulating around the hall twisted the photograph so that it appeared to be trying to escape from the barrel of the machine gun. It was an eerie sight.

One wall was covered with a montage of black and red posters of Fred Hampton, the slain Illinois Black Panther leader, designed to form the words "Live Like Him." The rest of the hall was decorated with banners, posters, and photographs of Eldridge Cleaver, Fidel Castro, Malcolm X, Ho Chi Minh, and Che Guevara. Minh and Guevara were the patron saints of the Weathermen. They probably received more adulation than most Catholics give St. Joseph and St. Anthony. If either one had a higher place in the Weatherman litany of revolutionary heroes, it was Guevara, so it was not surprising that his bearded face watched over the group from all angles of the ballroom.

Rock music blared over the loudspeaker system as the hall filled up with about 400 movement people: Weathermen, White Panthers, Running Dogs, contacts, and members of splinter groups that endorsed the Weathermen philosophy. The hall was in a black neighborhood, and there was some concern before the conference started that 400 whites invading a black neighborhood could lead to trouble. Therefore, black militants from the area were invited to attend. Those who came clustered together along the wall near the entrance.

A few wooden folding chairs were scattered around the large room, but most of the people sat on the floor or stood leaning against one of the walls. The room ended in a stage with a microphone standing alone in the center. On the wall behind the microphone there was a poster of a pig's head wearing a policeman's helmet. Off to the side of the stage was a counter that probably served as a bar when the hall was used for neighborhood dances, but now it was a snack area. A middle-aged black man was serving coffee, donuts, hot dogs, sodas, potato chips, and peanuts. According to his list of prices, he was not sacrificing profit for the sake of the revolution.

Mark Rudd set the tone of the meeting. He and Bernardine Dohrn were the most notorious Weatherman leaders. Rudd, a former Boy Scout in Irvington, New Jersey, had won fame as the SDS leader who engineered a two-month student rebellion that closed New York's Columbia University in the spring of 1968. However, the rebellion was not merely a student action. Rudd successfully aroused residents of nearby Harlem to fight "Columbia's racism" over a local issue and encouraged the students to protest the existence of the Institute for Defense Analyses on campus. This approach extended the rebellion from the usual "students versus school administration" to the broader context of "racism and imperialism."

Following this rebellion, Rudd wrote that Columbia proved the old SDS dictum: "People have to be organized around the issues that affect their lives." He also wrote that the media subjected the general public to a "barrage of propaganda trying to show that the rebellion at Columbia (as well as other rebellions) was due to campus unrest over archaic administrative procedures — or failure of communication among students, faculty and administration."

However, Rudd considered the media either ill-informed or afraid to admit the truth: "Every militant ... was there because of his opposition to racism, and imperialism, and the capitalist system that needs to exploit and oppress human beings from Vietnam to Harlem to Columbia."

Rudd said the Columbia rebellion trained many leaders who were now providing other local movements with leadership. Many of these "leaders" were in the hall now as Rudd paced back and forth, exhorting us to "raise the level of struggle." He wore Levi's, a denim jacket, and a large white cowboy hat. He recapped the Weathermen's rapid advance since its formation in June. Then he reminded us that this week "represented the birth of a much greater struggle, marked by the solidification of the revolutionary movement in the United States."

"Dare to Struggle! Dare to Win!" Rudd roared, quoting Mao Tse Tung. "And we can win. It may take time, but we will win." He pointed to one of the posters of Che Guevara. "Che supported our fight. He said it was important because we live 'in the heart of the beast.' "

I looked up at one of the photos of Che. I detested Che's methods, yet I also admired him. Che was a dedicated man. He once told a reporter, "At the risk of sounding ridiculous, every revolutionary has to be motivated by great love." I couldn't help wondering if Mark Rudd had enough "great love" to carry out a revolution. Or, for that matter, if anyone else in the room did.

Finally, Rudd stopped pacing. He stood in the middle of the room facing the crowd: "I'm monomaniacal," he said loudly. "And everybody in here should be monomaniacal." He paused for effect. Murmurs spread throughout the room.

"What do you mean?" someone shouted.

Rudd had their complete attention. "Remember Captain Ahab. He was monomaniacal. He was possessed by one thought-destroying the great white whale."

"We should be like Captain Ahab and possess one thought — destruction of this mother country." His voice rose to a ringing pitch, and as the sentence was ended, the hall erupted into a burst of cheers and applause.

"Right on!"

"Off the mother country!"

"Up the revolution."

Rudd was a hero. He seemed pleased with the reaction to his speech. As he moved over to the side of the room, he was immediately surrounded by a group of disciples.

I pushed my way through the crowd to the refreshment counter and bought a bottle of Coke and two donuts. I looked at the man behind the counter and wondered what he thought about this conference. Soon he had a crowd around the counter. Even revolutionaries get hungry.

I roamed around the hall again. Every few feet there was a group gathered in serious discussion. A girl from Seattle trying to find out how a problem on agitating riots was handled in New York; a guy from Boston giving tips on recruiting contacts. I joined a group discussing greasers.

"You have to assume the characteristics of the greaser," a guy from Chicago was saying as I sat down. "You have to be willing to wear your hair in the same fashion ... slick it back if necessary. Get a leather jacket. Hang out where they go. Get a bike. Learn to ride."

Greasers, along with the working-class element, were needed for a successful revolution. And Chicago, being an extremely large metropolitan area, had a lot of them.

The guy warned everybody about the hazards of recruiting greasers, however. "They consider us peace freaks or flower children and would just as soon stomp us as talk to us. You can't approach a guy in a street gang and immediately start talking politics." His statement made me think about the barroom incident with Barry Stein.

"Once you get to know them," the guy continued, "you'll find greasers make good allies."

I moved on. The guy seemed to understand street gangs better than anyone else I'd met in the Weathermen. And he was right. If they could get support from all the gangs in big cities, the Weathermen would have a substantial nucleus.

Time started to drag. It was only the first day of the conference, but I was already bored. My wanderings came to a sudden halt when Bernardine Dohrn appeared on the stage. She stood erect, like a high priestess waiting for her followers to quiet down. She was sexually appealing in long dark boots, a short miniskirt, and a see-through blouse with no bra. I moved closer.

Bernardine radiated confidence and displayed a poise that can be acquired only from countless public appearances. She was one of the most traveled of the Weather people, having visited Yugoslavia, Cuba, Budapest, and Hungary. Although she was born in Chicago on January 12, 1942, her parents soon moved to Whitefish Bay, Wisconsin, an upper-middle-class suburb of Milwaukee. At Whitefish Bay High School she was treasurer of the Modern Dance Club, a member of the National Honor Society, and editor of the school newspaper. After high school she spent two years at Miami University in Ohio and then transferred to the University of Chicago, where she also obtained a law degree in 1967. During her years at Chicago she became active in various SDS projects. In 1968, she was named interorganizational secretary for SDS. Like Rudd, she was one of the founders of the Weathermen.

When the crowd quieted down, she began talking; her words belied her feminine appearance. At one point she praised Charles Manson, the freaked-out cultist who killed movie actress Sharon Tate and seven others. "Dig it," Bernardine said of the Manson attack. "First they killed those pigs, then they ate dinner in the same room with them. Then they even shoved a fork into one's stomach. Wild."

Next, she criticized white revolutionaries for being afraid of fighting alongside blacks in the street. "We're honkies," she shouted. "We can't just stand around and talk about it; we have to get into armed struggle." She condemned our racist, chauvinistic society and urged the women to become more involved in all aspects of the movement.

After Bernardine spoke, we separated into smaller groups for more discussions. Bernardine and Rudd left the hall along with other members of the Weather Bureau; they were conducting private, high-level meetings in a motel not far from the ballroom. As I walked around the room, I saw Tom Udall sitting with a group, listening intently to what some guy was saying.

There were a lot of other high school students like Udall at the meeting, although when we invited him to come along, I really didn't believe there would be many young people at the council. I sat down with Udall's group. The discussion centered on urban guerrilla warfare.

"We have to be prepared for street fighting," one guy was saying. "We have to be ready for running gun battles with the police. Obviously, we have to increase our skill with arms, dynamite, Molotov cocktails. In particular, dynamite. This must be thoroughly understood. If any of you are totally unfamiliar with dynamite, pick up a handbook. I think there are some on sale here."

He said we'd have to learn to work in small action groups, or focals, of four or five, within the overall structure of the collective. "These will be our strike forces," he said. The speaker had been sitting Buddha-style on the floor, but he straightened out his legs, put his hands behind him, and leaned back, looking at the rest of us in the small circle.

Udall hunched forward. "Have you ever killed anyone?" he asked the speaker.

The guy stared at Udall. "Only in Nam," he said cautiously, "but I'll be ready when the time comes." Then he asked Udall: "How about you? Will you be ready?" But before getting an answer, he directed his attention to me. "Or you. Are you ready?"

I glanced over at Udall. He was waiting for my answer. I felt sorry for him. All he really wanted was a friend, someone to talk to, someone who'd listen to his troubles. I could see that this conversation excited him. I was sorry I had joined this group.

"We're waiting," the discussion leader said, interrupting my thoughts. "Are you ready, or are you one of the hankies who are afraid to fight?"

For Udall's sake, I wanted to say yes, but I couldn't. "I'm in a war," I said, using the movement rhetoric. "That means I'm ready to fight. If I have a gun and a pig comes after me, I'll shoot."

The speaker was pleased with my answer. He then turned to each of the others in the circle and asked the same question. Udall was pleased, too. I was sorry about that. He should have been home worrying about the Walnut Hills High football team.

Somebody else asked who our main targets would be. "The pigs," came the reply. "Police chiefs to start. But even better, the pigs who run the country. A well-organized program can turn this country into chaos. And that's when we get rid of the pigs."

"When?"

"We don't have a timetable. Maybe it will take a year. Maybe two. Maybe ten. But it will happen. We just have to be patient." When the discussion began to get repetitive, I excused myself and got up. I pulled Udall by the arm. He was reluctant to leave, but he did. "That was heavy stuff," he said as we walked toward the back wall, where two blacks were talking to a girl. "You dudes are serious," one said. "I dig it. I thought this was just going to be a honky freak-out, but it's not."

"That's what a lot of people thought, but we're real, man."

The night wore on. Udall came with me to get a Coke, but then bounced off to get into another rap session. He never said much. He just sat and listened.

It was after 10 o'clock when we left the hall. I got a ride back to the school with a group of people from Chicago. We stayed up rapping until about 2 o'clock. Then I couldn't take it any more and fell asleep.

The second day began much like the first. We reported to the hall about 10 o'clock for exercises that evolved into a practice session of karate; we had 300 people moving about the hall wiping out imaginary racist pigs. Some of the exercises were led by Tom Hayden, who was a celebrity because he was on trial in Chicago for his part in the demonstration at the National Democratic Convention. Hayden was connected with SDS, but he was not one of the Weathermen. After the exercises, rock music blared over the loudspeaker, and many people began dancing. The dancing stopped when a guy climbed up on the stage to start us singing Weatherman songs. He conducted the song fest for about 20 minutes, then left the microphone to anyone who wanted to speak.

Howard Machtinger, another signer of the original Weathermen position paper, grabbed the microphone. He was a graduate of Columbia University and began graduate studies at the University of Chicago's School of Science, but was kicked out. Machtinger was a weird but likeable guy who had a very strange voice and a large Adam's apple that bobbed around as he spoke.

He made a humorous speech, although his meaning was just as violent as the others.

"Everybody knows Superman's arch rival is Lux Luthor," he said. "And everybody knows that Superman always defeats his arch rival. How else would it be in a pig story?" He paused and glanced around the hall. "But Luthor always comes back. He never gives up."

"Since he never gives up, Superman never wins the war. He wins the battles, but never the war." He made a few weird gestures to animate the story, and everybody laughed. "Just like Lux Luthor, we won't give up. We're going to destroy Superman because, just like Luthor, we're willing to fight forever."

When Machtinger finished, he got a good round of applause. He couldn't arouse and capture an audience like Rudd, but he got his point across.

After Machtinger left the stage I joined a group from Cleveland. As it turned out, they were discussing police undercover agents. "They should be killed," someone said as I sat down. When I found out who they were talking about killing. I wanted to get up and run. This was getting personal.

"Before you can kill them, you have to catch them," the group leader remarked. "Our question is, how do you catch them? How do you tell if it's a pig? How does he act?" He looked straight at me when he asked the question.

How do I get involved in these discussions, I thought. But it was too late to back out. "It would depend on his mission," I said.

"Go ahead."

"Well, say he was sent into a collective to be a provocateur. In this case, he'd always be ready to lead others into some violent act. For example, he'd be the first guy ready to blow up the f—in' ROTC Building." The group was listening to me, so I continued more forcefully. "On the other hand, if the pig just wants to infiltrate a group, he's not going to say as much. And he probably won't take part in any demonstration where some form of violence is planned." The group was so interested that I began to think I had gone too far in my explanation.

"I think it goes deeper than that," one guy said. "There are a lot of pigs who grow beards and try to get into the movement, but they never really understand the philosophy. That's how they get caught. There are probably a few pigs in this hall right now, but nobody really deep in the movement."

"Why do you say that?" "Because the pigs won't live the life style. They may grow a beard, but they'll go home at night."

The guy was right for the most part. I supported him by telling the group about the cop in Cincinnati who tried to get into the collective. It got a good laugh.

Another person spoke up. "I don't agree. I think there are some pigs who can adapt to our life style. If we accept a generalization like the one you just stated, we can get into trouble. If we let our guard down, the next thing we'll know is that some pig is pointing a revolver at our heads. I wouldn't be surprised to find pigs in this room right now."

After leaving this short course on "How to Spot a Pig," I bumped into Eddie Schaeffer. I hadn't seen him since the night we arrived. He was leaving the hall with a couple of White Panthers and asked if I wanted to go along. I refused. I thought it best to stay around the hall, although I felt very confined.

The morning turned slowly into afternoon, and afternoon crept into evening. In between, a battery of nameless faces spoke into the microphone. Most of them just reinforced what Rudd or Dohrn had already said, although Ted Gold, a member of the Weather Bureau, spoke more about the need for Weathermen to have close ties with revolutionary groups in other countries that were fighting U.S. imperialism. Gold said the ultimate success of the Weatherman movement depended upon the success of other Third-World guerrilla forces.

Each speaker tried to initiate debate; each wanted to stimulate a deep discussion on a particular phase of Weatherman philosophy.

As the session came to a close, I found Naomi rapping about women's role in the revolution with a group from San Francisco. There were seven people in the group, and five were women. I joined in at the end of the discussion, but the only thing I was thinking about was food. All I had eaten were donuts. As the discussion broke up, I asked Naomi if she wanted a hot dog. My question startled her. She was deeply involved and hadn't thought about food until now. She agreed.

We got the last two hot dogs at the snack counter. I devoured mine in a few bites, but Naomi nibbled hers. She was still wound up with conference business. By the time we left the hall, our ride back to the school had already left.

"We can thumb a lift with someone else," I said. We were standing on the front steps. The night was cold, but not as bone-chilling as it had been. The sky was bright.

"No. Wait," she said, "let's walk."

"It's two miles."

"So, if we get tired we can thumb."

She put her arm through mine, and we strolled off. I wanted to ask her about Cleveland and the meeting with her future in-laws, but didn't; it was best not to show any concern. I looked down at her walking beside me, wondering how we would have reacted to each other if we had met under different circumstances. After a few blocks of idle chatter, she asked, "Do you think we're getting anywhere at this council?" She didn't wait for an answer. "I've been involved in the movement so long, I want to be sure we're going in the right direction. There's so much to be done. So many people who need our help. Do you think we can really accomplish anything here, Larry?"

I wanted to say no. To scream, for God's sake, no. Go home. Give up this idiotic idea about revolution before a lot of you get killed or injured or busted. But even if I did tell her that, she wouldn't have listened to me. She was dedicated to a cause.

What I said instead was, "We're getting to know each other's problems." She murmured something and walked another half block in silence before answering. "Do you realize how heavy this council is?"

Did I? If they did half of what was being talked about, there was going to be a lot of hell to pay in the coming months.

She continued. "I wonder how many of us are willing to make the commitment. We're talking about war. Picking up the gun. Some of us will be killed. Some innocent people will be killed. I know it has to be done, but are we going about it in the right way?"

I didn't know how to answer her questions. She was looking

for some reinforcement for her own philosophy.

"I've been in the movement all my life, Larry. My parents were dedicated communists. I guess they still are, but they gave up before they accomplished anything. Not only them, but their whole generation. Most of them are living the fat lives they were fighting against. They contribute to us now and then, but their movement is dead. It's up to us, Larry."

She stopped abruptly as if she had dwelled long enough on the past. She returned to the present: "You were in Vietnam. You saw how we're destroying the country for the sake of Nixon's puppets. But in North Vietnam, it's even worse. I was there. I saw the hospitals we bombed, the factories we blew up, the civilian casualties we caused. Just so some fat capitalists could get fatter."

"But the North Vietnamese people aren't giving up. They're winning the war despite all our propaganda. They're winning because they have spirit. I met a girl who had shot down one of our war planes. Imagine. A 14-year-old girl who had the nerve to stand in a field and shoot at a big, screaming, frightening jet. She shot it down, and the townspeople captured the pilot. It was wonderful to be with those people. They're taking on the monster and winning. And so can we. We have to have the spirit of that little Vietnamese girl. I was so proud of her, I had my picture taken with her."

When Naomi talked like that, I didn't understand her. I could take her through village after village where the Viet Cong had massacred the men, women and children, leaving their bodies ripped apart.

She continued to talk. "When we're ready, Larry, we can get all the help we need. And anything we want to carry out our mission. That's why we have to be sure we're going in the right direction now. We don't want to waste time with a false start."

By help, I assumed she was talking about North Vietnam and Cuba. There was an unspoken knowledge within the movement that, when the time came, we could get guns, ammunition, explosives, even training from other countries. And it made sense. What Third-World guerrilla force wouldn't contribute to overthrowing the U. S.?

"What did the Weather Bureau want to accomplish when they called this council?" I asked. I was feeling colder and tired as hell of all this revolutionary talk. I grabbed Naomi's hand and started to run. "Come on. It will help us warm up."

She started laughing, and followed along. We ran too fast, and she tripped off a curb, but I caught her before she fell onto the street. I held her close for an instant. It was unreal. We should have been coming back from a dinner date, not returning to an encampment of budding guerrillas.

Soon I saw the lights of the school cutting out little squares in the darkness ahead. We ran the last 100 yards. I was so cold, I couldn't feel the heat when we walked into the building.

Before we reached our classroom, we could hear Benedict's angry voice. When he saw me walk into the room, he snapped: "Where the hell have you been?"

"We missed our ride and had to walk back."

Naomi was taking off her coat. "What's the trouble?" she asked.

Bennett was still glaring at me. "I thought you were going to warn everybody about bringing grass up here." I was stunned. "I did. Why?" "That f—ing friend of yours got busted for smoking tonight." I knew he meant Schaeffer. "How did it happen?" "He and those f—ing White Panther friends of his borrowed a car and went for a ride. The pigs followed them a couple of miles outside of town and made the bust when they lit up. That's all we needed. Hell, this could give the pigs an excuse for breaking in on the sessions tomorrow. And if that happens, it won't look good for us. Any of us. They think we're a little weak in Cincinnati as it is."

Bennett was obviously more concerned about how the Weather Bureau was going to react than by the fact that Schaeffer was sitting in jail.

"How much bail does he need?" I asked.

"I don't know."

"It can't be much. Maybe we have enough bread to spring him."

Bennett turned away from the window. "I don't think we have $100 among us." I reached into my pocket and pulled out my money. It totaled $35. "Let's take up a collection. There's a couple of hundred people in the school. I'm sure we can raise enough."

Bennett didn't answer. I turned to leave the room. "Wait a minute," he said. "Even if we can come up with the bread, we're not getting him out." I didn't understand. "You can't leave him in the slam," I snapped.

He walked to the center of the room with a pensive look. "We have to," he said. "It will teach him a lesson. When I said no grass, I meant it. If this council is in jeopardy, it's because of him. Leave him there. And I mean it, Grathwohl."

Bennett stalked out of the room. Naomi came over to me. "He's right, you know."

Schaeffer was the feature topic of conversation for the remainder of the evening. I felt sorry for him. I could visualize him pacing his jail cell like a caged animal. It was a horrible thought. It was late when we went to bed.

The next morning I left for the ballroom earlier than the others because I was assigned to security duty at the front door. Bennett had volunteered my services. I always seemed to end up with duties like that because of my size. My instructions were to bar anybody who didn't have a valid pass or who wasn't accompanied by one of the Weathermen with identification.

People started arriving about 9: 15 A.M. A couple of local newsmen showed up early, looking for Mark Rudd. I wouldn't let them in, but I did tell them that an official statement would be handed out later. They moved over to the side of the steps and waited.

An unmarked police car with two plainclothes cops in the front seat cruised down the street to take a position halfway up the block. A television camera crew set up on the sidewalk to film. There was more action out in the street than inside.

The first Weather Bureau person to show up was Bill Ayers. Ayers, the son of the president of Commonwealth Edison of Illinois, had been involved with SDS since 1963, when he entered the University of Michigan. He had a reputation for being radical and violent. He walked up the stairs pompously and started to pass by me.

I held out my arm to block his path. He was a few inches shorter than me, but very broad.

"What are you doing, man?" he snapped.

"Where's your pass?"

He tried to shove by me again, but I moved in front of him. "Get out of my way," he shouted. I didn't move. He was furious. "Do you know who I am?" I pretended not to. "I'm Bill Ayers." I shrugged my shoulders. "You still need a pass." I was enjoying my work. At age 25 Ayers, along with Bernardine Dohrn, probably had the most authority within the Weathermen. Slowing him down was fun. The more furious he became, the more adamantly I demanded that he produce a pass. A crowd was collecting at the door by now because they couldn't get through. Most of them knew Ayers, so it was embarrassing for him.

He decided to get tough and threatened to knock me on my ass. I grabbed him by his jacket and pushed him aside, but before anything more happened, Eric Burns, who was in charge of security, came bounding out of the meeting hall. He vouched for Ayers, but I still feigned great concern about allowing him in without a pass. Burns said he'd take the responsibility, so I gave in. When they both finally disappeared inside, I turned back to checking the other passes, but I couldn't keep from laughing to myself.

The two reporters who were standing on the side of the door came back over to talk with me. I rapped with them for a while. I didn't think they believed the war council was serious, and I wished I could have let them in to see for themselves.

I was assigned to the door all morning. After the hall became crowded, I didn't do anything but sit on a folding chair in the small hallway separating the front door from the main ballroom. Nobody tried to crash in. Benedict's worry about a police raid was unfounded.

I also had security duty the last morning of the convention. By now we had lost about 100 conventioneers; the conference had become redundant. With a well-structured program, everything could have been accomplished in two days. However, the longer conference probably eliminated some of the movement people who were not absolutely dedicated. It also eliminated some of the fringe groups. The White Panthers had gone by the end of the second day, and I didn't see the people from the Bay area revolutionary group the third day. Even the few local blacks who had attended the first two sessions didn't come back. The conference had already made its point: we had to "pick up the gun and raise the level of struggle." The continued meetings only served to ram this slogan home. We left Flint on December 31. The spirit was high. Everybody had the feeling that we were on the verge of dramatic action. Everybody hung around the school until late in the day, rapping about the council. For all practical purposes, it turned out to be a fifth session.

It was New Year's Eve. Back in Cincinnati, my friend Brewer was planning a party. It had been a historic year. Neil Armstrong stepped from a space ship onto the surface of the moon and got a telephone call from President Nixon. But it was also the end of a violent decade: three major political assassinations and over 40,000 killed in the country's longest war. And here I was in a church school in the middle of a rap session about blowing up the country.

Chapter 10

Purges

As soon as we got back to Cincinnati, the purges began. Bill Ayers was in town to lead the dismissal of members who were not considered totally committed to the movement. When Ayers arrived, he called Bennett, Harmon, Spiegel, and Bittner to a special meeting in a downtown motel, where they could talk freely.

The meeting began January 2, 1970. While it was going on, Barry Stein took charge of the collective because Naomi was in Cleveland getting married to Bill Milton. The sudden promotion to leadership, even though it was temporary, greatly inflated Stein's ego. He had a difficult time adjusting to this newly assumed power, however. Consequently, it was a fairly easy trick to disappear for the afternoon to report to Murrish on the war council at his office. I did take extra precautions in getting there, though. I walked through two department stores, including McAlpine's, and browsed in a bookstore to lose anybody who might be following me.

My meeting with Murrish was extremely tedious. He made me go over and over all the incidents that had occurred during the four days in Flint, elaborating here and there on particular events. He questioned me very carefully about the speech Bernardine Dohrn made the first night although, judging from his questions, he already knew what she had said. My report was probably used to substantiate what had been turned in to other FBI offices. With Murrish doing the questioning, I certainly didn't leave out any details. He was a very methodical man. Every time I thought the meeting was over, Murrish would say: "Now, are you positive you don't remember anything more?"

"I'm sure." "All right, then. But before you go, tell me one more time about the sessions on the greasers. Just to double check." When he was finally satisfied, I felt drained. After closing his notebook, he pushed back in his chair. "Do you want another cup of coffee?"

"No more," I said in self-defense. I had already had five.

He asked about my job. I told him I had taken the week off between Christmas and New Year's day because it was usually slow at this time of year, anyway. People were bringing things back, not buying.

"What do you make at the store?" he asked.

"About $145 a week."

He was silent for a moment. "I'll try to get you some money."

I was surprised. I had never asked for any money, and he had never mentioned it before. "What for?" I asked. "You put in a good week's work for me. I'll try to reimburse you for what you missed at the store plus another $50 for expense money." Although I could use the cash, I didn't want Murrish to think I was motivated by money. I told him that. He said he understood how I felt, but insisted that I had earned the money. "When I get a check, you'll have to come in to sign for it."

Murrish stood up and shook my hand. "Good job," he said. "If you need any help straightening this out at McAlpine's, let me know. I'll be glad to call them. We appreciate what you're doing and wish more people were as concerned."

I thanked him. "You'll hear from me," I said, and left. I was glad to have the money. If I was going to stay in the collective, it was obvious I couldn't continue working at McAlpine's I considered taking Murrish up on his offer to smooth things over, but what good would that do in the long run? I decided to call the manager on my way back to the collective. I told him I was quitting. I didn't give him a reason and he didn't ask for one; he didn't exactly sound disappointed.

When I got back to the collective, Stein was romping about giving orders. As soon as I walked in, he grabbed me. "Grathwohl, I've got an important job for you," he barked, without even asking where I'd been.

"Your friend Schaeffer is back in town, but he says he's quitting."

The way we had treated him in Flint, I wouldn't have blamed him if he blew up the collective. I guessed that Stein was concerned about Schaeffer's decision because he didn't want anybody quitting while he was in charge. Stein had decided that Anne Walton and myself should go out to Schaeffer's house and talk him out of quitting. Why not, I thought. When I told Anne, she was eager for the challenge.

Schaeffer was staying at his parents' home in a suburban part of western Cincinnati. I had called Eddie to tell him we were coming, and he was waiting for us outside when we drove up. I stared at him as he came down the walk. He had his coat collar pulled up around his ears, and I couldn't see his face very clearly, but there was something funny about him. As he got closer, I started to laugh. He had a closely cropped haircut.

"What did you do, enlist again?" I joked as he reached the car. "F— you," he snapped, climbing into the back seat. He said the cops in Flint had cut his hair off.

We went to a quick-service drive-in restaurant not far from his house but, instead of eating in the car, we went inside and took a corner booth. We ordered hamburgers and Coke, then began rapping. Anne flung herself into the job of saving Schaeffer for the cause as if it were a personal crusade. She rambled on for an hour about why he was needed before taking a break, and that was a forced one; she had to go to the john. When she left the table, I asked Schaeffer a simple question: "Are you tired of all this?"

He didn't answer me, but I knew he was. Everything was settled. He was out. Anne returned and continued her same line again, but this time she didn't carry on as long, and we drifted off into politics in general. Then we drove Schaeffer home. When he got out of the car, all he said was, "I'll see you around."

The next couple of days were filled with arguments. It began when Stein heard we hadn't convinced Schaeffer to return. He got angry with Anne and me. Then he started blaming everybody for failing to execute his plans properly. The spirit generated during the council at Flint was disintegrating.

Then, on January 4 we were all called to a meeting at St. John's Unitarian Church. Naomi and Milton had returned from Cleveland the same day. They walked into the house carrying a color television set, a complete set of dishes for eight, silverware, and money. Naomi laughed as she produced the loot.

"I wonder if Che had color TV," I mused.

"We're selling it," Naomi snapped. Then she laughed.

We all left for the meeting together. It was being held in the same basement classroom at the church where I had attended my first Weatherman meeting. Karen Bittner and Mike Spiegel were waiting. I had expected to see Bill Ayers, but he wasn't there. I was wondering if he'd remember me. Then I noticed that Harmon and Bennett were missing also. I assumed that the three of them had gone off on another mission.

Karen opened the meeting. She began by building up the importance of the Flint council and how it was imperative that we raise the level of struggle. Of course, to accomplish this, we needed truly dedicated people who had only one goal on their minds. Then she made a startling announcement. "The collective has been reorganized," she said, looking around the room to study the reaction. "We felt it necessary to restructure ourselves so that we can move faster and more effectively." Then she added: "Bennett and Harmon have been purged from the Weathermen."

She went into a long explanation. She wanted all of us to understand that Harmon and Bennett had failed to move the collective forward, which jeopardized the entire movement. She praised Harmon for his past work. He had been instrumental in setting up the Denver collective. "But our political goals have changed quite a bit since John was in Denver," she said, "and he has not kept up with the level we're functioning on now."

Another factor was Harmon's refusal either to leave his wife and two children for the sake of the movement or to bring them into the collective. As for Bennett, he was "not political enough." In other words, he was nonviolent.

The room was quiet while Bittner explained the reasons for

the restructuring. Then she announced that Naomi had been elevated to primary leadership, alongside Spiegel and herself. The last statement shot an arrow through Barry Stein's ego. He had been priming himself to move up the ladder. I glanced over at him to catch his reaction, but he didn't show any emotion.

Hal Lincoln, however, did. He objected vehemently to the purging of Bennett and Harmon. "Who made the decision?" he demanded. "Why weren't we all consulted?" A collective was supposed to function on its own, yet it was apparent that the Weather Bureau was dictating the moves.

Spiegel defended the decision. So did Naomi. Debate was encouraged. It was better to have all the dissatisfactions aired now. It was impossible to move forward unless everyone had a complete understanding of the action and agreed with it.

Bittner reiterated that the plan to attack the local power structure aggressively would be impossible under Bennett and Harmon. They had failed to capitalize on any local issues in the past, so they could not be trusted to change in the future. Lincoln finally gave up his argument, but he was not pacified.

Bittner then turned to a new subject. She said that some of us would be sent to Cuba as a Venceremos Brigade. She announced that Arlo Jacobs was in charge of coordinating our activities with the Venceremos people.

The Venceremos Brigades were started by people in the United States who were sympathetic to the Cuban Revolution. Venceremos was a Spanish slogan used by Che Guevara, meaning "We shall overcome." The brigades were organized as work forces to help the Cubans harvest their sugarcane crop. Because the U. S. restricted direct travel to Cuba, members of the brigades had to take devious routes to reach their destination. Some traveled to Canada and then by boat to Cuba, while others went by way of Mexico. Weathermen seized the opportunity of going to Cuba. Not only could they actually work for a successful revolutionary government, but once in Cuba they had the opportunity to get professional training in weapons and guerrilla tactics. When Naomi was in Cuba, she was trained in the use of sophisticated weapons such as the AK47 machine gun and was given assurances that any serious revolutionary group in the U.

S. would get help when it was needed.

Bittner said it was still not determined who would be asked to go to Cuba, but that we should all regard it as a fantastic opportunity, especially the women. "Women aren't second-class citizens in Cuba," she stated. "The Cuban women fought alongside the men to overthrow a racist, chauvinistic government. And the Federation of Cuban Women is continuing to work to make the revolutionary economy as productive as possible. They're working for the whole society and not just the selfish family unit. Those of you who go to Cuba will enjoy a fantastic experience that will help you the rest of your lives."

It sounded like Karen was employed by a Cuban travel agency. After she finished, I was ready to pack my bags. Luckily, this was a fleeting desire. Karen ended the meeting by reminding us that tonight's changes were only the beginning of a new dedication to action and progress.

Our methods did become more violent. We started manufacturing small explosive devices, using cherry-bomb firecrackers reinforced with extra powder and adhesive so they'd stick to windows. By placing a lit cigarette over the wick of the cherry bomb, an individual had plenty of time to leave the area before the device exploded. This was a step forward for members of the Cincinnati collective. Up to this time, if we wanted a window broken, we merely threw a rock through it.

One night these cherry-bomb devices were used to blowout an entire series of windows at Indian Hills High School. However, some of the bombs were left by mistake in Tom Udall's car, and the police, acting on a tip from a witness, went to Udall's house, searched the car, and then arrested him. I didn't take part in the action, and I was really sorry to hear that Tom was busted. But his mother bailed him out immediately. He repaid her by stealing her car and driving to Yellow Springs, the Venceremos Brigade's rendezvous point, to join up.

As the month progressed, we purged Hal Lincoln, and Bill Milton quit. Lincoln became expendable because he constantly defended Harmon and Bennett after they were kicked out. On the other hand, Bill Milton had begun to display a lack of concern for movement activities. He was constantly making up excuses for not going on night actions, and he spent an increasing amount of time working on the car his parents had given him as a wedding present. This was ironic because, shortly before he quit, his car was ruined by a group of neighborhood greasers who threw stink bombs into it, slashed the tires, and smashed a side window.

The night Milton quit, he was in a gloomy mood. He packed his clothes, then went down into the living room to take the television set. When Jacobs and I saw what he had planned, we blocked his way.

"No way, man," Jacobs said. "That tube stays here. We already have a buyer for it."

Milton started to argue, but not too aggressively. He looked at Jacobs, then glanced over at me. We were both bigger than he was. Without another word, he turned around and left the house like a whipped puppy.

On January 15, the Weather Bureau assigned a tough-minded veteran SDS member, Dianne Donghi, to our collective. As soon as she arrived, I sensed I was in for trouble.

Naomi and Mike Spiegel picked Donghi up at the airport the night she arrived. When they got back to the house, I was sitting downstairs reading. It was extremely cold outside, and Dianne was wrapped up like an Eskimo. But when she took off her coat, I had to stare at her outfit. She was wearing a purple see-through blouse with no bra, grey Levi's, and boots. It took a while before I noticed the boots.

As soon as we were introduced, she showed such a keen interest in me that I was leery of her. "So you're Grathwohl," she said. "We have a lot to talk about. I've only heard about you through other sources."

Although I wasn't the only one she questioned during the next few days, she spent more time with me than anyone else. She wanted to know about my days running in the streets in Cincinnati, especially my bouts with the police. Then she questioned me at length about Vietnam. Although the questions were penetrating, she was always affable. She never demanded to know anything. However, I did find out through Murrish that she made attempts to check on my stories about the police by calling the juvenile record bureau, claiming to be an employer of mine.

One day when we were rapping in the kitchen, I said: "You don't seem to trust me."

She laughed, but didn't answer.

Right after Dianne arrived, several other new Weathermen were assigned to Cincinnati, including John Skardis, Robert Carter, and Carol Stanton. They all knew Donghi.

One night, when about ten of us were in the living room, Arlo Jacobs and Lisa Misel began accusing Naomi and myself of being monogamous. We denied it, of course. I said the charge was ridiculous because Naomi was married to Milton.

"Bullshit," Lisa said. "They got married for a good reason. To help all of us. But the relationship between you two is selfish."

Dianne didn't say a word during the criticism, but she watched our reactions very closely. She studied our expressions and listened intently to everything we said in our own defense. The session didn't last very long, and even Arlo and Lisa didn't push us very hard. It was because of Naomi. Everybody knew she was dedicated to the movement, yet they wanted to let her know that she wasn't beyond rebuke.

Two days later Naomi was assigned to Detroit. I went to the bus station with her and bought the ticket.

"I'm sure this is my fault," I said.

"It's not anybody's fault," she said. "We have work to do, and it can't be accomplished in Cincinnati. Our feelings as individuals can't be considered when you're planning for the overall good."

The call came for her bus. Naomi turned to me: "Give Dianne a chance. She's very skeptical of those who haven't been in the movement very long."

I kissed Naomi good-bye, then waited as the bus pulled off. She waved from the window, but then turned away abruptly.

Within a couple of days, Spiegel was also sent to Detroit, and Bittner left for the West Coast. Dianne was sole leader of the collective. She called a joint meeting between our group and the White Panthers in a "safe" house across town. She said it was important that everybody attend.

The meeting was held in a third-floor apartment of an old tenement building. I got there about 7:30 P.M., a half hour before we were scheduled to begin. Several people had already arrived. The apartment belonged to a contact of the White Panthers who was out of town. I arrived in the middle of a criticism session of a new girl in the collective named Lynn. She was a former dancer in a chorus line in Las Vegas and had been in Cincinnati only a few days. Evidently, she had spent the afternoon in the apartment with two of the White Panthers. Dianne and Carol Stanton were denouncing her for "balling any guy who was around" and "giving into the appetites of male chauvinists." They sounded like the nuns at St. Mary's, who were always warning us about the evils of sex. Before they were finished, Lynn ran out of the apartment.

"Let her go," Dianne commanded. "She's not tough enough. We can't use her." By now the living room was crowded and filled with the noise of idle chatter. People were sitting on the chairs, sofa, and floor, and I noticed a small box being passed around. I didn't pay much attention to it until I realized that each person was removing a small capsule, popping it into his mouth, and swallowing it. It was LSD.

LSD is a hallucinogen, which scares me. I had smoked marijuana, but I had never dropped acid or taken any harder drug, and I didn't want to begin now. I glanced around the room as the box made its way toward me. Dianne Donghi was on my right, sitting cross-legged near the living room doorway. She was pretending to be absorbed in a conversation with Carol Stanton, but I noticed she was watching me. She was extremely interested in my reactions.

LSD was popular on many campuses, but it wasn't used much by the Weathermen. I tried to recall everything I had read about LSD. The drug affects each individual differently. Although most users can continue to carry on a conversation, others have distorted visions or terrifying thoughts. Basically, LSD expands a person's sense of perception. Everything becomes more vivid, magnified-colors, the lines on another person's face, the palm of your own hand. I also knew that many societies take hallucinogenic drugs as a way of life. In Saigon, I had seen old men sitting for hours puffing on their opium pipes. And many Indians in Mexico and the Southwest conduct their religious ceremonies around mescale, or peyote, an hallucinogenic drug made from the dried tops of cactus plants.

The small box with the LSD reached me. I took a capsule, then passed the package along. I looked out of the corner of my eye at Donghi; she was watching me. I popped the capsule into the corner of my mouth and leaned forward in my chair and dropped my head so it rested between my two hands. All the while I watched Dianne. When I saw Dianne turn her head to answer a question, I moved my fingers onto my mustache, cupped my hand slightly, and spit the capsule into the palm of my hand. I didn't think Dianne saw what I did. I hoped not. After a few minutes, I pushed back in my chair again and crossed my arms, slipping the capsule into my shirt pocket.

I relaxed. Judging by what I had read, it would take about an hour before the LSD would have an effect on everybody. I knew that whatever was coming later would involve me. All I could do was wait.

The conversation continued. Revolution was on everyone's mind. A young guy we called Bear was pushing back while sitting on an old kitchen chair, when all of a sudden the back leg cracked, and he went crashing to the floor, his legs flying upward. One of the White Panthers who had been watching Bear began to laugh. He couldn't stop. As Bear untangled himself from the chair, the White Panther laughed even harder. His laughter trailed off for a few moments, but then he started all over again.

The inquisition began slowly, moderately, almost like any other criticism session we had. Dianne Donghi began it by criticizing the two White Panthers who had been in bed with Lynn that afternoon. They were male chauvinists. They had taken advantage of Lynn, which reflected the racist chauvinistic society we lived in.

Voices criticizing others or expounding on the revolution rang out from everywhere. For me, time dragged. But I was sure that for them, time didn't exist. They were in another dimension.

An hour passed. A girl on the floor was rocking back and

forth, staring at the crack on the wall. The guy who had laughed at Bear was still laughing. The general conversation had grown meaner, more violent. Carol Stanton was criticized for being too hard on Lynn. Then Anne Walton turned on me.

"You should have defended your sister," she said accusingly. "You didn't say anything. You just sat there." At first I didn't know what she was talking about, but then I realized she was talking about the verbal attack on Lynn hours before. Arlo Jacobs joined in. "He never says much. He just follows." Then he addressed me directly. "You're afraid of responsibility." "Afraid of making decisions," Dianne Donghi shouted. "Why are you afraid? Why do you hold back?"

Voices of accusation were screaming at me from all sides. I was surrounded by vicious sounds coming at me like a rapid-firing machine gun. I didn't answer. I sat motionless in the chair, trying to stay calm, appear unconcerned. But as the voices grew more vehement, I felt a twinge of fear creeping over me. I wasn't afraid of any of them individually, but collectively they could be dangerous, especially under the influence of LSD.

A White Panther pulled a switchblade knife from his pocket, snapped it open, and started flipping it into the floorboard in front of him. The periodic thumping of the knife as it sliced into the floor began ringing in my ears.

The verbal assault went on. Dianne Donghi was the instigating force. She continually introduced new subjects, supplied new ammunition. I still didn't answer, because I didn't know what to say. My hands were tightening around the arms of the chair. My throat was getting dryer and, even though the room was cool, I was sweating.

Dianne Donghi got up from the floor by the door and wandered around the room. Then she came over and stood in front of me.

"Who are you, Larry Grathwohl?" she screamed. "Where did you come from? What's inside you?" She sounded angry, vicious. She stared at me wildly.

I continued to look straight ahead; my eyes fixed on the leg of the sofa across the room. Dianne hollered again, repeating herself. "Tell us who you are, Larry Grathwohl. Tell us why you joined us."

The room had quieted down now. The others realized that this was getting serious. They began to close in around me. I continued to stare straight ahead, but I could see the faces all around me.

"Do you hate us, Larry?" a voice asked. "I think you hate us. I know you hate women." The voice belonged to Anne Walton. She was standing over my right shoulder, so I couldn't see her, but I knew it was she. Then she moved around in front of me. She had worked herself into a frenzy. She was so outraged, her hands were trembling. She had grabbed the knife the White Panther had been tossing and was pointing it at me.

"You're a pig, Grathwohl," she said. Dianne Donghi took over now. "Pig, Grathwohl. Pig. You've been lying to us."

My heart was beating faster now. My mind was running wild with thoughts. Did they really know who I was? If they did, how did they find out? I recapped what had happened since Donghi came to the collective. She couldn't know anything about me other than what I had told her. She came in suspicious of everybody, me especially. But this had to be a bluff. Donghi was acting on a hunch, a hunch that someone with my background wouldn't change his basic concepts.

I had two choices. I could leap up and run for the door or play out the bluff. If I acted fast, I could probably get away because they weren't expecting it. But if I did, I'd be through in the movement. I kept thinking of the cop they caught in Chicago. I didn't feel like taking a beating. I could hear Dianne's voice above the others, yelling at me. I decided to bluff it out. Donghi wasn't going to force my hand.

I had to do something before they all worked themselves to such a pitch that they'd strike at me without thinking about it. They were all yelling "Pig!" with a fury that was increasing.

"You killed for the pigs in Vietnam!" Donghi screamed. "Why should we believe you're not still a pig?"

The mention of Vietnam brought Anne Walton into the action again. "You killed Vietnamese women," she hollered. "You killed women and children." As she yelled, the knife flashed in front of my face.

Somebody started making a noise like a pig. The noise was quickly copied.

"We have a pig!" Donghi shouted to the others. "He doesn't defend himself. He must be a pig."

"When are pigs good?"

"Roasted."

"Roast pig. Roast pig," came the chant.

The only one not shouting was the girl who was rocking back and forth. She was like the calm in the center of a tornado.

As the chanting grew louder, I acted. I pushed up on the arms of the chair, lifted my body off the chair, and swung my legs up onto the seat. I stood up on the chair with the psychological advantage of towering above them.

Then I shouted. "I'm a pig! I'm a pig!" This took them by surprise. The chanting stopped. I screamed louder: "You're right. I am a pig!" All eyes were staring at me. I had their attention, but I had to capitalize, fast.

I leaped off the chair, landing in a crouched position on the floor. I stayed in this position and moved rapidly around in a small circle. "Oink. Oink. I'm a pig!" I screamed. Then I remembered the LSD capsule in my pocket. If it fell out, I was through. I made rapid little advances like a wild boar toward the crowd standing around me, and they retreated. It took them by surprise and kept them off balance.

"Sure I'm a pig," I screamed again. "But what are you, bitch?" I shouted, glaring at Anne Walton. "What have you done for the Vietnamese you accuse me of killing?"

Then I shouted: "You've done nothing but squeal like a pig!" I had to keep the initiative.

I straightened up rapidly and threw my arms out as if stretched on a cross. "I'm a pig because I killed for the pigs in Vietnam. I was on the payroll of a monster that was destroying innocent men, women and children."

"Have any of you ever killed innocent people? No, but I have. I admit it. I was part of a napalm-spitting monster. Napalm that charred little children to death."

I let my arms fall down to my side. The room was still quiet. I hoped I hadn't overplayed my part. I looked around the room, preparing for a last statement. "That's why I'm a pig," I said, and flopped back into my chair.

Nobody said anything for a few moments, then there were murmurs about the revolution. Everybody drifted away from me. The acid test was over. I had won.

We stayed in the apartment for another hour. My eyes were very tired. I could just about keep them open. Daylight started breaking through the window. I looked out at a cold, rainy day. But later, when we finally broke up, I stood on the street, lifted my face, and let the rain fall on it. I felt alive.

Chapter 11

Underground

Two weeks after the acid test, I was chosen to become part of an elite group of Weathermen organized to select and destroy major targets. This new phase began when Dianne Donghi got a phone call February 9 from the Weather Bureau in Chicago, directing her to take her six best people and report to Cleveland immediately.

The call came early in the morning when most of us were still asleep. Dianne woke me up, saying that it was important that she talk to me. I pushed her away a few times, but she was persistent. When I finally went downstairs to see her, I was still groggy from my heavy sleep.

I started to rinse out a cup in the sink so that I could pour coffee in it, but Dianne told me to forget about my stomach until after our talk. "Put on your coat," she ordered. "You need some fresh air to clear your head. We'll take a short walk."

Outside, she apologized again for being rough on me, especially during the acid test. "I hope you understand, but I had to be sure about you. I came to Cincinnati knowing that I could count on Spiegel and Jaffee because they've been so close to the movement for a long time. But I had to find out about all the others for myself."

I tried to act nonchalant. "Don't be Mister Cool," she said. "If you hadn't come off so f—ing well, you wouldn't be here right now."

I didn't ask her to explain what she meant. We were around

the block before she talked about the phone call that got me out of bed.

"We have to go to Cleveland," she said. "It's very important. You're the first one I've told. I'm going to bring five others, so we'll need transportation. Get Arlo to help you with that. We're going to leave as soon as we can, but I only want the seven of us to know where we're going."

She was excited about the meeting. Being called to Cleveland obviously meant something big, but she wasn't sure exactly what it was — or at least she didn't admit it.

When we got back to the house, I found Arlo in the living room counting the money he had been soliciting on Calhoun Street and around the campus for the Venceremos Brigade. He had over $1700, all of it collected in less than a month. I told him about the call to go to Cleveland and the need for a bigger car.

"I'll call the minister," Arlo said. "Maybe I can switch our Corvair with him for a few days." Arlo pushed the money back into a paper bag and got up. "Tell Dianne I should be ready in a couple of hours."

The others who were coming with us were Carol, Stanton, Kathy Sanchez, Robert Carter, and John Skardis. By noon we were on our way to Cleveland. Arlo was successful in borrowing the minister's large Ford, but with seven people it was still crowded. I was glad to get out of our apartment. The place smelled horribly. There wasn't any water pressure in the toilet, so it couldn't be flushed after it was used. But nobody seemed to care. They all used it, anyway. I welcomed the trip to Cleveland.

On the way, we speculated on the urgency of the phone call. Dianne didn't say very much, which led me to believe she knew a lot more about the reason for this meeting than she claimed.

We arrived in Cleveland just as it was getting dark. When Arlo pulled the car over to the curb in front of the collective, Dianne asked me to run in and find out where we were staying. She had been told that a "safe" apartment would be at our disposal.

John Fuerst, one of the primary leaders in the Cleveland collective, was waiting for us. He came out with me and squeezed into the front seat of the car. He directed Arlo to an old, wooden-frame duplex house in a rough part of the city, not far from the collective.

"This place is safe," he said. "We have access to a few apartments when we need them. The couple who live here are away for a few days, but I have extra keys. We just ask you to be careful of the furniture. The people who rent the apartment are good friends."

We climbed the stairs to the second floor and entered a three-room apartment that was inexpensively but neatly furnished. Arlo said he wanted to rest before heading back to Cincinnati. The rest of us got into another rap session about the meeting. Soon we got around to admitting that we were hungry, so Fuerst and I went out to get pizza and Coke. I also needed cigarettes.

We stayed up rapping until well after midnight. We got up early the next morning, but spent most of the day sitting around speculating about what was going on. We were being given ample time to prepare ourselves psychologically for whatever commitment we would be asked to make.

About 10 o'clock, Fuerst came over to get Dianne Donghi. They left and didn't return until 4 P.M. Then Dianne asked me to go for a walk with her. We probably could have talked just as well in the kitchen, but she needed to make a mystery out of what she was going to say.

We walked by old warehouses, two cheap rundown hotels, a pawn shop, a liquor store, and two crowded bars. On the next block there was a small hole-in-the-wall food counter that had a service window facing the sidewalk. I told Dianne to wait a minute while I bought two ice cream cones. She thought I was crazy, but she took the cone, and we walked along licking the ice cream. A seedy-looking guy in a skid-row bar stared out the window at us. I waved to him, and he lifted his beer glass to me.

"Our commitment is getting very serious," Dianne was saying as we passed the bar. "We're reaching a point where somebody could get killed-a point of no return."

Then she asked: "Are you willing to leave Cincinnati?" Her question caught me by surprise, so I had to ask her what she meant.

"Are you willing to go to another city to carry out our work, or to as many cities as it takes to win? What I'm trying to find out is: are you willing to travel freely without much notice?"

I hadn't thought about this before, but I had to say, "I'm ready to do anything that will help."

This answer pleased her. "Good. I can't explain anything to you now, but you'll understand before we leave here. It's important that you be ready to commit yourself totally to the revolution. You have to be ready to hit and run."

I assured her that I was.

When we got back to the house, it was dark. My hands were extremely cold. John Fuerst was waiting for Dianne. He said that Mark Rudd and Linda Evans, another member of the Weather Bureau, were holding a meeting of the primary leadership. He took Dianne and left.

When Dianne got back, she said we all had to leave early in the morning for an important meeting. Then she started rapping with me about the revolution. We finally fell asleep on the floor in front of the fire.

About an hour later, we were awakened by someone shaking us. I looked up into the face of Barry Stein. Dianne was taken by complete surprise. "What are you doing here?" she demanded.

Stein wasn't at the collective when we'd gotten the phone call to come to Cleveland, and Dianne hadn't made any attempt to contact him. "I figured you weren't able to get in touch with me, so I came up anyway," he said.

Dianne looked right at him: "We didn't try."

Her abrupt answer shook Stein. He didn't say anything. All he did was stare at us. Dianne then ordered him to go back to Cincinnati. Stein started fumbling for excuses to stay.

"It's late," he pleaded. "Let's talk about it in the morning." But Dianne was firm. "You'll leave now," she said sternly. "We'll talk when I get back to Cincinnati." Stein started to protest again, but she shut him up. "We'll talk when I get back to Cincinnati," she repeated.

Stein left almost as suddenly as he had appeared.

The next morning, after our usual donuts and milk breakfast, Dianne led us on a two-hour trek to our meeting place. She refused to give us any hint as to where we were going. All she would say was that it would take a while to get there. We started out by using the Cleveland rapid transit system. Then we took a bus. Next we walked. I hadn't done so much walking around in cold weather since I was in the army. By this time we were in a residential area of Cleveland. The houses were built on good-sized plots of well-groomed land. The neighborhood looked rich, even in the drabness of winter.

Dianne was looking at the house numbers as we walked along. Finally we turned into a low, ranch-style house. She opened the front door, and we went inside without ringing the bell. John Fuerst and other members of the Cleveland collective were already there. We were directed to a small room off the expensively furnished living room. A short, heavy-set man with gray hair came in to welcome us and said that his wife had left a snack in the kitchen for us. He then told us to make ourselves at home and apologized that both he and his wife had to leave. He was a professor and had to get back to the campus for an afternoon class.

Shortly thereafter, Linda Evans and Mark Rudd joined us. When they came in, we were all in a general discussion on the revolution. I was arguing the feasibility of expecting the working class to join us. "The working class doesn't think they're oppressed," I said, using my stepfather as an example. "He's content to have his beer in front of the television set. If you talk revolution to him, he'll laugh in your face."

"Then you're saying revolution is impossible," one guy snapped.

I didn't want to be an antagonist, so I backed off my position mildly."No, I'm not. What I'm saying is that it will take time to get the working class behind us. We can't do it by just sitting around talking."

"Right on," another voice said. "The man's right on target."

I looked around. Mark Rudd had been listening to our conversation and was supporting me. Then he suddenly cut off the group discussion. "We're going to continue this on an individual basis upstairs. We want you to come up one at a time to rap with one of us." We continued our group discussion as individuals disappeared up the staircase. When each person came down, he was ushered into the living room by Dianne Donghi, who was standing at the bottom of the staircase. The interviews were averaging about ten minutes each. Dianne finally called me. The first room on the right, she said. I went up the carpeted staircase to a large, nicely decorated bedroom. Linda Evans was sitting in a chair on the far side of the room near the window.

"Close the door," she said as I went inside. I could hear Rudd's voice in the other room.

I sat down on the bed and leaned back on the pillow. Linda began by reviewing my reasons for joining the movement. She knew a lot about me.

"The only mark that seems to be against you is that you've failed to develop your leadership qualities," she said. "We hope this will change. We want everybody to live up to his potential."

I listened without answering. Then she added: "You were at Flint, so you know that we're beginning a second phase of activities. We have to become more aggressive."

She told me Dianne had given me an excellent recommendation, which is why I was at this meeting. "Some of the others from your collective are already more active," she said, referring to Naomi and Spiegel. "What we're asking from you is total commitment," she said, looking directly at me. "I mean a commitment to kill if necessary, or be killed. Can you give us that commitment?"

"I'm with you." She paused a moment, then stated: "The Weather movement is going underground."

I was surprised. My first reaction was that the decision would hurt them. They had been building broad support on many campuses, but now they were throwing this away in favor of a small, active group. It would make them harder to catch, but it would also keep them from growing rapidly.

"You seem surprised," Linda said.

"I am."

Linda explained that the Weathermen had become convinced they could accomplish more working in small focals, or action groups, in an underground environment than they could by being an open movement. In preparation for this phase, many Weathermen had to be purged so that a fighting force could be organized. Weathermen would now operate in focals of three to six individuals within the framework of a collective in target cities. On any particular action, each focal would be given only enough information to carry out its part of the assignment. This policy would protect other members as well as themselves. Collectives in each city would be responsible for selecting and destroying targets. However, if needed, they could call on the national Weather Bureau to send in additional help.

After Linda finished explaining the new structure, she said I would be assigned to either Chicago or Detroit. The Cincinnati collective was being disbanded in favor of a heavy concentration in three major areas: the East Coast, centering around New York; the Midwest, centering around Chicago and Detroit; and the West Coast, centering around San Francisco. I left the room, amazed at the plans.

Later, when the individual interviews were finished, Rudd spoke to the group. "We don't want to become terrorists," he emphasized. "We don't want to destroy a building unless it has meaning. All our targets must be symbols of authority, either on the local, state, or federal level. Our targets can be people as well as objects. Policemen, police cars and buildings are prime targets on the local level. All federal buildings from courthouses to the ROTC facilities are prime targets, as are high government officials such as the Secretary of State, the Vice-President, the Secretary of Defense. Naturally, other prime targets are the White House, Capital, Pentagon, and Defense Department. When plans are formulated, these buildings will be hit."

Then we discussed the possibility of kidnapping high government officials for ransom to finance our activities. Rudd warned us again that we could be killed in carrying out these new assignments. "Offing pigs is one thing," he emphasized, "but we don't want to injure innocent people. We can't afford to turn the masses against us. We need their help. Remember, we have to concentrate on symbols of authority."

We stayed in the house rapping about the underground for a few more hours. The enthusiasm was fantastic. It was suggested that the first federal target should be Vice-President Agnew. This would prove to the country that we were to be taken seriously. No possible target was discouraged, but the person who suggested it had to be ready to show how it could be accomplished.

"Our main objective is to cause enough chaos in the system that it will be ripe for an overthrow," Rudd instructed. "But at the same time, we have to select assignments that we can execute without getting caught. We can assassinate any official if we're willing to sacrifice ourselves, but we want to strike and get away."

We left the house late in the afternoon and returned to the apartment. The only thing we had had to eat during the meeting was carrot sticks and ice cream left by the woman who owned the house. Everybody was excited and anxious to get moving. Arlo Jacobs was waiting for us when we got back. He looked haggard after his marathon driving stint, delivering people going on the Venceremos Brigade, and he was now ready to take us back to Cincinnati. Dianne called him aside to tell him what he had missed.

Back in Cincinnati, we began working rapidly to disband the collective. Each of us at the Cleveland meeting was given certain assignments. My job was to get in touch with the White Panthers and explain our new position to them. Then I had to talk with several of our contacts. Dianne Donghi was taking care of the members who had not gone to Cleveland. Some of them would be assigned to other cities to set up aboveground collectives so that we could keep in touch easily; others were told they would have to continue working for the movement on their own. Still others, like Barry Stein, were being dropped.

The White Panthers didn't agree with our new position and felt we were only hurting ourselves. Tom Udall had gone on to Cuba, so I just told the other contacts that the revolution was called off. Many accused us of copping out.

My hardest job was getting to see Murrish. I was extremely busy with movement activities. I managed to call him the first day we got back to tell him about the decision to go underground. This was news to him; no other office had reported it. Murrish was extremely interested in the meeting with Rudd and Evans. I couldn't talk long, but I did assure him I'd get in touch before the next day. He was peeved that I had gone off to Cleveland without telling him, but I explained that there hadn't been any time. The decision to go underground had confirmed my original fears about the Weathermen.

Later that same night, Dianne told me I was assigned to Detroit with Arlo. Dianne was going to Chicago. She said Stein was very bitter about being dropped and asked me to watch him closely until I left Cincinnati.

It took us a couple of days to make arrangements for everybody to get his proper assignment. During this time I was in contact with Murrish twice, both times by phone. When I told him I was going to Detroit, he said he was concerned for my safety, but that he would work out some arrangements with the FBI office there. He also told me I was the only one working with the FBI who had been accepted into the underground Weather movement. All the other FBI contacts had been purged by the Weathermen. "Be extremely careful," he said. "If you run into any trouble at all, get out." He told me to use the code name "Allen" when contacting the Detroit office.

We had to rent an extra car to help us clear up all the business in the city. The day before Arlo and I were to leave for Detroit, we took Dianne to the airport for her plane to Chicago. She was carrying a twelve-gauge shotgun with her in a guitar case. She had had the gun with her since she arrived, but this was the first time I had seen it. As she climbed on the plane with the case, it reminded me of a scene from a movie about the gangsters in the 1920s. She also had a .38-caliber revolver that she had left at the collective by mistake. Instead of going back for it, she asked me to wrap it up and send it by Greyhound to Chicago. I told her I would put it on a bus the next day. When I got back to the house I wrapped the revolver in a large box. Then I called Murrish; after I explained about the revolver, he said he needed a photograph of Arlo Jacobs. I told him I'd bring Arlo to the bus station at about 10 in the morning when I shipped the package. All the FBI would have to do was to have somebody there with a camera.

The morning Arlo and I were ready to leave for Detroit, he shocked me. He said we were going by way of the Ohio State and Dayton campuses. "We were told to get up there as soon as possible," I said. "Why are we stopping?"

"We're going to need help, and I can get it at Ohio State," Arlo said, acting smug. "Since we're driving to Detroit, why not accomplish something along the way?"

I didn't like the way Arlo was acting. I had to know what he had planned. "Look," I said. "We've been ordered to Detroit for something big. I don't think we should be stopping off just to socialize or play games."

Arlo snapped at me. "This is no game. We can pull it off. All we need is a little help."

"What the hell are you talking about? I want to go to Detroit, and you're giving me riddles."

This angered Arlo. "We're going to fire-bomb the computer complex at Dayton University," he blurted out. "The complex does a lot of work for the government. It's a natural target."

This stunned me. "Have we got enough help?" I asked, for lack of anything else to say.

Arlo said he was counting on a couple of guys at Ohio State to get the dynamite for us. We had plenty of help at Dayton, although Arlo admitted that neither his friends at Dayton nor those at Ohio State knew of the plan.

"You don't waste any time, man," I said to Arlo. "We go underground, and you get right into it." Arlo was pleased with my comments. My thoughts were to get away from him so I could warn Murrish. It wouldn't take us long to drive to Dayton, so I assumed Arlo was planning the attack for tonight.

"You sure we have enough time to plan this?" I asked.

"No sweat. There are two dances on the Dayton campus tonight. One is an ROTC ball, and the other is sponsored by an antiwar group. All we have to do is cause a little diversion and then hit the complex."

Arlo was serious. Evidently he had given the plan enough thought to check on the scheduled events. How could I warn Murrish? Then I remembered the rented car out front.

"Jesus, Arlo, I have to return that car," I said. I was hoping he would volunteer to bring it back, but he didn't.

"No problem," he said. "I'll follow and pick you up."

We walked out of the barren apartment and clicked the door locked behind us. Both cars were parked near each other. "Let's go, man," I said as we reached the street.

I sprinted to the rented car, turned on the motor, and took off. Arlo was right behind me. My only chance was to get to the car rental office with enough time to spare to call Murrish. I ran two yellow caution lights, but Arlo stayed right with me. I started to weave in and out of traffic to pick up a few minutes. Finally I got a break. Arlo got stuck at a light. I ran a red light and one stop sign before ripping into the car rental garage. I dashed into the office, tossing the keys and papers onto the counter. There was a phone in the corner, but a man was walking toward it. I pushed past him and grabbed the receiver, dropping in a dime at the same time. The phone at the FBI office seemed to take a long time to answer. When the receptionist finally spoke, I said: "Give me Murrish, quick!" Another delay. Murrish wasn't at his desk. Find him. Find him. I looked across the room and out the window. Arlo hadn't arrived yet. Murrish was on the phone. I fired out the plan and hung up. When I walked back to the counter for the receipt, Arlo was pulling up out front.

On the way to the Ohio State campus, Arlo outlined his plan. I listened carefully, injecting negative thoughts here and there without looking overly anxious to block the action.

When we got to Ohio State, a guy just back from one of the Venceremos Brigades was holding a press conference in the student union building. He was very impressed with himself and with what he had done for a struggling nation despite threats of reprisal from the U. S. government. I listened to his speech while Arlo went off to find his friends. Arlo returned alone. His friends had left campus for the weekend. At least that was one break.

But Arlo was still convinced we could carry out the plan. I stressed the urgency of getting to Detroit and questioned the wisdom of planning a major assignment without clearing it with our new leadership. "Suppose this is already planned as a target by another group? We could screw it all up. If the complex is so important, somebody must have it on their list."

I was getting to Arlo with this argument. Back in the car I continued to stress the need for careful planning in order to carry

out this action. He was weakening, but he still was insistent that
we could pull off the attack. Finally he agreed to wait until we
got into Dayton before we would definitely commit ourselves to
executing his plan. Halfway to Dayton the car began to swerve
violently and almost went out of control. Arlo had to fight to
keep it on the road. Finally he managed to pull it to a stop. We
got out and found that the rear axle had snapped. Another good
luck omen, I thought. But Arlo was determined to push ahead.
We pushed the car well off the road and left a note on it saying
we were going for assistance. Then we stuck out our thumbs and
started hitchhiking to Dayton.

Just as I thought luck was running with me because nobody
was stopping for us, a large Ford came screeching to a stop, and
the driver waved us over to the car. He was going through Dayton.

"Yessir," he said. "I'll have you there in no time."

The driver was a middle-aged man with a protruding stomach. He was a private detective on his way to St. Louis. He
had just helped a small manufacturing company in the Midwest
break up a union threat. He didn't explain all the details, but it
sounded like he had used some high-pressure and devious tactics to keep the company employee leaders from joining a large
national union.

I could tell Arlo was seething inside. I figured if I popped
off about the need for unions, the guy might not take us to the
campus. I tried to get him mad. "You're a f—ing strikebreaker,"
I said.

Arlo hit me in the ribs to keep quiet. He wanted the ride into
Dayton. It was getting late. I had to anger the guy without getting Arlo mad at me. But no matter what I said, the guy would
answer me with some innocuous phrase like, "I gotta make a
living, son."

He dropped us off right on the campus. I went into the
campus restaurant while Arlo went looking for Jim O'Hara, the
Weathermen contact I had met on the Washington trip, and Tom
Scanelli, an SDS leader at Dayton.

The three of them joined me in the campus restaurant. Arlo
had briefed them on his plan on the way over, but they didn't

agree with it. Both were protesting, and their reluctance to go along would make it easier to change Arlo's mind. I proposed that we use this trip to Dayton as a planning session and then come back to hit the complex some other time. Both Scanelli and O'Hara favored my idea. I could tell that neither of them wanted any part of the bombing, were even uncomfortable talking about it. Arlo criticized them for not being properly prepared. He claimed they should have been ready to execute an emergency plan.

I backed Arlo. "You guys should have thought of this yourselves," I said.

Using the fact that nobody was prepared as an excuse, I convinced Arlo to postpone the attack. However, since we were on the campus, Arlo insisted on disrupting the ROTC ball scheduled for that night.

We left the restaurant and went over to Scanelli's apartment just off the campus to work out some details. Scanelli called Larry Brown, the Black Panther leader on campus, and a few other radicals from Antioch College. They agreed to join us. We were about a dozen.

At 10 o'clock we drifted over to the student union building where the two dances were in progress. The ROTC had the main floor, while the antiwar group was in the basement. There were about 150 at the "antimilitary ball" in the basement, dancing to a four-piece band. Scanelli knew many of the people in the room, so he took over the microphone when the band took a break.

"This is a perfect example of the injustice in this country," he yelled into the microphone. "We're the ones who want to stop the war, and what happens? We get put in the basement. And who gets the ballroom upstairs?" He jerked his thumb up and down at the ceiling. "The war-mongers, that's who. The ROTC pigs who are going to make a career out of killing Vietnamese so Dow Chemical can get rich."

Scanelli got a favorable response from the audience, though nobody was ready to charge out of the room to battle with the ROTC. So then he shouted: "What should we do? We can't let the warmongers get away with this." He looked out at me. He wanted me to take some action, but I was hesitant. Finally, I thought, what the hell, I could justify starting a fight if it prevented a bombing.

I raced up to the microphone and grabbed it away from Scanelli. "Hell, we've been listening to these guys long enough. Let's go. Let's go stomp those f—ing pig bastards." Then I shoved the microphone aside and ran toward the door. Others were shouting and yelling behind me.

About 50 of the dancers followed me as we raced up the stairs and to the ballroom. Five guys in army uniforms, holding police-like billy clubs, were standing in front of the door. I veered off to the side, and Arlo joined me.

"Nice going," he said to me. "For awhile, I didn't think we were going to get them." The guys with the clubs moved out to meet us. As they did, one of them was punched on the side of the head. The doors of the ballroom swung open, and the doorway quickly filled up with walking uniforms. The scuffle turned into a shouting match, but most of the action was just pushing and shoving.

Soon Arlo was satisfied and suggested we cut out before the campus police arrived. We got Scanelli and the rest and took off. We ended up in Scanelli's apartment for a rap session, and I turned on Arlo for not telling any of us about his plan until the last minute. As I criticized Arlo, I was laughing inside. A potentially violent night had been held down to a minor incident. I was ready for Detroit.

Chapter 12

Detroit

I arrived in Detroit the day after our demonstration at the ROTC ball. Arlo had hitchhiked back to pick up the disabled car and would be following as soon as he could get it repaired. Instead of immediately telephoning the number Dianne Donghi had given me, I checked into a YMCA to spend a night between clean sheets and enjoy a steak dinner and a few beers. The next day I called the collective, and Naomi answered the phone. I told her I was at the bus terminal. She and Beth Wales, whom I met for the first time, came down to pick me up in the same 1962 Chevy we had had in Cincinnati.

My reunion with Naomi was cordial, but not emotional. Naomi said she was glad that I was assigned to Detroit, but then quickly reminded me that I was a day late. I told her about the side trip to Dayton University, exaggerating my participation while criticizing our contacts there for not being better prepared. She listened without commenting. When I finished, she asked when Arlo was due to arrive. Bill Ayers needed the $1700 Arlo had collected for the Venceremos people to help defray expenses in Detroit.

As we drove over to the collective, Naomi discussed our reasons for being in Detroit. She said it was an extremely racist pig city where the blacks not only were oppressed by the police, but were exploited by three of the world's leading purveyors of capitalistic injustice — General Motors, Chrysler, and Ford. The city was considered ripe for revolution.

141

Detroit was one of the first cities the Weathermen became active in after splitting from SDS in June 1969. Two early Weatherman demonstrations that were highly publicized in the underground press occurred in Detroit. The first, referred to as the Metro Beach Riot, happened in July 1969. At that time the Weathermen were beginning to recruit for the National Action in Chicago. As part of this program, about 30 of them roamed around the public beach carrying Viet Cong flags and handing out leaflets. When the Weathermen planted the red flags in the sand at the beach, a fight broke out with other young people, many of whom belonged to a motorcycle gang in Detroit. The melee exploded into a riot that the police had to break up. Weathermen claimed the demonstration was a success because it proved to the greasers that movement people were ready to fight for their cause and, as a result, they won the admiration of the motorcycle gang, many of whom became allies.

The second action, which took place in August, was conducted entirely by Weather women. Nine of them captured a sociology classroom at McComb Community College to protest what they termed the school's racist admissions policies. The women charged that the college wanted to train white females only for secretarial positions, so it made entrance requirements very difficult for blacks. At one point in the demonstration, according to New Left Notes, two males in the classroom got up to leave. However, the women attacked them with karate chops. Their occupation of the classroom ended when the police carried them screaming from the building. All nine were arrested for assault and battery and being disorderly.

Naomi took me to 1412 Pearson Street. Our collective was a four-room apartment on the second floor of an old tenement house. The absence of furniture made it resemble the other collectives I had been in. There were also two other apartments in town because we had 17 people assigned to the Detroit area.

We spent most of the week in political discussions, reaffirming our commitment to the movement and getting ourselves emotionally ready for action. However, I did manage to slip out on Wednesday afternoon to meet Carl O'Gara, my FBI contact in Detroit, in a downtown restaurant. I had found a way to call him on Monday to let him know I was in town. He suggested we meet.

After leaving the collective, I walked along the embankment of the freeway for a half mile so I could see if anyone was following me. Then I hitchhiked a ride into town. I got to the restaurant before O'Gara, so I had time to order a sandwich and coffee. We didn't have much food at the house, and I was hungry. I had already lost 12 pounds since joining the Weathermen. Our eating habits didn't exactly meet dietary specifications.

O'Gara was a pleasant person to work with. He asked me where the collectives were located, who was living in Detroit, what our specific plans were. We rapped for about an hour, and I promised to call him at least every other day. Like Murrish, O'Gara gave very little information in return for his questions. In the long run that was safer for me. For the same reason I was never told who the other infiltrators or informers were. If trouble occurred, I might be inclined to seek help from another agent, which would blow his cover. However, Murrish had told me that I was the only infiltrator who had made it into the Weatherman underground. He told me that so I'd be extremely accurate in gathering information, since it would be difficult to cross-check now.

Our apartment was so crowded, nobody questioned me when I returned from my meeting with O'Gara. One of the women had her four-year-old daughter living there with us. The young woman was named Melody. Her husband wasn't in the collective. The little girl was a frail, pensive child. She obviously didn't have any playmates, and she wasn't enrolled in school. She just hung around the house all day, going outside on occasion to play alone in the small courtyard. I felt sorry for her.

During the week, I also became friendly with Dianne Oughton, a very sweet-looking girl from an extremely rich family in Illinois. Dianne had been involved in the movement for seven or eight years. When I first met her, it was hard to believe she could be dedicated to violent action. But she had an honest conviction that revolution was the only solution to curing the ills of suppressed classes. She hated injustices, yet could rationalize violence as a means of righting them.

About a week after my arrival Bill Ayers called an important meeting at Wayne State University. Naomi announced that I was expected to attend, along with Linda Herbert, Beth Wales, and Marsha Brownstein. There was always some nervousness about holding planning discussions in the collective. We assumed the police didn't know where we lived and couldn't bug us, but Ayers wanted to be absolutely sure. We had to be free to talk, so he called this meeting for the university.

Dianne Oughton drove us over to the campus. It had been snowing off and on in light flurries all day long.

We went into a large classroom that had a big table at the front of the room facing rows of desks. Bill Ayers was sitting at the head of the table, as if presiding over a committee meeting for General Motors. He waved us to take the chairs around the table. He looked at me. "Where's your f—ing friend, Arlo?" he demanded, as if I kept track of Arlo's wanderings. "He's got $1700 we need." Obviously Ayers was counting on using the money Arlo had collected for the Venceremos people to run our collective.

When we were all seated, Ayers said we had been called together to make plans to select and destroy targets that were symbols of authority. If necessary, we would kidnap government officials for ransom and assassinate others when it was politically expedient. The Weathermen were now a fighting force.

We had aggressive units in New York, Buffalo, Boston, Philadelphia, Chicago, Detroit, Cleveland, Denver, San Francisco, Oakland, Berkeley, and Seattle. All these collectives had enough dynamite, blasting caps, and gunpowder to carry out all assignments; when necessary, temporary units would be established in other cities to implement certain projects. When traveling, we would be contacted, if needed, by the Weathermen name, "Delgato." For example, I'd be paged at an airport or bus station as Larry Delgato. Marion Delgato was a legendary figure in Weatherman circles. He was a five-year-old boy who supposedly placed a concrete slab on a railroad track, derailing the train. I had always been amazed that a five-year-old boy could lift a slab heavy enough to do such damage, but since the story was accepted, I didn't question it. Now I had two code names: Delgato for the Weathermen and Allen for the FBI.

Then Ayers turned to our assignment. "This group is going to be a fighting focal. You will work together within the structure of the Detroit collective." As soon as Jacobs got into town he'd join us, and so would Wendy Schramm. Schramm was raising money by marrying Mark Stivic. They were both due back in Detroit by the weekend.

Ayers pushed his chair back, stood up, then leaned forward, looking at each one of us. "You're a focal; therefore you need a target. And before we leave here today, you'll have one."

I looked at my companions. Whom or what would they select?

"Agnew!" came the first nomination. Ayers studied this possibility. "That's fine," he said, "but is it practical now? I mean, will he be in Detroit within the next few weeks? What can we do that will apply here?"

"How about the mayor. What's his name?"

"Gribbs."

Again Ayers pondered the suggestion.

"That may be good. The blacks are definitely suppressed in Detroit, and Gribbs isn't doing anything to alleviate the situation." Someone added: "He just appointed something called the Detroit Renaissance Committee without any blacks. The NAACP is pissed off." Ayers shook his head. "All right," he said. "We have Gribbs. Any other suggestions?" I was sure Ayers had a target in mind and wanted us to reach the same conclusion. It was typical Weathermen strategy. If we were going to be the ones who had to carry out the mission, we had to convince ourselves.

The General Motors Corporate headquarters building was named. "GM is one of the largest racist capitalistic pig companies in the world. Its only black employees are on the assembly line, working like slaves."

"That's good," Ayers agreed. "But is there something else, something closer to the black community that we can strike out at for them? Remember, our targets should be simple. The masses must grasp our message immediately."

He paused to accept more recommendations.

"Why not the police commissioner?"

Ayers was smiling. We had obviously touched on the target area. "Let's discuss the police," he said. "What's going on here that focuses on everything we've been talking about?" There was silence while we tried to think about what was going on in Detroit. "Of course," someone broke the silence. "The trial of the pigs who murdered the three blacks in a motel a couple of years ago."

"Right on," Ayers said. "The pigs are on trial in Flint. They murdered three black brothers for no reason, and we all know nothing is going to happen to them. The trial is a farce, like all establishment trials."

During a riot in Detroit in July 1967, three black men were killed at the Algiers Motel. A police investigation showed that they were shot at close range; that the Algiers Motel was well over a mile from the center of the riot area; that the police at the scene didn't make an official report of the incident. Eventually, three policemen were arrested. They were on trial now in federal court for conspiracy to violate the civil rights of the three dead men.

To Ayers, the three policemen on trial were only vehicles through which he could attack the system. Weathermen had to thrive on local issues, just as on the national level they had to take advantage of the war in Vietnam. Without issues, revolution was impossible. Ayers hammered on the desk. "Where did those pigs get the money to hire decent lawyers? The Police Officers Association put up the money. The pig officers can't afford to have their foot soldiers found guilty. It wouldn't look good for them. Somebody might get the idea to investigate the racist pigs who give the orders."

Ayers had narrowed in on our target: The Detroit Police Officers Association Building.

"Right on."

"We blast that f—ing building to hell," Ayers said." And we do it when the place is crowded. We wait for them to have a meeting, or a social event. Then we strike."

While our focal was concentrating on the officers building, another unit was making plans to destroy the Thirteenth Precinct, the station house where the cops involved in the incident were assigned.

"Any objections?" Ayers asked.

There were no objections, so Ayers took a large, flatly folded paper from his coat pocket and opened it in front of us. It was a street map of the officers building and a description of the area surrounding it.

"This is it," he said, pointing to the map. "It's a two-story brick building." Then he turned to me. "Grathwohl, take a look at this diagram. You haven't said much tonight."

I leaned over and looked at the map. Ayers waited a few seconds, then asked, "How much dynamite will it take to blow that up?"

I kept my eyes on the map, trying to think of an answer. How the hell did I know how much dynamite it would take? But I knew Ayers thought of me as an expert in explosives and weapons because I had fought in Vietnam. In addition, I was a greaser; therefore, I was used to violence.

"Well, what's the answer?" he snapped. "Thirteen sticks," I finally said. "That will blow the hell out of the building." "Okay," he said. "You'll get it. How about using a shape bomb to get more force?"

This time I answered right away. "No problem."

Then he said, "What I want you to do is cut the dynamite sticks open with a knife to get the powder out."

I looked up at him, amazed. "You're crazy," I blurted out. "You let me know when you're going to do something like that, because I'm going to be far away from here."

This remark annoyed Ayers. "We'll talk about that later," he snapped. "We have other details to go over now."

He warned us to plan every move very carefully. He didn't want anybody to get caught. To protect all of us, each individual would know only as much as he had to about the mission. The person who would actually place the bomb would not be selected until the last minute. That way, if the pigs busted any of us, no one would be able to tell the whole story.

Some of the details that we had to work out were possible disguises, a getaway car, the best time for placing the bomb. Ayers assigned Marsha Brownstein and me to case the building as soon as possible. "Study this map so you'll both have a mental picture of the area before you go over there," he said. "Weigh all the details carefully before making a recommendation on how we should act." Ayers said he'd be responsible for getting all the material we would need.

When Ayers finished talking, Naomi said that the six of us would work out of an apartment on Forrest Avenue. She recommended that from now until after the mission we stay together as much as possible. We were still expected to be over at Pearson Street for meetings with her or Bill, however.

Our Forrest Avenue apartment was on the second floor of a run-down three-story building. It had no more furniture than the Pearson Street place, but a lot more room — two big bedrooms, a living room, and a kitchen.

As we walked into our new apartment, my head was still spinning from the meeting. I had to get the information to O'Gara. Marsha and I decided to case the building the next day, so that would probably be the best time to call O'Gara. All I had to do was think of an excuse to leave her.

The next day Marsha and I sat in a small coffee shop on West Grand Boulevard, staring across at the Detroit Police Officers Association Building. The building was nestled almost in the center of a block that had a National Cash Register office on one corner and a Howard Johnson's on the other. There was a small, eight-foot-wide alley between the officer's building and the Red Barn Restaurant next to it. We sat drinking coffee and watching for two hours, but nobody went in or out of the building. Then we got up, left the coffee shop, and strolled up and down the sidewalk across from the building. We went down the alley into a parking lot in the back and noticed the expressway was a short distance away. It wouldn't take a car long to get from the lot to the expressway, especially at night. Although it was early afternoon, the Red Barn Restaurant was fairly crowded. Any bomb placed on the alley side of the building would surely rip through the Red Barn, injuring or possibly killing several people.

"What do you think?" Marsha asked as we walked down the alley for a second time.

"This place will crumble easily. It's an old building. But I'm worried about that restaurant. There's a lot of blacks inside who could get injured if we put the bomb in the alley."

"Good point. We'll have to discuss that with Ayers."

I had to get away from Marsha to call O'Gara, so I stopped walking. "Look," I said, "we got a good idea of what this area is like, but we still don't know what events are going to take place in the building during the next two weeks. And I don't think we can walk right up and ask them. We have to get this information, and there are only a couple of ways of doing it."

"What do you suggest?"

"One way is to check the local newspapers. Very frequently social events or important meetings will be listed on the women's pages. There are only two newspapers in town, the News and the Free Press, so we could go over and ask to see their back issues." Marsha thought about this for a moment. "We could spend all afternoon in the newspaper office and not find anything."

I looked down at the sidewalk, pretending to analyze her comment. "You're right," I finally said. "We can't afford to waste too much time. But if you take one newspaper and I take the other, we can get it done fast."

She agreed with this idea. I was relieved. It was the only plan I had. As it turned out, the two newspapers were within walking distance of each other. Once we got into the area, Marsha went to the Free Press building, and I hurried off to the News. Time was important. I found a phone booth and quickly dialed the FBI. O'Gara wasn't at his desk, but he was expected back shortly. I hung up, annoyed. Why wasn't he in when I called? Then I went inside and asked where I could go through the back issues. I had to go through the motions, just in case Marsha got through first and came down to find me. I waited 15 minutes and called O'Gara again. He had come back, but wasn't at his desk. The time it took to locate him seemed like an hour to me. As soon as I heard his voice, I began talking. As I explained the plan to O'Gara, I kept looking out from the phone booth at the door leading into the lobby of the newspaper office.

O'Gara warned me not to initiate any action. He didn't want me to be a participant, just an observer. He also wanted to catch us in the act of placing the bombs. As soon as I knew the time and day, I was to call immediately. He said he'd ask the police to cancel any activities in the building for the next couple of weeks, but that obviously couldn't be done at the Thirteenth Precinct building. Knowing the exact day was extremely important.

I assumed the Weathermen would try to blow up both buildings on the same night, but this was just an instinctive guess. A double strike would cause greater impact and actually lessen the chances of getting caught. If one explosion preceded the other, the police would be on guard all over the city.

After hanging up, I hurried back to the reference room. My book of newspapers was still open on the table. I took a little more interest now, and found a calendar of events. If anything was scheduled for the DPOA Building, it wasn't listed, which was good news. I hadn't been back at my desk long before Marsha came in. "Having any luck here?" she asked. From the tone of her voice I could tell she hadn't found anything. "Just a couple of more pages," I said.

Outside it was snowing lightly. I turned my collar up as we stepped out into the cold air. "We wasted an hour, but it had to be done," she complained. I agreed.

When we got back to the collective, Ayers was waiting for us. He was anxious for a report and called us into the kitchen for a conference. He was pleased that we had taken initiative to check through the newspaper files.

"Let's get down to details," he said. Arlo had arrived with the money, and Wendy Schramm was there, so our focal was complete. Now we had to work up a plan of attack. Molotov cocktails and firebombs were ruled out because they had to be thrown, which meant the chance of getting caught was greatly increased. The bombs had to have delay mechanisms so that the individuals had plenty of time to get away. And they obviously had to placed without our being seen.

The plan we worked out was actually quite simple. Two of us, a male and a female, would attend the late evening show at the movie theater around the corner from the police building. Naturally, the two would be dressed in "straight" clothes, in order to blend in with the crowd. Near the end of the movie one of the two would go into the washroom and assemble the bomb. The device, including a burning cigarette, would be placed inside a paper bag, then carried out of the theater when the movie was over. It was a two-minute walk from the theater to the alley beside the police building. Many other people would cut through the alley to get to the parking lot. On the way down the alley, the person selected would place the paper bag containing the bomb in the doorway on the side of the building and leave.

I objected to leaving the bomb on the side of the building. "We'll blow out the Red Barn Restaurant. Maybe even kill a few innocent customers — and most of them are black."

Ayers didn't appreciate my remark. "We can't protect all the innocent people in the world. Some will get killed. Some of us will get killed. We have to accept that fact. That bomb is going to be placed on the side of the building." He glared at me for questioning his authority. "Have you cased the building at night yet?" he asked me.

"No."

"Well, you'd better get on that. We want to be sure that enough people leaving the theater use that alley so that it won't look unnatural for two of us to be walking around there late at night."

I nodded in agreement.

"Now let's talk about the bomb." He spread a diagram of a bomb out on the kitchen table. "All of you have to learn to make these, so you might as well begin now."

In a sense I was standing in a crude bomb factory. Ayers was holding a diagram that showed thirteen sticks of dynamite, wrapped tightly with wire. An M-80 firecracker was set into the sticks to act as the detonator. The exceptionally crude part was the timing device. This was merely a lit cigarette that was supposed to burn down and then ignite the wick of the firecracker; the firecracker would then explode, setting off the dynamite.

"What do you think of it, Grathwohl?" Ayers asked.

It was a primitive device that could work, but Ayers had forgotten one thing. The wick of a firecracker is waterproofed, and it normally takes more heat to light it than could be supplied by a burning cigarette, especially when the entire device is enclosed in a paper bag. There was an excellent chance that the bomb as devised wouldn't work. Also, the simple design of the bomb would make it fairly easy for the police to dismantle once they found it.

I looked at Ayers. "It looks fine. You seem to know what you're doing."

Ayers smiled.

After talking about the bomb, Ayers confirmed the fact that both the DPOA and precinct buildings would be attacked the same night. "We want both bombs to explode as close together as possible," he said.

We went over the plan several more times before Ayers broke up the meeting. He reminded me to check out the area at night and then told me that Mike Spiegel wanted to see me over at Pearson Street. When I got there, Spiegel was waiting for me in the kitchen drinking coffee.

"Sit down," he said. "We have a problem that you can help with."

I pushed my chair back up against the wall. "What is it?"

"When you came back from Vietnam, what outfit did you say you served with?" I became cautious. Why did he want to know? "I was a DI at Fort Campbell." Mike shook his head. "No man, not that. Weren't you with another outfit for a little while?" I couldn't figure out what he was getting at. "Yeah. I was with a vehicle-maintenance group."

"That's what I thought. You took care of the trucks, cars, jeeps."

"If you want to call it that. I did very little mechanical work."

"But you did some."

"Sure. Some. But I'm not a mechanic." I was wondering what idea Spiegel had now. He put his coffee cup down on the table. "You may not be a mechanic, but you're going to have to do." I didn't know if that statement was a compliment or not. "Do for what?"

"I want you to hold a series of clinics on car maintenance. Suppose something goes wrong, and we have to take off from the pigs. If we get out on the highway or in the back road somewhere, we can't afford to stop at a gas station for minor repairs. We have to be able to do it ourselves. We have to be self-sufficient in every respect." Spiegel was so determined to conduct auto-repair clinics, I decided not to argue with him. Anyway, I didn't want to develop a reputation for being negative.

"Look man, I'll do what I can," I volunteered. "I think you're right. When you're ready, let me know. I'll give a course in auto mechanics that nobody will forget." Spiegel laughed. "Hell," he said, "don't get carried away. Let's go into the other room. Ayers wanted us to join them when we were through."

The living room was crowded. Spiegel and I climbed over a few people to get to sitting room on the floor in the corner. Ayers was conducting a session to reiterate what we should and shouldn't do now that we were an underground organization. Much of the material he was covering came from the Minimanual of the Urban Guerrilla and from Revolution in the Revolution. As we walked in, Ayers was giving tips for survival. He was covering the major danger facing all of us, pig spies. Their only punishment should be death. This would discourage others from trying to infiltrate our groups. Statements like that never helped my nervous system.

Ayers reminded us about the danger of keeping address books, notebooks, plans, maps, or any written information. "Memorize what you can, then throw the paper away. The pigs can't convict us if they don't have any evidence."

Then he opened up the meeting to a discussion of recent accomplishments of the Weathermen and other revolutionary movements. Bombings had grown more frequent from Seattle to New York. Obviously, not all the attacks were organized by Weathermen, but that was incidental. We encouraged other groups to follow our lead. Among the violent acts in the last ten days were exploding dynamite at a municipal building in Cleveland, which injured a judge, and setting fire to an ROTC office in Boston.

Yet, on the national level, we were slow to act. We had three avenues open to us: destruction of national buildings and power plants; kidnapping government officials for ransom and publicity; and assassinations. Assassinations had to be used only when it was politically expedient. Killing national figures could turn the masses against us. But there might come a time when an assassination would throw the country into utter chaos and open it up for full-scale revolution. When that time came, we would go all out to get our target.

Kidnappings had to be considered as a real possibility. A successful kidnapping where ransom was paid, political prisoners freed, and the subject released unhurt would gain us a tremendous following. These acts would prove that we were unstoppable even by the federal pigs. As our image grew stronger and brighter, the government would look increasingly inept and stupid.

Whom should we kidnap?

Vice-President Spiro Agnew. A prime subject because he was part of the administration, although it would be difficult because of the number of secret service men who usually accompanied him. If the time was ripe, however, an all-out assault on his entourage could be condoned. Some would die in getting him, but it could be worth the price.

Presidential aide Henry Kissinger. A much more likely target. He might be the person closest to the President we would be able to get. Kissinger traveled frequently, which opened up many opportunities when he was vulnerable. We might even capture him in another country with the aid of our friends. A careful reading of The New York Times would disclose his travel plans.

Secretary of Defense Melvin Laird. Also an excellent choice. He was responsible for our war machine. It might even be possible to take him at home by a well-organized attack.

The President's Communications Director, Herb Klein. Probably the easiest person in the administration to get. The only disadvantage was that not enough people would respond to his kidnapping. But he was definitely a prime target. He was the mouthpiece for corruption.

Ayers said that each of us should work out detailed plans on how each individual mentioned could be kidnapped with a minimum of danger to the Weathermen. Nothing was to be in writing. The list could be expanded by any of us, although we had to be prepared to give reasons why new subjects should be added.

Next we discussed national symbols of authority: buildings, air bases, or power stations that could be identified with government suppression of blacks, browns, poor whites in this country and around the world. The floor was open for suggestions.

The Pentagon. It was the symbol of our military war machine. It had to be bombed. An explosive device strategically placed might also "off" a warmonger general.

The White House. The home of the chief imperialistic pig, It, too, had to be destroyed to prove how vulnerable it was. The Capitol. The major symbol of our imperialistic government. It was a prime target. The Department of Justice. Since its name was a contradiction of its performance, it, too, had to be attacked.

The Washington, Lincoln, and Jefferson monuments, although foolish symbols of our society, were not prime targets. The masses attached too much sentiment to them, which could cause adverse reaction should they be destroyed.

Outside of Washington, D.C., we were already striking at federal buildings, courthouses, and ROTC buildings. But we should also concentrate more on air bases, especially those harboring B-52 bombers. "Wright-Patterson Air Force Base outside Dayton is a good example," Ayers said. "This would be close for us, yet it carries national exposure."

The mention of Dayton pleased Arlo. "Don't forget the computer complex there," he said. "It has a lot of government contracts. We have our people casing it now."

Wright-Patterson was especially ripe for attack because of the B-52 strikes in Vietnam. An attack on the air base would be a blow against our military war machine and a boost for our friends, the Viet Cong. It would show them that people in this country support their cause.

"Getting on an air base wouldn't be easy," I said.

Naomi answered me. "Getting past those male chauvinist pig guards would be simple. Any woman can do it. All we need is a short skirt, make-up, and a flirtatious smile. If they want to f —, we let them."

"We can get all the weapons we need from our friends," Ayers said. "Or we can knock off an armory. Hell, the military is so screwed up they wouldn't miss a few guns anyway."

"No target is invincible," Naomi said. "If we make up our minds to destroy it, we can."

Ayers interrupted her. "The Tupamaros do it every week. So

can we. And it's important for us to take on these major targets. Anybody can pipe-bomb a police car, but we have to go beyond that stage."

Everybody agreed that national acts were needed to convince the masses that we were serious. Once they gained confidence in us as a viable fighting force, they would join us.

"How do we bomb the White House?" Marsha Steinberg asked. "Don't they have guards searching people as they go in?"

Ayers began to answer the question, but Naomi interrupted him. "It's not a thorough search. Anyway, the guards are males. We playoff their chauvinism. Any woman can get by with dynamite taped to her thighs. If two or three of us carry a few sticks each, it will be very simple."

The women would also carry two pocketbooks, one inside the other. The larger one would have a plastic waterproof lining. Once inside the White House or other building, the women would go to the ladies room and assemble the bomb inside one of the stalls. They would place the bomb inside the pocketbook with the waterproofing and put the unit inside the toilet tank. A timing device would give them sufficient time to leave. The only problem would be to select a strategically located ladies room, one close to an office.

The most unbelievable thing about the discussion was that everybody in the room was serious. They even made me believe that each target mentioned could be successfully destroyed.

As the session slowly began to taper off, individuals continued to discuss certain possibilities privately. Dianne Oughton was sitting next to me. When there was a lull in the conversation she said, "Do you think it's possible?"

"What's possible?"

"The air base in Dayton. Do you really think we can attack it?"

I glanced around the room to see if anyone was listening to us, but most of them had left or were standing. We were still sitting in the corner. "No," I said. "You can't get to that base without an all-out commando raid."

She was silent for a moment. "All this talk can seem so foolish. I don't know if we're doing any good or not. I've been around a long time. Much longer than you, Larry. And I'm not sure any longer."

She had expressed doubts to me before, but usually only one or two words. She had great concern for people, and the thought of destroying them was bothering her. She was losing weight, and I attributed this to her nagging doubts. She was for change, but I don't think she condoned the violence.

I talked with her a while longer. Then Naomi came over to join us. "I haven't seen much of you lately," I said as Naomi sat down on the floor next to us. "We've both been rather busy," she said. She glanced over at Dianne, then added, "I understand your project is going very well."

I nodded. By now I wasn't in the mood for more politics.

"Can we talk alone?" Naomi asked.

Dianne stood up. "I was just leaving," she said. I watched her walk over to Bill Ayers, who was standing near the door. Then Naomi told me that Dianne Donghi had been arrested in Chicago on a gun violation charge.

"But the lawyer got her released right away."

Jesus, they can't keep anyone in jail nowadays, I thought. "What happened?" I asked. I had to show some interest.

"She's not sure," Naomi explained. "But she thinks Barry Stein may be trying to get her for letting him go. He was bitter when it happened, you know. But when you have to purge somebody, you take the chance that they may come back to try and get you."

Nothing was mentioned about my mailing the gun to Dianne in the first place, so I brought it up. "I wrapped that gun myself," I said. "Then Arlo and I dropped it off at the bus station. How could Stein know what was going on?"

Naomi didn't answer my question. She changed the subject.

"You know, when this project is completed, you may be sent somewhere else," she said. I assumed that would happen. "Do you know where?"

"No. But if it does happen, it's to help develop your leadership qualities. You're still weak in that area." She didn't say any more, so I didn't push her for answers. We talked a while longer on general subjects. Then she asked:

"You going back to Forrest Avenue?"

I looked at her.

"I thought I'd crash here tonight."

She agreed. We went into the other room to bed.

When I got back to the house, a meeting was going on. The women were talking about their role in the general structure of Weathermen. They now were objecting to the name Weathermen being applied to the group as a whole. The group, they protested, should be called Weather People, Weather Movement, or Weather Machine. Then, within the group, there would be Weathermen and Weatherwomen.

This was the strongest stand the women had taken since I was a member. However, in the last few months they had been demanding more authority on all levels. They were also taking more initiative on their own. They were avowed defenders of women's liberation, belittling the "equal pay for equal jobs" slogan as being childish and insignificant in comparison to the total women's movement. Women should be completely independent. Some of them even said that men were unnecessary for sex. Sex for pleasure could be enjoyed between two women just as much as between a man and woman, and if men didn't accept women's liberation, they would have to do without women. Any man who believed in women's liberation had to agree with this. A liberated man would refuse to accept women as sex objects and could enjoy sex with other men.

One woman admitted that she eventually wanted a baby, but only through artificial insemination and only if it was a female. This led to a discussion of the role of the family in a revolutionary environment — the relationship between parent and child. The consensus was that the family didn't have a place in their society. Loyalties to families held the movement back. It made revolutionaries more concerned about their dependents than about the cause. Children should be reared in communes, where father and mother figures substituted for the parents.

As the discussion continued, I watched Melody. She appeared to be dedicated to the movement, but she also had great affection for her four-year-old daughter, who was trying to sleep while lying across Melody's lap. Slowly the discussion turned into a criticism of Melody.

"What about Melody's child?" Naomi asked. "We all live here together, but is she holding us back? Would we do more if Debby lived in a commune with other children?"

Beth Wales agreed. "One way or another, Debby has to restrict us. We don't want to hurt her, so we ease up on our plans." "The child should go," Linda Herbert said sternly. "She's been here too long as it is."

Melody had tucked her legs up under her and wrapped her arms around Debby, who was looking at us through sleepy eyes. For the past month we had been her aunts, uncles, friends; yet here we were, talking about having her live somewhere else. It must have been confusing and frightening for her.

Melody defended her little girl. "She's no trouble to any of you. She takes care of herself. She's never in anybody's way." Melody was gripping Debby more tightly now.

The tempo of the criticism increased as each person built a case against Debby's living in the house any longer. Melody's eyes started to fill with tears. Debby was obviously scared.

Why couldn't they just call Melody aside and tell her to move out? Why subject the little girl to this? I just sat there listening without speaking out for Melody. Melody was being forced to make a decision, and I couldn't do anything about it, regardless of how cruel the process was.

"There's a commune near here that will accept Debby," Marsha said. "We can bring her over tomorrow."

"No!" Melody screamed. "No!"

"Come here, Debby," Marsha coaxed. "Come over here."

Debby only buried herself deeper into her mother's arms, crying softly. I wanted to jump up and grab both Melody and Debby and run out of the room. Take them out of this weird place. I was ashamed and saddened by what was going on. Yet I couldn't do anything. If I did, I'd be on the wrong side.

As time moved on, Melody began to relent. She wanted to stay in the collective. Finally, she gave in. They could take her daughter in the morning. I felt lousy inside. These were intelligent people; most of them had a true concern for helping those they considered oppressed, yet they could still rip apart a mother and daughter. It didn't make any sense.

The next day I made an excuse to go to the Veterans Hospital for my malaria. I had to get away to see O'Gara, and the hospital was a good place to meet. Dianne Oughton volunteered to drive me into town. I didn't want to draw any suspicion, so I pretended to be pleased to accept her offer. On the drive, Dianne was questioning the movement again. She seemed to be in a completely confused state of mind. When we got to the hospital, she pulled into a parking space, and turned to talk to me.

"You're a funny guy, Larry."

"Me? Why do you say that?"

"Because everybody likes you. You avoid criticizing people. Everybody else enjoys those meetings, but I think you hate them. I think you'd rather just go out and do something without all the talk."

I had to laugh when she said that.

"You're right. I didn't know it showed. Those long meetings can get boring."

"I know what you mean. I've been in this movement a long time. I've seen people starving in Latin America because of us. Our oppression is real, but I'm not sure we're going about fighting it in the right way. What do you think?"

I couldn't think of anything to say except: "You have to do what you have to do."

She reached over, putting her hand on mine.

"I'm leaving Detroit," she said. "But maybe we can get together when I get back." "Fine," I said, opening the door. She volunteered to wait for me. "No thanks. I may be a while. I have to fill out a lot of papers." I walked across the lot to the front walk. I heard the horn as she drove away. I turned and waved good-bye. Inside, I went to the phone booth and called O'Gara.

On Saturday night, February 21, Beth Wales and I went back to take another look around the DPOA building. We walked up the street in front of the building, then turned down the alley into the parking lot. The building was dark.

"Those pigs don't seem to use the building very much," Beth commented. "They don't have time for that," I said. "They're out roughing up the greasers. That's their sport." Beth laughed. "Or roughing up the blacks. The f—ing pigs are the same all over."

We went back up the alley and walked around the corner to the movie theater to check on the time the movie was over: the first show got out about 8:30 on weekdays and 9:30 on weekends. Since it was 9 o'clock, we went into Howard Johnson'S to wait for the people to begin pouring out of the theater. I drank two cups of coffee before the first group left the theater. Some of them walked into Howard Johnson's, but others continued around the corner. We paid the check and left. We joined the crowd as it moved down the block, then into the alley next to the DPOA building. Beth and I strolled along, arm in arm. Halfway down the alley we stopped, and she placed her pocketbook on the ground, while pretending to fix her shoe. Then she straightened up, picked up the pocketbook, and we continued on to the parking lot. If a car had been waiting for us, we could have gotten away without anyone noticing what we were doing in the alley. Instead, we turned around and retraced our steps. The sidewalk along the boulevard was almost deserted now. The movie crowd would be our key to success. We could mingle with them without being obvious, plant the bomb, and make an easy escape.

When we went back to Pearson Street, we reported to Ayers. We all sat on the living room floor while he asked questions. "I still think we should put the bomb in the back of the building," I protested.

"Stop worrying about those people in that restaurant. That's not your concern," Ayers snapped. "You can't build a revolution worrying about a handful of people."

He went over the entire plan three times with all of us. "We have all the materials we need," he told us. Then he began a rap session about the movement expanding rapidly.

"We need support in other cities. We have to move fast to keep the pigs confused." He was leading up to something, and I didn't like it. When he was finished, he made a shocking statement: "You people are finished with your assignments in Detroit. You did a good job, but as far as you're concerned, the project is finished."

Then he told Wendy Schramm and Linda Herbert and me that we were being sent to Madison, Wisconsin, along with Mark

Stivic. Madison was to be our training ground in urban guerrilla survival.

We weren't the only four sent out to form an active focal. Arlo was assigned to another city with three companions. Only Ayers, Naomi, and probably one or two Weather Bureau members knew where each focal was assigned.

"You're going out on your own. Get your own supplies. Pick two targets, hit them fast, then get out. If you get in a jam, call the house here. There's no need to spend more than a few weeks in Madison. When you've finished there, we have other cities for you."

I was stunned. I couldn't leave. I still didn't know what day the bomb would be placed.

"Why can't we finish the job we started?" I protested.

"Consider it finished," Ayers said, smiling.

"It's not fair to cut us off like that."

Ayers thought a moment before answering: "I appreciate your dedication, Grathwohl, but as far as you people are concerned, the project is finished."

"When do we leave?" Linda asked.

"First thing in the morning," Ayers said, reaching into his pocket for money to give to us so we could get to Madison. How the hell was I going to get to O'Gara?

Chapter 13

Trying to Stop the Bombings

I didn't sleep well the night we were assigned to Madison. For the next two weeks or a month I would be virtually cut off from the Detroit collective — and from any further information on the DPOA plan.

I had to get in touch with O'Gara to tell him that I would no longer be able to supply details needed to prevent the plot. The only way to delay my departure was to fall back on the malaria excuse. It might work because everybody knew Dianne Oughton had recently driven me to the Veterans Hospital. It had to work. I couldn't think of any other way to stay in Detroit. At breakfast I complained of starting to feel sick. I suggested that we wait until Monday to leave so that I could go back to the Veterans Hospital for pills or a shot. Arlo and his group had already gone, so that morning only Wendy, Linda, Mark, and I were in the house. We discussed my proposal for a few minutes, but the other three decided to leave that morning anyway. I was to stay over and meet them at the student union building at the University of Wisconsin in Madison the next day at 7 P.M.

As soon as they left, I packed my bag and took a cab to the Veterans Hospital. I waited there awhile, then called another cab to take me into town so that I could check into a hotel. I called O'Gara from the hotel and he came right over. While I was waiting, I took a shower. The dirt that poured off me was unbelievable. It was the first time I'd felt clean in three weeks.

When O'Gara showed up, he had his supervisor with him. The supervisor seemed annoyed at being dragged out on a Sunday to meet a hippie freak, regardless of what the freak was working on. He was very condescending. I started by explaining that I had to leave for Madison, and therefore wouldn't be able to keep them informed about the bombing plots.

"Who said you could go to Madison?" the supervisor asked.

"What do you mean, who said I could go?"

"Have you gotten clearance from Washington?"

I looked at him in disbelief. "No. I forgot to call Mr. Hoover this morning," I said sarcastically. I could tell this angered him, but he managed to control his temper. "We'll have to send an airtel to Washington immediately to get clearance for you, but being Sunday, we probably won't get an answer until tomorrow." I looked over at O'Gara to see if his boss was serious. O'Gara must have read my mind, because he motioned for me to calm down.

The supervisor opened a briefcase and removed a legal-size pad.

"You claim to know a lot of Weathermen," he said. "Who are they?"

I was confused by his line of questioning, but I decided to play his game, at least for a while. "Well, I met most of them, I guess." "You guess?" "I know. I've met Mark Rudd, Bill Ayers . . . " he cut me short. "Don't tell me," he said. "Write them on this pad." He held the pad out. I went over and took it, then went back and sat on the edge of the bed. I started writing, then stopped. Who the hell was this guy to test me? I got angry.

"Bullshit," I said, getting off the bed. "What the hell do you think you're doing to me? If you want to know the names of all the Weathermen I know, read the goddamned files in your office. I'm sure there are copies of all my reports. I'm not wasting my time writing out another list."

I could see O'Gara was horrified at my outburst, but I was too angry to care.

"I've been living in hellholes so you guys can get information, and you ask me whom I know. Don't you ever talk to your agents?"

The supervisor wasn't expecting my attack. I was acting outside the rule book written for infiltrators. But I wasn't just one of his hired hands. "I don't owe you guys anything," I yelled at him. "I didn't come crawling to you offering to sell information. Believe it or not, I'm doing this because I want to help stop those crazy bastards."

The supervisor didn't say a word during my tirade. O'Gara finally calmed me down and turned the conversation back to the DPOA plot. I told him it would be wise to keep a surveillance on both buildings every day during the next week, although I thought the bombings would take place on Thursday.

"Why do you say that?" the supervisor interjected.

"Just a hunch. Or, you might say, an educated guess." I could tell he was completely dissatisfied with my answer. I gave him all the other details I had, even the names of those I thought were going to remain in Detroit. They stayed about an hour, then O'Gara suggested they leave.

On the way out, the supervisor told me that he would send O'Gara back the next morning with "clearance for you to proceed."

I almost went into another rage. O'Gara saw my reaction and hurried the supervisor out the door. When they left I went out for a few beers and a steak, thankful I didn't have to work for that supervisor.

When O'Gara came back the next morning, he gave me traveling expenses totaling $120 in cash, for which I signed a receipt, and said Washington approved of my plans.

It was close to 7 P.M. when I got to Madison, so I took a cab from the airport to the student union building, hoping I wouldn't be too late for the meeting. I walked over to a table where Mark, Linda, and Wendy were sitting. "Hello, people," I said. "How's it going?"

"Fine, man, fine," Mark greeted me with a handshake.

They wanted to know how I made out at the Veterans Hospital. It was a perfect opening for setting up an excuse for getting out of Madison after I had had time to ruin our effectiveness here.

"Hell, those f—ing bureaucrats refuse to treat me any more because they don't have my records."

"What kind of crap is that?"

"What are you going to do?"

"I have to go back to Cincinnati, fill out a lot of papers, and get some kind of card that will let me get treatment in other cities." They all sympathized with me. "Now you know how a poor black woman feels when they force her to sign away her soul just to get welfare money," Wendy said.

They had made arrangements to spend a few days with a group of hippies living near the college while we looked for an apartment. We rapped at the student union for an hour, then returned to the pad and went to sleep.

The next day each of us went out on our own looking for an apartment to rent, stores we could rip off for food, and places we could get dynamite. We also were searching for an old car to buy. We had discussed stealing one, but decided against using a hot car. The cops could pick us up right away.

The only specific assignment Ayers had given us was to try to get in contact with a group that called itself the New Year Gang. In January, the group had stolen a small two-propeller plane, flown over the army ammunition plant in Baraboo, Wisconsin, and dropped homemade bombs. The bombs landed in the snow and hadn't gone off. But Ayers thought the stunt was fantastic and wanted us to get in touch with the group, so part of our activities that first day was to make discreet inquiries around the campus.

This freedom during the day gave me ample time to call Tom Fadden, my FBI contact in Madison. Fadden wasn't overjoyed that he had a group of four instigators running around town planning to blow up buildings. He had enough trouble with campus radicals already. I told him we wouldn't cause any serious trouble as long as I could prevent it. Then I asked him about the Detroit bombing plot, but he hadn't heard anything yet. I told him I'd keep in touch.

Later, when I was walking up the main street in town, an arm grabbed my shoulder and a voice from behind said: "Larry! What the hell are you doing here?"

The voice was familiar. I turned around. Barry Stein was standing there, smiling at me. "What d'ya say, man?" he said, holding out his hand. I shook it.

"You're a long way from Cincinnati."

"I like to travel."

Stein laughed. "Come on man, what are you doing here? What have you got planned?"

"Same as you, man. Touring." Stein looked at me, disbelieving. "Hey. You can tell me. What are you up to?"

I didn't answer him.

"Okay, man, okay. Have it your way. Don't tell me. But look. I'm staying in town; why not come over when you get time?" I said I would. He gave me his address, then turned and left. We had a meeting that night to select our primary target. Stivic reported that he had found a construction site where we could rip off enough dynamite to carry out any mission. We began our discussion by listing buildings on campus and federal property in the area. Both the armory and an ROTC classroom building were nominated. Then somebody suggested the home of the judge who was trying a case against radicals in Milwaukee. Next came the army ammunition site in Baraboo that the New Year Gang had tried to hit. This suggestion sparked general interest. Somebody else had already tried and failed, so by succeeding we would boost our reputation. We discussed the possibility, and Stivic suggested an alternative to attacking the plant directly. He had discovered that the Baraboo plant was kept in operation by a nearby electric power station. He suggested it would be easier to knock out the power station, thus effectively shutting down the munitions plant.

After another hour of discussion we agreed on the power station as our target. I volunteered to case the area the next day while the others tried to get us a pad. When our business was settled, I casually mentioned that I had seen Barry Stein. A complete silence enveloped the room.

Stivic was the first to speak. "What did you say to him?"

"I said hello."

"That's all you said, just hello?"

"Of course I said more than that. What of it?"

Mark, Wendy and Linda all began to criticize me at the same time. As far as they were concerned, Stein was a walking threat to our plans in Madison. He could identify us as Weathermen, which he might do in retaliation for being purged. He might tip off the police. By implying more than he knew, he could destroy our effectiveness.

"Look," I snapped in defense, "I turned around, and he was standing there looking at me. What could I do, ignore him?"

"We have to off him," said Stivic. "It's our only way out."

The others agreed with him. If they didn't get rid of him, he could ruin the entire operation.

I couldn't believe my ears. These people were seriously talking about killing a man in cold blood just because he knew they were in town. If I hadn't known better, I'd have sworn they were drunk or high on acid. But they were cold sober.

"What do you think, Larry?" Wendy asked. I looked at her blankly. I had heard more compassion from GIs about killing Viet Cong. I couldn't take the conversation seriously.

"Hell," I answered. "I never did like Stein anyway. You girls hold him down and I'll tickle him to death. Or maybe we can chop him up and feed him to a bowl of goldfish. Then we could send the goldfish to pig Hoover."

Wendy and Linda laughed, but Stivic berated me for trying to be funny. This was a serious matter, and I had to help. I was a Vietnam vet, so it would mean nothing to me to go out and kill Stein, they thought. I knew they were waiting for me to volunteer to carry out the assignment. Finally I decided to test their courage. I reached into my pocket and took out a book of matches, ripped off four from the pack, then tore one in half and placed all of them in a row in my hand.

"Okay," I said. "We off Stein. The person who picks the small match does the job." I said it without laughing, Humphrey Bogart style.

I shoved my hand in front of Mark.

"You first."

When he hesitated, I moved on to Wendy and then to Linda. I moved my hand without giving them time to make a decision. As soon as each one hesitated, I put the matches in front of the next one. "All right," I challenged them. "If you don't want to pick, I'll go first." I paused after making the statement. "Wait a minute," Wendy said. "Maybe we have been too hasty. After all, Barry was one of us. He still might be on our side."

"Why not talk with him first?" Mark added. "You always got along with him, Larry. Why don't you and Linda go talk to him? If that doesn't work, then we can pick the matches."

I glanced around. Everyone agreed.

Linda and I went to see Stein the following day. We talked to him as a brother in the movement and didn't threaten him. He admitted he would have been concerned if the positions were reversed and promised not to say anything about us. He even agreed to ignore us if he saw any of us again on the street.

While we were talking to Stein, Mark and Wendy found us an apartment. It was a one-room loft in an old three-story wooden building. We moved in immediately. The room had only one light, a bare bulb hanging down from the middle of the ceiling. The only furniture was an old wooden dresser in the corner of the room.

We spent the rest of the week making plans. Linda and Wendy had decided to steal pocketbooks from the girls' dormitory at the university. They wanted credit cards and checks. They planned to cash the stolen checks, using the credit cards as identification. They'd also charge as many items on the cards as they could, then sell the goods for cash. This would finance our activities. They planned to begin this operation on Saturday when the stores were busy and the salesclerks didn't have much time to spend on each customer.

On Friday night, March 6, the four of us were eating at the campus cafeteria when Barry Stein saw us and started over.

"I thought you told that idiot not to talk to us," Stivic said when he saw Stein coming in our direction.

Stein was making a foolish move, I thought. He was going to start the debate about killing him all over again. I was hoping he'd walk past us, but he didn't. He came over to the table, leaned in to us, and whispered in a very solemn voice: "Is it true? Is Rudd dead?" His question startled us. "Rudd dead! What the hell are you talking about?" I asked.

"The explosion," he said. "I heard Rudd was killed in the explosion."

An image of the Detroit police station being ripped apart with Rudd caught inside flashed through my mind. Although I hadn't heard anything, I jumped to the conclusion that that was what Stein was talking about.

"You mean in Detroit?" I asked.

"No, in New York," Stein answered. "You mean you haven't heard? It's been on all the radio news broadcasts." "Tell us what the hell you're talking about," Stivic demanded. A Weatherman bomb factory in New York City had blown up that afternoon, killing three people who were as yet unidentified. The rumor was that Mark Rudd was killed in the explosion.

The news stunned all of us. Wendy suggested we call the house in Detroit for information. We permitted Stein to stay while we got the information.

When Wendy returned from making the phone call, she looked pale and shocked. She sat down without saying a word, shaking her head. Then she finally said: "They were all blown apart, heads and arms ripped off their bodies. It must have been horrible."

I wanted to know who was killed. Wendy looked at me. "One of them was Dianne Oughton," she said.

"My God," was all I could whisper. I was sure the others were as stunned as I was. The other two victims were Ted Gold and Terry Robbins. I had met both at the war council in Flint, but I didn't know either one very well. But Dianne's death was a shock. I had been looking forward to seeing her again.

The police were looking for Cathlyn Wilkerson because the house the bomb factory was in belonged to her father, who was away on a vacation. It was a $200,000 town house on Eleventh Street in New York City'S Greenwich Village. The blast rocked the entire neighborhood, even ripping the wall out of the house next door, owned by the actor Dustin Hoffman. The basement of the town house, which was used as the bomb factory, had 57 sticks of dynamite, 30 blasting caps, wire, clockwork timing devices, and pipe.

What a way to die, I thought. None of us said anything for

a long time. We all realized a similar accident could happen to us. After Stein heard the details, he left. Nobody said good-bye to him. We were holding a private wake for three dead people. Our enthusiasm for blowing up the power station temporarily vanished. We didn't discuss revolutionary tactics that evening. And the plan to try and cash the stolen checks was postponed. The accident not only saddened us, but frightened us. It took us until Sunday night before we began seriously discussing our project again. Wendy and Linda decided to put their part of the plan into operation Monday.

As a precautionary move, I taped one of my army dog tags to the inside of my boot. If an accident like that happened to me, I wanted the police to be able to identify my body. But my main concern was to bring our activities in Madison to a halt as quickly as possible. I started my counter-plan by initiating criticism of Mark Stivic for being monogamous. This was a diversionary tactic to keep our discussions away from the target. I accused Stivic of thinking more about Wendy than about our mission in Madison. Surprisingly, Wendy took my side in the criticism.

"Hell, if Larry even looks at me, you get jealous," she said. "I don't belong to you or any other man."

Our harangue continued for over two hours. When it was over Stivic went out alone for a walk, while the three of us went to sleep. I felt sorry for Stivic because I really believed he wanted to be married to Wendy, but he had chosen the society he was living in, and right now it frowned on monogamous relationships.

That ploy was just a beginning.

The next morning I called Tom Fadden, my FBI contact, and told him about Linda and Wendy's plans to cash the stolen checks or use the credit cards. He said he'd alert the local police, who would warn the major department stores in town. Then he told me that the bombs in Detroit had been placed on Thursday night. Local police detectives and FBI agents had spent all week watching the DPOA building. They had roasted me for sending them out on a wild goose chase. Thursday night had started out the same way. The crowd from the first showing at the movie theater came out. As one man walked down the alley to the parking lot, he paused to light a cigarette. It was windy in the alley, and the man had difficulty keeping the match lit long enough for the cigarette to light. He moved in closer to the building to escape the wind. At that point, he was almost jumped by two Detroit detectives and one FBI agent, but fortunately, the match held its fire, and the man strolled off, not knowing how close he had come to arrest.

The crowd from the second movie session moved down the block and through the alley without any hesitation. The agents thought another long night had passed without an appearance from the bombers. As the police were getting ready to call it quits, they noticed in the alley a brown paper bag that wasn't being pushed along by the wind. They raced across the street.

Inside the bag a cigarette had already burned down, and the wick of the firecracker was starting to sputter. The police easily dismantled the bomb. Then they immediately called the Thirteenth Precinct. A search of the station turned up another bomb neatly wrapped in a waterproof bag inside the toilet tank in the women's rest room. There were 44 sticks of dynamite in the two bombs.

"Your information was right on target," Fadden said, "but nobody saw who placed either bomb. So, obviously, we didn't make any arrests."

After talking to Fadden, I hung around the city for a couple of hours before going back to the apartment. The story of the bombs in Detroit scared me. They could easily have gone off, killing a number of people. Yet, whoever placed them got in and out without being seen.

When I walked into the apartment, Mark was waiting for me. He was very upset and distraught.

"Where the hell have you been?" he said. "I've been looking all over for you. We've got problems." He was pacing around the room as he spoke, using up nervous energy.

"Wendy's in the slam." He seemed on the verge of crying.

"Where's Linda?"

"She's in, too. The pigs busted both of them this morning."

They were arrested trying to cash a forged check in one of the department stores. A salesgirl delayed them long enough to make a call to the store's security force, who called the police. Fadden hadn't wasted any time in alerting the stores, I thought.

"What are we going to do?" Stivic repeated several times. "We don't have enough bread to bail them out." "Call Wendy's mother. She's got enough bread to get them both out," I suggested.

For some reason Stivic was against it.

"No, I can't do that. It's impossible." He started tossing out other ways of getting the money. "Let's go out on the street for handouts," he said. "You go out on the street for handouts," I snapped. "You have the solution, but won't use it."

Stivic stormed out of the room. We spent the next two days arguing, while Wendy and Linda sat in a jail cell. This was a real break. It had destroyed our effectiveness in Madison. Even if we did get Wendy and Linda out of jail, I could argue that they'd be watched so closely that we couldn't carry out our plan. The focal was destroyed, at least temporarily. But I was sure someone else would go after the same targets.

When I returned to the apartment the second afternoon, Naomi was sitting there waiting for me. I was surprised to see her. She was upset at our failure. "How did this get so out of hand?" she demanded.

I recounted all our moves since arriving in Madison, including our discussions about Barry Stein. She didn't comment on the Stein incident, but was furious at me for not taking charge of the situation. "We can't salvage anything now," she said. "Why didn't you get in touch with Wendy's mother right away? Why did you listen to Stivic?"

She took over immediately and made telephone calls to Wendy's and Linda's parents. Within two days they were both out on bail and back at the apartment.

As soon as we were all together again, Naomi launched into another criticism of the bungled assignment. She tore into all of us, but especially Stivic. She blamed him for blocking my suggestions. I grabbed the opportunity to turn the blame away from me and keep the attack focused on Mark. I suggested that Stivic's monogamous attitude toward Wendy had held us back. Subconsciously, he didn't want Wendy to get hurt, so he had purposely delayed my positive action. My theory began a long criticism of

Mark, which continued for several hours. Before the day was over, Stivic was purged from the Weathermen. This rationalized our failure in Madison and paved the way for Wendy, Linda, and myself to operate in other cities. I had already made up an excuse to return to Cincinnati, however, and Naomi said she would give me two weeks.

"I'll call you after that with another assignment," she said. I gave her the phone number of my mother's house.

She told Wendy and Linda they would be assigned to other cities, reminding them not to worry about the charges brought against them in Madison. "They're too insignificant," she said. "Your parents may be out the bread they put up for bail, but so what?"

When I got back to Cincinnati I walked into my mother's unannounced. She was upset over my appearance. She said I looked like a typical hippie bum. I assured her that I wasn't in any danger, but I don't think she believed me. I visited Donna and my father-in-law. He had been very helpful over the past few months by supporting Donna and Denise. He was proud of what I was doing, but Donna was upset. She didn't want me to get hurt.

I also telephoned Murrish. He was surprised to hear I was in the city and asked me to come over as soon as I could.

Murrish was upset that I would be away from the Weathermen for two weeks. "Suppose Naomi doesn't call? How are you going to get back? How will we know what they're planning or where they are?"

Murrish's demanding attitude was a change from the past. He was more excited now, more concerned with my involvement with the underground. At other meetings, he had always been reserved, even to the point of questioning my continuing.

"We were the first office to turn in the information about the Weathermen going underground," Murrish said, "and now it's important that we continue to be informed of what's going on."

I suspected that the town house explosion had galvanized the FBI into taking the Weathermen seriously. It stimulated public reaction by showing how dangerous the Weathermen could be. This must be adding pressure on all agents to find out what was going on. I spent three hours with Murrish reviewing the past three months. As I was leaving he said, "Call me as soon as you hear from Naomi."

The only activity I took part in during those two weeks was a rally at Fountain Square in downtown Cincinnati led by radical students at the university. Since several of the leaders had been Weathermen, I was welcomed like a conquering hero. After a lot of speeches, the American flag was torn down, and a Viet Cong flag put in its place. There were a few fights, but no major acts of violence.

When Naomi finally called me at my mother's house, I gave her the number of a telephone booth on the street corner and went out to wait for her to call again. She was afraid that my house phone was tapped.

"You feeling better?" she asked when we spoke the second time.

"Fine. I'm ready to go."

"Great. We have an important assignment in Buffalo. I want you to get there by April." "What's happening?" "You'll find out more when you arrive." After hanging up, I called Murrish. He told me to come right over.

This time he was acting like my boss. Murrish had never been that way before.

"When are you leaving?" he said.

"Tomorrow."

"Very good. When you get to Buffalo, I want you to contact Chuck Green or John Maynard. In fact, I'll have them meet you." These instructions were unusual. Murrish normally hadn't told me to go anywhere. I had always been on my own.

"Another point, Larry, we appreciate what you've done, but we want to make it official now. We want to put you on the payroll." The only time Murrish had talked about money before was when he gave me $500 a month for services in February.

"From now on we'll pay you $600 a month and up to $500 in expenses," he said. "And we'll expect you to provide frequent reports, almost daily, on all activities."

He said the FBI was expecting indictments against many Weathermen, stemming from the riots in Chicago. Once these were issued, arrests had to be made. Murrish wanted me to give the whereabouts of everybody on the indictment list when it came out. He was talking to me as a hired hand.

When the instructions were over, he told me I was the star performer in the photos taken at the demonstration in Fountain Square by the Army Intelligence. He didn't say why Army Intelligence was there, but they definitely had an interest in me because I was a Vietnam veteran. Naturally, the FBI didn't admit to knowing anything about me.

The next night I boarded a bus for Buffalo.

Chapter 14

The Cover is Blown

I arrived at the Buffalo bus terminal at 7 A.M. on April 1. It had been a 12-hour ride from Cincinnati, and I was tired when we pulled into the bus dock. I was wearing a Levi jacket, Levi's, and a headband to keep my hair from falling into my eyes. My only baggage was an old army duffel bag that I had been carrying around since we went underground.

After getting off the bus, I walked through the station and out the front door, following Murrish's instructions. I paused a moment, lit a cigarette, then turned right. As I neared the corner, a car pulled up next to the curb, moving slowly along with me as I walked. A man in his late 30s rolled down the window.

"Get in, Grathwohl," he said, as the car came to a stop.

As I climbed into the back seat, he lifted a walkie-talkie up to his mouth. "We got him. You guys can go home." "How many other agents did you have out there?" "Eight," the guy said. "We wanted to make sure you weren't followed. Somebody picked you up as soon as you got off the bus. The others were spotted around the building watching anybody who showed even a slight interest in you."

Then he introduced himself as John Maynard; the driver, Chuck Green, was in his late 20s. "You guys are starting the day early, aren't you?" I said.

They didn't answer. We drove around the city for a half hour while I gave them a rundown on the latest activities of the Weathermen. Buffalo, like many other cities, was having trouble on its college campuses, including a series of fires at the state university.

I didn't know if any specific act of violence in Buffalo was connected with Weatherman agitation, but I did know we had an underground collective in the city. It was also a gateway city into Canada for Weathermen, as well as draft dodgers.

The agents dropped me off a block from the collective. I threw the duffle bag over my shoulder and walked down the street to the apartment, which was in an old three-story, red-brick building. I went up the stairs to the second floor and knocked on the door.

"Who is it?" came a voice I recognized as Robert Carter's.

"A friend, Larry Delgato," I said, using my code name.

The door opened. "Well, goddamn!" Carter said. "Come on in."

Dianne Donghi was sitting in one of the three battered old chairs in the living room. Furniture, I thought, that's a step up. The three of us sat around and rapped a while about what we'd been doing. I suggested getting some breakfast, and we went to a pancake house four blocks from the apartment.

During breakfast they told me they had been testing homemade explosives in the woods. They were also manufacturing a supply of pipe bombs that could be jammed in the tailpipes of police cars. They were safer than Molotov cocktails because they allowed time to get away. If a person threw a Molotov cocktail at a patrol car, he had to turn and run from the scene. Obviously, this increased his chances of being caught.

Then Dianne said abruptly, "Nixon is supposed to come to Buffalo or Niagara Falls. We're going to organize a welcome for him." I almost choked on a mouthful of food. Trying to sound as casual as possible, I asked, "We going to try and off him?" Diane put the fork down.

"No," she said after a pause. "But we're going to have a nice demonstration. Maybe hit some of the local pig cars in the area where he is. Something to draw attention to us, without getting us caught. We can hit the local pigs because the secret service pigs wouldn't be watching them."

"Who else is here to help us?" I asked.

"Naomi," Ward said. "That's the focal. The three of us and Naomi. And Ayers will be in tomorrow night, but I don't know how long he's going to stay."

I didn't like the plan. It wouldn't be as easy to disrupt as Madison. These people were a lot more experienced and calmer.

After breakfast, Dianne suggested we take a walk over to Buffalo State University so we could continue talking. It was cloudy when we left the restaurant. Halfway down the block, she said: "We have a main target, but we're going to need more help. We'll also need heavy explosives."

I listened as they outlined a wild plan to blow up the power station at Niagara Falls. They estimated it would take 20 to 30 people and at least 100 pounds of dynamite. I thought the entire idea sounded stupid, even with help.

"It's an ambitious plan," I said. "But we need more people."

"We'll get them," Carter commented.

We talked about Niagara Falls until we reached the university. As a professional soldier, I was delegated to go to Niagara to figure out how many people we would need, how many pounds of explosives, and how we could get in and out with the least number of casualties.

We went into the campus club at the university's student building, ordered coffee, and sat in a booth. Our conversation returned to the Nixon trip.

"We can't be content with just a demonstration against pig Nixon," Dianne said. "We have to do something dramatic."

Carter agreed. We were discussing alternatives when Naomi joined us.

"You're looking good," she said to me. "I hope the hospital put you in good working condition." She was smiling. I laughed. Naomi had just gotten back from New York, where she was ripping off money to finance our Buffalo focal. As usual, she wouldn't mention specific details of what she was doing.

"What did you decide on Nixon?" she asked.

"Nothing yet," Carter said.

"We don't have much time."

"Offing the pig cars seems our most logical target," Dianne commented.

There was a lot of work to be done. We had to know exactly where Nixon was going, the route he would be taking, and how many local police would be used. The closer we could get to Nixon, the more effective our plan would be. As an alternative, we agreed to settle on the Niagara plan or any other explosion that would draw attention to us while Nixon was there.

We sat in the campus club for almost two hours. Then we started to break up. Carter and Donghi had things to do, so Naomi asked me to go downtown with her. She wanted to check something at the library. When we left the campus club, it was raining, so we ran over to the student parking lot and hitched a ride.

It was a pleasant afternoon. Naomi was loose and casual, not so completely wrapped up in the movement and her concept of being a revolutionary. Late in the afternoon we had a hamburger, then started back to the apartment. We took a bus to within a few blocks of our street. It had stopped raining, but our clothes were still damp.

As we walked the last few blocks, Naomi asked what I thought about the Niagara Falls target.

"It's ambitious," I said.

She smiled. "Don't evade the question. What do you really think? Can it be done?" "I think it's stupid." I expected sharp criticism for my negative reaction, but when none came, I went on. "I think it can be done, but you'd need 50 armed people attacking in commando style."

We had gone another half block before she said, "I agree with you." Then she changed the subject back to Nixon. "If we can come close enough to scare him, we'll have accomplished our objective."

When we got back to the apartment, Carter and Donghi were waiting for us and, after more discussion, Naomi and I begged off and went to bed.

Bill Ayers was a day late in arriving, but when he got there, he had the distinction of being a federal fugitive. The government had gotten indictments under an antiriot law against 12 Weathermen who had helped organize the Days of Rage in Chicago. In addition to Ayers, those indicted included Mark

Rudd, Kathy Boudin, Bernardine Dohrn, Jeffrey Jones, and Linda Evans. Both Ted Gold and Dianne Oughton, who were killed in the Greenwich Village explosion, were named among 29 coconspirators.

Ayers was in a jovial mood when he came into the apartment. "I'm on the pig list," he said. "If the rest of you work hard, you can make it, too." Then he laughed.

Ayers was positive he'd never be caught, but he was just as confident that the government couldn't win the case even if he was busted. "The seven in Chicago were acquitted of the antiriot act because those federal prosecutors are incompetent," he said. "Hell, I'll bet Bernardine could make a fool out of them in court, and she doesn't even have that much experience."

He made a few more jokes about the pig list before getting into a serious political discussion. As the result of a recent Weather Bureau meeting, several changes in strategy and philosophy would be implemented. I wondered if the meeting had been held in Chicago because on March 30 newspapers had reported that the FBI had raided an apartment there, finding enough explosives to "blow up a city block," as a police spokesman said. In addition to the explosives, the raid also netted rifles, shotguns, a revolver, and guerrilla warfare literature. The superintendent of the building identified several Weathermen from FBI photos, including Dohrn, Boudin, and Ayers, as being in the apartment. So I assumed that's where the latest Weather Bureau meeting had been held.

"First," Ayers was saying, "we're going to change our strategy. For the last couple of months we have had many small focals working in a number of cities across the country. Now we're going to concentrate on the major metropolitan areas on both coasts so we can solidify our power. New York and San Francisco will be our major bases. We'll remain active in Chicago, however, and possibly in the Denver area."

He said the decision to concentrate on the major coast cities was made because of the vast number of working people in these areas who were ripe for the revolution. "The blacks, the Puerto Ricans, the poor whites, and the Mexicans in those areas represent a tremendous segment of the population. By rallying them to our side we can bring down the cities. Once this is accomplished, it will be a simple matter to get the rest of the country to fall in line."

"What about our projects in Buffalo?" Carter asked.

Ayers said they'd be postponed, but not cancelled.

"You still have a few days left up here," he said, "and any major project in the works will be considered for a later date."

His next announcement concerned social philosophy within the Weathermen. "Monogamous relationships will no longer be banned," he stated. "If two people are working in harmony for the revolution, they can have a close relationship as long as it doesn't take precedence over the movement. If it does, the relationship will have to be terminated. We believe people can work and live together for the common goal."

Ayers enjoyed delivering these dicta to his subjects. He paced around the room emphasizing certain points by throwing his fist into the air in the power salute.

When he finished outlining our new codes, he tore into a fiery criticism of the passiveness of most members of the organization. "Too many of you are relying on your leaders to do everything," he said sternly. Then, in a departure from relating individuals to specific acts, he mentioned the park police station bombing in San Francisco.

"It was a success," he said, "but it's a shame when someone like Bernardine has to make all the plans, make the bomb, and then place it herself. She should have to do only the planning." He charged us to become more aggressive in working out details and executing plans by ourselves.

Then he announced that he and Naomi had to go to Canada for an important meeting with friends. He suggested that the rest of us spend our time getting false identifications. We were to collect as many as we could in the event that somebody else needed them. Naomi said she'd make a phone call to the booths on the corner every night at 9 o'clock if they could get away. We could give a report on our activities at that time.

The next day I went off to the public library to check old newspaper records of people who had died as infants about the same time we were born. Once I got a list of names, we planned to go to the Bureau of Vital Statistics claiming to be relatives and requesting birth and death certificates. Once we got a birth certificate, drivers' licenses and credit cards were easy to get. This took longer than stealing identification, but it was more efficient.

I called FBI agent Maynard from the library to tell him that Ayers would be back in a day or two. He wanted to know why I didn't go to Canada with him.

"They didn't invite me."

"Why didn't you ask to go?"

"We're a paramilitary organization," I explained. "When Ayers says I stay in Buffalo and collect IDs, I stay in Buffalo." I was getting annoyed.

"You should have offered to pay your own way and gone, anyway," Maynard retorted. Then he told me to stay at the library because he and Green were coming over to discuss something extremely important.

In about half an hour, a librarian came up to me in the reference room with a message to go downstairs. In a small office, Maynard and Green were waiting. The first thing they discussed was a system to arrest Ayers when he returned from Canada.

"Just don't burn me," I said. "These people think they're being followed all the time, so they might not suspect anything if you pick Ayers up on the street."

"Don't worry," Green said. "We'll take him when you're not around. We just want you to keep us informed about him."

They decided to put a stakeout in front of the house beginning that night. Since I'd be talking to Naomi every night at 9 o'clock, I agreed to call the FBI headquarters if Ayers wasn't returning. In that way they could call off the agents so they wouldn't spend an entire night in a stakeout for nothing. If any of the others on the list of 12 wanted in Chicago showed up, I agreed to leave the house as soon as possible to give them a call.

I thought our meeting was over, so I got up to leave.

"Wait a minute, Larry," Maynard said, "we have one more thing."

He began by asking me questions about the Weathermen's international ambitions. Actually, all he was doing was verifying facts he already knew: some members had been to North Vietnam; some had met with various guerrilla groups in Cambodia; some were trained in Cuba; Ayers and Naomi were presumably in Canada meeting with the Quebec Liberation Front; and attempts had been made to contact Arab guerrilla outfits.

After reviewing the various Weatherman attempts to establish international ties, Maynard said he wanted me to do something that could be extremely beneficial to the FBI, but could also be very dangerous to me. I agreed to cooperate.

"We want you to come with us to meet somebody," Maynard said. "We'll explain on the way."

Green left first to get the car and move it around to the side of the building. I left the room next, with Maynard following a safe distance to be sure nobody was watching me. Once in the car we drove around the city, out onto an expressway, then back, reversed directions, and headed toward Lake Erie. When we were out of the city again we headed into a wooded area, and turned down a dirt road. While we were driving, Maynard and Green began telling me about the mystery man waiting for me. He was an Arab guerrilla. My meeting was to be in strict confidence. They refused to tell me why he was in the country, how he got in, or where he was going. Obviously he was working for the United States, but before I could ask questions, the car pulled to a halt near an old shed on the lake.

We got out of the car and walked to the dilapidated boathouse. We creaked the door open and went in. Two men were inside. One was introduced as Ali Baba and the other I presumed to be an agent, although we were not formally introduced.

"We want you to get to know each other," Maynard said. "We'll be outside."

Ali Baba was in his 30s, fairly tall and aristocratic-looking. He was dressed in a shirt and tie and spoke English with a British accent. He wanted to know as much about the Weathermen as I could tell him, including names of the leaders and whether I thought they were dedicated to revolution. If a contact were to be established between the Arab guerrilla movement El Fatah and the Weathermen, he wanted to be the one to make it. That way he could pass along information to the U.S. Government.

He suggested I become more aggressive in pushing the Weathermen to make international ties. This would enhance my chances of being sent on foreign missions, and I might be able to arrange to meet Ali Baba, thus creating a link with the Arabs.

Then he gave me a warning. "These Arabs are professionals. Many of them may be the same age of your leaders, but they do not play games. They think nothing of killing if it has to be done to reach a goal. By comparison, Weathermen are amateurs."

I asked him why a group like El Fatah would want connections inside the United States. "They want to prove that they can strike anywhere," he said. "This gets their message across to the world. What better place to strike than the United States?" After a pause, he continued. "There is talk of doing something at the World's Fair in Spokane in 1974. El Fatah considers this a perfect platform. If they go through with it, it will be violent."

As we talked, the lake water splashed up against the dock outside, and the wind whipped through the cracks in the wall, making it chillier and damper inside than out. But for security reasons, we had to do our talking within the shed.

Ali Baba said the Arabs also planned to strike at the next Olympic Games in 1972. "I don't know exactly what they've planned, but there definitely will be a demonstration of terrorist force."

We talked for awhile longer, and then Maynard came back into the shed. "We'd better get both of you back," he said.

I shook hands with Ali Baba. On the way back in the car, I started to ask questions. "Is Ali Baba working for the CIA also?" I might as well have been shouting out the window. Neither Maynard nor Green acknowledged that he had even heard my voice.

"Where's he going now?" I asked about Ali. Still no reply. I never figured out the exact reason I was introduced to Ali Baba, but it was obvious the FBI wanted me to cooperate with him should the need arise.

They dropped me off near the library and reminded me about calling the office if I heard that Ayers was not coming in that night.

I was the first one back to the apartment. Carter and Donghi came in separately within a half hour. Shortly before 9 o'clock I went out to wait for Naomi's phone call. It came on time. They wouldn't be back until at least tomorrow. I quickly put a dime in the phone and called the FBI.

"Take off the stakeout," I said.

We spent the next day going through the files again for names that we could use in false identification papers. When I checked in with the FBI, Maynard was mad. The stakeout had been on all night, and Ayers hadn't shown up.

"What the hell were they doing there all night?" I said. "I called in about 9 o'clock." Maynard didn't answer. Whoever took the message had never passed it along.

That night was a repeat of the first. Naomi said they wouldn't be back. I called the FBI again and told them to make sure the message got through to the guys on the stakeout.

Ayers and Naomi arrived about noon the next day. Ayers was pleased with the meetings in Canada, and he was getting a later flight to New York City. I assumed that the stakeout was back on, so I didn't make any attempt to leave the apartment to call the FBI. They could follow Ayers to the airport and pick him up there. I listened smugly to Ayers, knowing that in a few hours he'd be in jail.

Ayers conducted a short meeting to review our strategy. When the meeting broke up, Ayers made a remark about "our international contacts." I grew extremely interested and pushed him on that point.

He bragged about new contacts with the Quebec Liberation Front, the Irish Republican Army, and El Fatah. When these groups were added to the Cubans, North Vietnamese, and Chinese, the Weathermen had an impressive list of foreign guerrilla groups to work with. Ayers said that these contacts would be strengthened to show Weatherman solidarity with the Third-World people. I wondered if Ali Baba or one of his contacts had met with them. That might have been why Maynard was so anxious for me to go to Canada. I wanted to press Ayers about El Fatah, but he obviously felt he had said too much already. About an hour after Ayers left, I suggested that I go out and buy a six-pack of beer. I used a phone in the delicatessen to make a call to Maynard.

"Did you get him?" I said when Maynard answered.

"Get who?"

"Ayers. Who else?"

There was silence on the other end. Then Maynard exploded. "You mean Ayers came back, and you didn't call us?" "Call you! What were the guys out front doing, sleeping?" I raised my voice, and the grocer looked over at the phone booth. Maynard told me the stakeout had never been put back after being called off the night before. They thought I'd call in when Ayers arrived.

"Christ," I said. "He's probably on the goddamn plane."

Maynard was angry. He hung up.

I was depressed when I started back to the apartment. Ayers had escaped, and it might have been my fault, although I didn't admit that to Maynard. It was his fault, though, for not having the stakeout in position during the day.

That evening, we made plans for closing up the apartment and leaving. When we were alone, Naomi told me I had a choice of going to New York or Washington.

"Normally I wouldn't tell you this, but Wendy Schramm and Linda Herbert are in Washington. In New York you'll be working with Dianne Donghi and Carter. I know you get along with all of them, so you can have your choice."

I took New York. "There'll be more action there," I said.

The next day, my job was to pack the explosives we had stored in our bedroom closet. There was enough dynamite, blasting caps, and black powder to blow up a good-sized building. We also had a shotgun, which I think was the same one Dianne had in Cincinnati. I put the explosives in the back of our tan Chevrolet. Carter and I were driving the car to a farm near New York where the explosives would be stored until we needed them.

Naomi and Dianne were leaving by plane that morning. I took them to the airport. Naomi purchased a ticket with false identification and a stolen checkbook. While Dianne and I were standing near the gate, Naomi quietly slipped away. She never came back. Dianne told me not to worry about it. We were being followed, she said, but as far as they could make out, there was only one person.

Carter and I both had false identification. I had told Ayers I needed a set for myself because I was wanted on a charge stemming from a demonstration in Cincinnati. Carter got me an almost perfect match. My new name was Tom Neiman, and I was from Long Island, New York.

On the way down the New York Thruway, a state trooper pulled me over for speeding. Carter, who was asleep in the back, woke up when the car pulled off the highway. The trooper looked at my driver's license. Luckily it was clean, or, I should say, Neiman's was clean. My hands were trembling, but I kept them down near my lap so the trooper wouldn't notice. He didn't search the car, which surprised me, especially because of my looks. He just gave me a warning and let me go.

"Take it easy the rest of the way," Carter said. "I don't want to end up in jail for just carrying that stuff."

Ayers, Donghi, and Naomi were already in New York when we got there. I stayed with Donghi and Naomi at an apartment near Columbia University that belonged to a friend. Ayers joined us later to explain that Donghi, Carter, and I would act as a focal and form others under us. He said we were not the only Weathermen active in the city, but it was not necessary at this time to know who the others were. We'd be charged with selecting our own targets. One of the primary targets we discussed was the police headquarters on Centre Street in downtown New York.

But New York had many symbols of imperialism. Some had already been attacked, including Mobil Oil Company, Sylvania Electric, General Motors, and IBM. The federal buildings on Foley Square were also in our plans.

When I went out for cigarettes the next day I called Terry Roberts in the New York FBI office. His name was given to me by John Maynard before I left Buffalo. I told him where we were staying, and that Bill Ayers was in town. I also told him that our focal had a tentative meeting with Linda Evans, one of the Weather Bureau people wanted for the Chicago riot. Roberts said to keep in touch. When I called him the next day, he said it was urgent that we meet. I had to get away from the Weathermen for at least a day and a half. I was to meet the FBI Saturday night at the Americana Hotel.

I spent the next two days trying to think of a reason for leaving. I had daily meetings with Donghi and Carter. We were planning for our meeting with Linda Evans. We held many of the meetings on a park bench in Washington Square. With New York University Law School looming in the background, we were planning how to tear down our judicial system. At one point in the conversation Donghi said we needed $500. At first I let the remark pass, but then it occurred to me that this was my excuse. I led us into a discussion on how we could get the money. After much debate, I declared: "I think I can get it. That old army friend of mine in Buffalo will give it to me. He owes me a favor. I'll call him."

Donghi agreed. I went off to make the call. I stayed away for half an hour, and when I returned, I said: "Okay, I'm going to see him. He invited me up for the weekend, but I told him I could make it only for Saturday night. I'll be back Sunday night with the money."

On Saturday afternoon I took a series of subways, then a bus, to make sure nobody was following me. Then I checked into the Americana Hotel. As I got on the elevator, two guys followed me. One was dressed in a shirt and tie, wore mod glasses, and a stylized hair comb. The other had on a sport shirt and jacket. I was registered in a room on the 17th floor, but I pushed 19 when I saw the others get on. As the elevator started up, the taller one said:

"Aren't you on 17, Grathwohl? I'm Terry Roberts," he said, sticking out his hand.

The other guy pushed the 17th floor button.

"That's Ken O'Neil," Roberts said.

When we got off the elevator we walked to the far wing of the building. "What about the people in the other rooms?" I said. "Don't worry," Roberts said, "we rented all six rooms in this wing of the building."

When we got into the room, Roberts opened a can of beer and poured it into a glass. "Have a drink," he said. "We'll have some food sent up later." The room had a large sitting area in it. I took one of the large comfortable chairs.

"Okay," I said, "what's so important?"

"We have to make an arrest," Roberts said.

"You had Ayers, but you missed him."

"That's in the past. This time we won't miss."

"Why make an arrest now? The only person on the list of 12 in the city now is Linda Evans." "That's who we'll take." I didn't like the idea. If they broke into the meeting with Linda, they would have to take all of us. If they let me go, my cover would be blown. "You're going to burn me," I complained. "This isn't our decision, Larry. We need an arrest."

"Why, for Christ's sake? Why not wait until we get all of them together, or at least Ayers, Rudd, Dohrn, or Jones? Ayers and Dohrn are really the ones you want. Rudd has a lot of publicity because he overthrew Columbia, but Ayers has more power."

Roberts shook his head as if agreeing with me.

"You may be right, Larry, but as I said, this decision came from the man in Washington. We need an arrest. The purpose of this meeting is to set it up."

I was angry as hell. I had spent months working into my position. Roberts let me storm around to release my tensions. "You have to arrest me, too, then," I said. "That's our only chance to retain the cover."

"We're thinking along the same lines," Roberts said. Then he broke into the conversation to ask me if I was hungry. "Hell, yes. I haven't had a decent meal since I've been in town. Let's go to a good restaurant." I started to get up. "We're not going anywhere," O'Neil said. "This hotel has a restaurant and room service. You just tell us what you want."

I ordered a shrimp cocktail, a large steak, and a bottle of wine.

"You're eating like a condemned man," Roberts commented.

"I am, man. If we blow the bust, I could be very dead."

Roberts didn't answer.

After dinner, I suggested we go for a walk.

"You can stroll around the room," O'Neil said, "but that's as far as we go until we get this arrest plan down."

We got back to work. The meeting with Linda Evans was taking place that week, but I didn't know where. As soon as I was told, I'd call Roberts.

If I was with Linda at the time of the arrest, I was to fight back. That way I could be busted for resisting a federal officer. When they picked up Dianne Donghi, they would claim that they'd been following her since she came into New York, which naturally led them to me and Carter. If possible, they would try to throw any suspicion about an informant onto Robert Carter.

I still didn't want them to make the arrest now. Linda Evans was a member of the Weather Bureau and wanted for Chicago, but we could get more of them if they let me go on. I made one last plea. It didn't work.

"I'll tell you one more time, Larry. These orders came from Washington. We're making an arrest."

The next few days I was tense, nervous. The agents had given me $300 to turn over to Dianne Donghi. I had promised $500, but this was better than nothing. On Tuesday, I was told that our meeting with Linda Evans was scheduled for Friday morning. The night before, we would check into the Greenwich Village Hotel in lower Manhattan. I would meet Linda at a nearby coffee shop at 10 o'clock the next morning and bring her back to the hotel.

I managed to get away to call Roberts, but as I was coming out of a candy store where I made the phone call, Robert Carter walked in.

"I forgot to ask you to get me some Life Savers," he said.

Was he following me? Did he suspect something? I had to be careful. "Wait a minute, and I'll walk back with you," he said.

The next two days went by slowly. Then on Wednesday night, Dianne came into the apartment and said our meeting had been changed. "We're going to see Linda tomorrow morning instead of Friday."

I should have suspected they'd do something like this. They were paranoid about security. It was already 6 P.M., but I had to get out to call Roberts. I waited about an hour, then started searching around for my cigarettes. I went over to my jacket and dumped the cigarettes from the pack into my coat pocket. I then removed the empty pack.

"Hell," I said, "anyone here got any smokes?" I knew they

probably didn't.

"I may," Donghi said.

I waited tensely for her to look.

"No. I thought I did."

"I'm going out to get some."

Donghi walked back across the room to get her coat.

"I'll go with you." She picked up my coat on the way back. She carried it loosely. I watched every step. If the cigarettes fell out of the pocket, I was gone. If they had talked about killing Barry Stein for recognizing them, they'd off me right on the spot. Then she tossed the coat the last few feet to me. I could visualize the cigarettes flying all over the room, but they held firm. I put the coat on, and we started to leave, but as we neared the door Carter asked Donghi to stay.

"We have to go over our plans for Linda," he said. "We can fill Larry in when he gets back."

Saved. I went out fast before she changed her mind. I hurried to the candy store. It was closed. Then I remembered a bar around the corner. As I reached for their phone, it occurred to me not to call Roberts at all. I could claim the meeting switch came at the last minute, and that I hadn't had a chance to call. That way the arrest couldn't be made. But I changed my mind. It wouldn't be fair to him. I'd have to go through with the plan. I made the phone call. When I hung up, I got some cigarettes out of the machine and threw the ones in my pocket away. I went back up to the apartment.

It was a long night. We rapped for several hours. Then Carter said he had to leave to meet friends at Columbia. It was decided that I should meet Linda and bring her over to the Greenwich Village Hotel for a meeting. We would check in later that night.

In the morning I walked over to the restaurant. Inside, one of the agents I knew was sitting on a stool at the far end of the counter drinking coffee. I sat down near the door. When the agent signaled for another cup, and I heard the counterman asked incredulously, "You don't want another one, do you?" I figured he'd been sitting there for a long time.

About 10 minutes later Linda Evans came in. She sat at a booth and ordered bacon and eggs. I joined her.

"How are you, Linda?"

"Oh, hi. Have some coffee with me," she said.

Then, by prearranged signal I took off my sunglasses and put them down on the table. As I did, the agent got up off the stool and walked outside. Linda and I talked about nothing special while she ate breakfast.

"Dianne and Carter are waiting for us at the hotel," I said.

As we walked outside, we saw a linen truck parked in front. We turned left and strolled by the truck. The driver got out and went around to the back. Then up ahead, Terry Roberts stepped out of a doorway.

"FBI," he said. "Please stand where you are."

I grabbed Linda, turned around and started to run. The driver of the truck ordered us to halt. I ran right into him, hitting him on the side of the head and knocking him down. We turned the corner and kept running, until one of the agents tackled me and another jumped on top. Two others had Linda. They put handcuffs on me, picked me up and pushed me against the wall to frisk me. Then they put Linda and me in the back of a car and took us up to the FBI office on 67th Street.

We were taken into separate rooms. Then they took my cuffs off and gave me a cigarette. Roberts told me that Dianne was arrested in the hotel room about the same time, but Carter wasn't around. This could possibly look good for me. It could throw some suspicion on Carter.

When I finished the cigarette, they put the handcuffs back on me, and led me upstairs to photograph me. They timed this move to coincide with Dianne's leaving the photo room. We passed each other without saying a word. After we were photographed, they took us downtown to Foley Square for arraignment. We were all taken off in separate cars, handcuffed. At the federal building I refused to answer questions. The commissioner set my bail at $5,000 for assaulting a federal officer. Dianne Donghi's bail was set at $10,000 and Linda Evans' at $50,000. Then we were all taken downstairs to the holding cells. Linda and Dianne were put in one cell, while I was left standing out front against the wall, within their view.

I asked to go to the bathroom, but the marshal wouldn't let

me. I stood there half an hour. I felt strange, trapped. I had wild thoughts. Suppose the few agents who knew who I was suddenly died? What would happen to me? I was scared. Then one of the marshals searched me again. When he took off my boots, he found the dogtag I had taped in there after the explosion.

"Ha," he said. "I thought your name was Neiman."

Before I could answer, the chief marshal, who had been told I was working with the FBI, snatched the dogtag out of his hands, looked at the name and threw the tag on the desk.

"That guy is Neiman," he said.

Donghi and Evans watched. I could tell from the expressions on Linda and Dianne's faces that their thoughts were the same: "Why didn't the chief marshal question the dogtag? Why did he insist Grathwohl was Neiman?"

The incident was a mistake. My masquerade as a Weatherman was over. The FBI had just lost a valuable undercover agent.

Chapter 15

Aftermath

The following day I was released, and the charges of assaulting a federal officer were dropped. But it took nearly three years for my life to return to normal. Ironically, for part of this time I was a fugitive from both the government and the Weathermen.

After my usefulness an an undercover agent was over, the FBI asked me to continue to work for them because of my knowledge of Weathermen strategy. I was also probably the only FBI contact who could recognize most of the Weathermen on sight. In these respects I was still valuable to them, a sort of professional observer. I attended demonstrations, rallies. And I was used on surveillance of suspected Weatherman collectives. So that it would be harder for the Weathermen to identify me, I shaved off my beard and mustache. I was apprehensive on some of these assignments because I knew what the Weathermen had done to the undercover cop in Chicago. But I also knew that in most cases FBI agents were nearby.

Weatherman violence continued. To draw attention to their philosophy, they began issuing what they termed "communications from the underground." The first one was released on May 21, 1970. It said Weathermen "are adopting the classic strategy of the Viet Cong and the urban guerrilla strategy of the Tupamaros to our situation here in the most technologically advanced country in the world."

Twenty days later, on June 9, in a second letter from the underground, Weathermen took credit for blowing out the second floor of the New York City Police Headquarters on Centre Street. The blast seriously injured seven people while shredding desks, mangling lamps, tearing doors off hinges, and shattering glass everywhere.

The method of planting the bomb followed Weatherman strategy that had been discussed in collectives I had lived in. One of the desk officers reported that he had seen a young woman who appeared to be pregnant walking around headquarters not long before the explosion. She obviously had gone into the ladies room, removed the dynamite taped to her body, quickly assembled a bomb, placed it in the toilet, and then left.

Later the same month I testified before a federal grand jury in Detroit about the plot to blow up the police association building and the Thirteenth Police Precinct. It was there I first met Guy Goodwin, Chief of Internal Security for the Justice Department. I later had to report to Goodwin as a material witness against the Weathermen.

As a result of my testimony, on July 23,1970 the grand jury handed down indictments against 13 Weathermen on charges of conspiracy to bomb and kill in four different cities. They were Linda Evans, Mark Rudd, Bernardine Dohrn, Bill Ayers, Kathie Boudin, Cathlyn Wilkerson, Russell Neufeld, Jane Spielman, Ronald Fliegelman, Arlo Jacobs, Dianne Donghi, Naomi Jaffee, and, unfortunately, Larry Grathwohl.

My indictment made headlines in the Cincinnati newspapers and on television news broadcasts. I had a hard time convincing my mother that I really was working for the FBI and not against them. I knew my name would be included on the indictment list as an effort to reinstate me with the Weathermen, but it didn't work. However, my role would have to be explained in any subsequent court case. Technically, I was a fugitive.

Then came the irony. The Weathermen circulated a "wanted" poster for me "for crimes against the people." This charge was amplified in the August 21 issue of the underground newspaper Berkeley Tribe under a two-page story entitled: "The Most Dangerous Police Agent Ever to Infiltrate an American Revolutionary Movement." The article said agents like me should be "wiped out."

The FBI asked me to work in San Francisco because the Bay area was a hotbed of radical activities. I knew there was a danger of being recognized, but I was confident I could keep out of sight. In the fall my wife and daughter joined me, and we tried to make another go of our marriage. Although I was still doing certain assignments for the FBI, they helped me get a job with the Pacific Gas and Electric Company. Being indicted, and therefore a fugitive, had its drawbacks when trying to get a job or even a loan to buy a car. Individual agents sympathized with me, but they knew it would be a long time before my name was removed from the list. Once the federal bureaucracy makes a decision, it's hard to change it.

In early 1971, Weathermen bombed two of the major targets discussed at almost every session in the collectives I had lived in–the Capitol and the Pentagon. It was found that both bombings were executed in the same manner: young women entered a ladies room, assembled a bomb, deposited it in the toilet tank, and escaped before the detonation. Following these bombings, the Weathermen became quiet. This led to speculation by many FBI agents and other law enforcement officials that the movement had petered out. I was not convinced. One major reason for their inactivity was the winding down of the war in Vietnam. Weathermen build their power by inflaming controversial issues, and they realize that there are certain times when the political or economic climate within the country is not ripe for revolutionary action. They therefore use this period to regroup and plan for the future.

After all, their philosophy goes, Lenin, Castro, and Mao Tse Tung had to wait many years before history was ripe for their successful revolutions. So, too, the Weathermen are prepared to wait.

As Weatherman activities waned, requests for my services by the FBI also declined, so in 1971 I moved back to Cincinnati. With the help of the FBI I was able to move around freely, even though I was still on the indictment list. I took a job with a lumber company. I worked there for over a year, but all the time I had to keep in touch with the FBI and Guy Goodwin at the Justice Department. He was preparing a case against the Weathermen, and I was to be a witness. I also had to be prepared to testify at other federal or state grand juries as needed. I did return to San Francisco for another federal grand jury on October 3, 1972. My part was to testify that there was a Weathermen conspiracy in the country.

It wasn't until early in 1973 that my life became freer. Charges against me for my role in the Detroit plot were finally dropped. I still had to keep the FBI posted as to my whereabouts, however.

In September Howard Machtinger, one of the Weathermen leaders at the war council in Flint, Michigan, was finally arrested by the FBI, three years after he was indicted on conspiracy charges stemming from the Days of Rage in Chicago. The FBI alerted me to the arrest. If there was a trial, I would have to testify.

They didn't have to worry about a trial. Machtinger jumped the $2500 bail. The New York Post quoted Machtinger as explaining, in a letter to his friends, that he had to return to the "underground" to continue his fight against U.S. imperialism. The statement supported my contention that they were regrouping.

Then, on September 29, a time bomb blasted out four rooms at the International Telephone and Telegraph Corporation offices on Madison Avenue in New York City. The Weatherman underground took credit in a telephone call to The New York Times. Weathermen claimed they had planted the bomb in retaliation for the crimes ITT had committed against Chile.

Shortly after this attack, I began reading reports that the government was going to drop charges against all Weathermen. Goodwin assured me this was not true.

But on October 15, 1973 the reports started coming true. The government dropped its case against those Weathermen indicted by the grand jury in Detroit. I was angry. I was also irritated that I had to read about it in the newspapers. I didn't understand it. According to the Justice Department statement, charges were dropped rather than to disclose "foreign intelligence information deemed essential to the security of the United States."

I thought of my brief encounter with Ali Baba in Buffalo, and wondered if he had supplied part of the "foreign intelligence information" referred to. Neither the FBI nor the Justice Department would discuss this with me.

To give up on the Weathermen would be a mistake. They are more dangerous now than when I first met them. I told Goodwin I would be ready to appear in court as a witness in any other case. He arranged for me to appear before the Senate subcommittee.

I have kept a close watch on revolutionary activities committed in the 1970s. In fact, I am counseling police and government agencies on terrorist and urban guerrilla organizations to help law enforcement officials to understand the thinking of the revolutionaries they are up against. I want to give them the benefit of my experience.

The irony of Weathermen thinking or philosophy is that they probably couldn't live in the society they would impose on the U.S. should the revolution succeed.

Most Weatherman planning and strategy goes into implementing a revolution and not into setting up a viable government afterward. However, when they did discuss this post-revolutionary period, their plans were frightening. Their society would make George Orwell's 1984 a pleasure to live in.

Weatherman doctrine calls for complete control of all individual thought and movement. Once the revolution has been won, a central committee will be appointed to run the country. Naturally, the committee will consist of Weathermen leaders. But it will also include members of other revolutionary organizations, especially black and Mexican and Indian groups. Whether some of these central committee members will be more equal than others was never made clear, but I suspect that would be the case.

While the central committee is being formed, Weathermen will go about the necessary task of eliminating everybody who was in power before the revolution. This means killing them. Politicians and police will be the first to go. The exception will be clergymen. Weathermen recognize the danger in immediately attacking religious foundations; however, they are committed to do this in time. This methodical elimination of those prerevolutionary leaders will help prevent a counterrevolution.

The second step in this process is to "isolate" those citizens who were against the revolution, but were not members of the ruling class. This isolation is to be accomplished in education camps. These citizens will be herded into camps to be taught about the revolutionary government.

For the poor and working class who rose up to help make the revolution a success, the Weathermen will unleash a steady barrage of revolutionary propaganda through controlled newspapers, radio, and television. Of course, most television programs involving sports will be eliminated. Watching football on television while sipping beer is a total waste of productive time. In the Weathermen's society, spare time activities must be politically motivated.

However, the Weatherman political philosophy doesn't come to grips with the question of how this new society will be supported. They immediately turn off all conversations about the economics. "We'll work it out," is a typical remark when the economy is discussed.

Their models for our new society are China and Cuba, with North Vietnam getting a good rating. Many Weathermen have visited either North Vietnam or Cuba, and they are determined to set up a similar government here, even if it takes a century. Russia is not considered a good model of socialism because the Weathermen believe the USSR is becoming increasingly involved in the capitalistic way of life.

In essence, the Weathermen's government will be one of total control over each individual in the society. In Weathermen terminology, this new society will be "one people working in total unity." This means an elimination of all the individual freedoms we are accustomed to having; it was my absolute belief in the freedoms offered by our form of government that drove me to fight the Weathermen in the first place. Even though I am no longer in the underground movement where I could help prevent violence before it happened, as in Dayton, Detroit, Madison, and Buffalo, while creating as much disunity as possible, I am still working against Weathermen and other radical conspiracies. Their way of life is not mine.

Larry Grathwohl continues to speak and write about his experiences with the Weather Underground. He lives in Cincinnati and has three grown daughters. To schedule interviews or appearances, please go to the book's website:

bringingdownamerica.com

Made in the USA
San Bernardino, CA
12 March 2014